Special Operations
in the Age of Chivalry
1100–1550

T0311306

WARFARE IN HISTORY

ISSN 1358-779X

Series editor

Matthew Bennett, Royal Military Academy, Sandhurst

This series aims to provide a wide-ranging and scholarly approach to military history, offering both individual studies of topics or wars, and volumes giving a selection of contemporary and later accounts of particular battles; its scope ranges from the early medieval to the early modern period.

New proposals for the series are welcomed; they should be sent to the publisher at the address below.

Boydell and Brewer Limited, PO Box 9, Woodbridge, Suffolk, IP12 3DF

Previously published volumes in this series are listed at the back of this volume

Special Operations in the Age of Chivalry

1100–1550

Yuval Noah Harari

THE BOYDELL PRESS

First published 2007
The Boydell Press, Woodbridge

Reprinted in paperback 2009

ISBN 978-1-84383-452-6

The Boydell Press is an imprint of Boydell & Brewer Ltd
PO Box 9, Woodbridge, Suffolk IP12 3DF, UK
and of Boydell & Brewer Inc.
668 Mt. Hope Avenue, Rochester NY 14620, USA
website: www.boydellandbrewer.com

The publisher has no responsibility for the continued existence or
accuracy of URL's for external or third-party internet websites referred to
in this book, and does not guarantee that any content on such websites is,
or will remain, accurate or appropriate

A CIP catalogue record for this title is available
from the British Library

This book is printed on acid-free paper

Printed in Great Britain by
CPI Antony Rowe, Chippenham and Eastbourne

Contents

Illustrations

between pp. 52 and 53

Maps

Genealogical table

To Alon, Beni, Martin, and Steve.

Preface

THIS book is a first attempt to study the conduct and role of inland special operations in the age of chivalry. Since at present there are neither academic studies nor popular history books on this subject, it aims to fill both gaps, and to contribute to the scholarly research of medieval and Renaissance warfare while simultaneously presenting the subject in a lively way for a general readership.

The book is divided into two parts. The first chapter, an analytical overview of special operations in the period 1100–1550, has two main aims: first, to outline the dominant characteristics of special operations during the period, and to relate the subject to several central debates in the scholarship of medieval and Renaissance war; second, to introduce some of the peculiar realities of war in the age of chivalry to non-professional readers who are interested in special operations but have little prior knowledge of medieval and Renaissance military history. The second part, comprising chapters 2–7, presents a number of special operations conducted between 1098 and 1536. This part too is aimed at a non-professional readership, and consequently forgoes analysis in favour of narrative. For similar reasons, footnotes and the discussion of sources are kept to a minimum.

✦ ✦ ✦

This book has been written in the midst of the ongoing war between Israelis and Palestinians. The landmark military events on both sides of this war were mainly special operations, though of different types. On the one side, Palestinian terrorist cells undertook pinpoint strikes against Israeli population centres and national symbols, and on the other side, Israeli special forces kidnapped and assassinated Palestinian terrorists, commanders and politicians. Though ethically and politically the two types of operations might be separated by a very wide gulf, militarily they can be grouped together under the umbrella term of 'special operations', as will be explained below.

While writing this book I was therefore well aware that special operations can be far different from their clean and glamorous image in modern popular culture. I accordingly tried to present a rounded picture of these activities, seeing them in their wider context rather than as memorable examples of heroic derring-do, in the hope of contributing to a more balanced and critical discussion of the issue.

Acknowledgements

THIS book is dedicated to the teachers who nurtured my love of history and who taught me how to engage with the human past in an insightful and judicious way.

I would like to thank Alon Klebanoff, who supervised my high-school project on the longbow in the Hundred Years War, for setting me on my academic course. His example and guidance were decisive influences in my choice of an academic career. Though more than a decade has passed and though I have been privileged to spend much time in several of the leading universities of the world, I have yet to meet someone with such a detailed knowledge of military history and with such love and enthusiasm for the battles and soldiers of bygone days.

I would like to thank Benjamin Z. Kedar, who was my mentor at the Hebrew University and supervised my BA and MA studies, for laying the firm foundations of my academic abilities and even of my academic personality. I would like to thank him for the long hours he spent both in class and outside it imparting to me the crafts of an historian, carefully correcting my steps in my first research projects. Yet I would like to thank him even more for giving me along with those firm foundations also free rein and active encouragement to go beyond the well-trodden paths of historical research, and wander through the wilder fringes of that kingdom.

I would like to thank Martin van Creveld, who together with B. Z. Kedar supervised several of my initial scholarly projects, for providing me both with broad historical visions and with the occasional brutal push in the right direction. I am particularly indebted to him for warning me against the pitfalls of narrow-mindedness and of self-obsession, which threaten to enclose scholars in a sterile academic bubble. The present book resulted from several discussions I had with him, and he has also read and commented on the initial drafts of the book's first chapters. I cannot pretend, though, that the book even approaches the standards he has set, for compared to his own projects, it is little more than an entertaining hobby-horse.

And I would like to thank Steven J. Gunn, who supervised my doctoral studies, for helping me to bring together the skills and knowledge I accumulated, and for showing me how to bridge the enormous gap separating historical theory from the practicalities of writing. Without his dedicated and selfless assistance, I could not have transformed the fleeting and ephemeral ideas in my mind into a corporeal doctoral dissertation. The hours we spent together in performing this alchemical exercise have been an invaluable lesson, and made the composition of the present book far smoother.

The book could not have been written without the kind and generous guidance of these teachers. I hope they will enjoy it, and would find something to be proud of in it.

✦ ✦ ✦

I am also grateful to my schooldays history teachers, and in particular Danny Fesler and Dafna Haran, for fostering my initial love of history, and for some of my best hours at school. Thanks are also due to Sarai Aharoni, my good friend of many years, for her ongoing intellectual stimulus, and to Jonathan Lewy, for his references and insightful comments concerning the Nizari sect.

I was fortunate in having two excellent research assistants, Ilya Berkovich and Eyal Katz. I am certain that if Ilya sets his heart on it, he would soon make a name for himself as an outstanding scholar. As for Eyal, it seems he is going to help people in a far more direct manner as an occupational therapist. I hope he will never have to help the victims of special operations.

I am greatly indebted to the Yad Hanadiv Fellowship Trust for their generous support of this research project, and in particular to Natania Isaak, who made it a pleasure as well as a privilege to enjoy the Trust's generosity.

Finally, I would like to thank my family for its emotional and material support, and in particular to Itzik, my spouse and life-companion, who also did an excellent job preparing the book's maps.

Special Operations, Strategy, and Politics in the Age of Chivalry – An Analytical Overview

The Definition of Inland Special Operations

A 'special operation' is a combat operation that is limited to a small area, takes a relatively short span of time, and is conducted by a small force, yet is capable of achieving significant strategic or political results disproportional to the resources invested in it. Special operations almost always involve the employment of unconventional and covert methods of fighting. It is these methods that enable a small investment of resources to produce a disproportionate strategic or political impact.[1]

For example, in January 1327 Queen Isabella of England and her lover Roger Mortimer overthrew the unpopular King Edward II, and shortly after murdered him in prison. They then ruled as regents for the fourteen-year-old Edward III, Isabella's son. As Edward grew up, his mother showed no signs of relinquishing power in his favour. Contrariwise, she and Mortimer strengthened their hold on the crown, and strove to create an independent power base for themselves. On the night of 19 October 1330 William Montagu infiltrated Nottingham Castle – where Isabella, Mortimer and Edward were staying – through a secret underground passage, at the head of about two dozen men. Acting on behalf of the young king, Montagu took the couple's guards by surprise, and seized the Queen and her lover. Mortimer was executed, whereas Isabella was forced to retire to her country estates. Edward thereby became ruler of England. This pinpoint strike by a handful of men, which took a few hours and cost almost no money and very few lives, accomplished what otherwise might have required a full-blown civil war, a substantial treasure, and thousands of lives.[2]

Special operations such as the raid on Nottingham Castle are different from espionage operations and psychological warfare – which can also produce significant strategic and political results with very limited resources – because they involve the use of force.[3] The difference between 'special' operations and 'regular' combat operations is more complicated. In their execution, special operations are frequently similar to combat operations that involve the use of surprise and subterfuge. In their impact too, regular combat operations could sometimes have strategic and political impact disproportionate to the resources invested in them.

For instance, in 1199 King Richard the Lion-Heart of the House of Plantagenet was winning his war with King Philip August of the House of Capet, securing the Plantagenets' Continental possessions, and hampering his rival's plan to unite the Kingdom of France. Just then a ploughman uncovered a gold and silver treasure in the fields of Châlus castle. The lord of the castle, Achard, confiscated the treasure, but was upended by his own lord – namely King Richard – who demanded the treasure for himself. Achard refused, and the outraged Richard quickly laid siege to the castle, refusing the offer of surrender made by its defenders. The small castle was defended by a few dozen men and women at most. As Richard was preparing the assault, a crossbowman from the garrison shot him in the shoulder. Richard's wound became infected, and after a few days gangrene carried the warrior king off the political map of Europe.

Within five years the Plantagenets lost Normandy, and within ten more years they lost all the rest of their Continental possessions save Gascony, whereas Philip August laid the foundations for the unification of France under the Capetians. Thus the defence of Châlus, an operation conducted with extremely limited resources, profoundly changed the strategic and political situation in western Europe, and helped reshape European borders for centuries.[4] However, we would not think of the defence of Châlus as a special operation, because Richard's death was a chance outcome, probably unintended even by the defenders – who were all put to the sword in retaliation for the king's death.

The difference between special operations and regular combat operations lies therefore not in their execution or in their impact, but in the *preconceived* matching of impact and execution. Unlike the killing of Richard the Lion-Heart, special operations such as the raid on Nottingham Castle are planned, and they are planned so that the same resources employed in ordinary operations can produce extraordinary results.

This definition is valid only for inland operations. Naval special operations are excluded from the book because they were very different on both the strategic and operational levels. Particularly in long-distance naval warfare the above definition cannot clearly differentiate special from regular operations. This is obvious for example in the case of long-distance piracy. Thus in 1523 the French pirate Jean Fleury seized a treasure fleet sent by Hernando Cortés from Mexico to Spain. Fleury was operating more than 2,000 kilometres from his base, leading a self-sufficient force of a few hundred men. He seized a fortune in gold and silver, and his operation had even more important psychological consequences. Was it a 'special operation'? According to the above definition, it certainly was. But if so, then almost all medieval and Renaissance piratical undertakings were special operations, and since these comprised a very significant portion of all naval operations, it would mean that many medieval and early modern naval struggles – and above all the struggle over long-distance trade between Europe and the Indies – were in fact 'special operations wars'.

This is a very interesting suggestion, but only in-depth research dedicated to naval strategy and naval operations could do justice to this problem. Since the task I have undertaken is already quite formidable, spanning about five centuries and more than one continent, I have decided to leave naval special operations for future research.

Special Operations in Contemporary Warfare, Culture, and Scholarship

In recent decades the importance of special operations and special forces has increased dramatically. Few countries lack special forces, which are usually considered the cream of the army, and are lavished with attention and resources. Special operations have become an integral part of strategic and political thinking, so that when governments and armies examine their different options in times of crisis, special operations are habitually included in the menu.

Special operations have been a particularly important option when the military targets in question are of the following types:

(1) **Infrastructure.** Waging war in the twentieth century has increasingly depended on industrial, communication, and transport infrastructure. Consequently the capture and destruction of bridges, dams, communication centres, factories, and laboratories could affect a country's ability to wage war at least as much as the destruction of armed units. Since infrastructure facilities are 'soft' unarmed targets, small forces which could never hope to defeat large enemy combat units could nevertheless achieve important strategic results by attacking these facilities. These may of course be guarded by the enemy, yet since the target of the attack is the facility rather than the guarding unit, if a way is found to avoid or neutralize the guards, it is still possible to achieve important results with a limited investment of resources.

A classic example is the German attack on Eban Emael (1940). A few dozen German glider troops secured the vital bridges over the Albert Canal by neutralizing Eban Emael fort, which contained more than ten times their number of Belgian soldiers. Though they did not defeat the Belgians, the German raiders prevented them from destroying the bridges, without which the German advance into Belgium would have been stopped and the German campaign plan jeopardized.[5]

Industrial infrastructure could be of even more value. One of the key links in the Nazi nuclear programme was the Norsk Hydro power station at Ryukan, Norway. A plant attached to the station produced almost all the heavy water then available for German nuclear research and production. Several bombing missions and special operations were conducted by the Allies to destroy the plant, without success. Finally, in February 1943 a special unit managed to sabotage the plant and halt production. The Germans tried to ship to Germany whatever heavy water the plant had already produced, but the ship carrying the water was sunk by another special operation. Though these two operations were not responsible by themselves for Germany's failure to produce nuclear weapons, they certainly contributed to this failure. Needless to say, the strategic and political consequences of this failure are incalculable.[6]

(2) **Weapon systems.** The technologization of late modern war has led to the introduction of ever more sophisticated weapon systems, whose cost and military impact have risen dramatically. The production and maintenance of a single weapon system such as a nuclear missile or a major warship could consume a significant percentage of a country's resources, whereas the introduction or destruction of just one such weapon system could alter strategic and political power balances. Such weapon systems have occasionally proved vulnerable to special operations, which could thereby produce an important impact with limited means. For instance, a significant portion of the special operations conducted during the Second Gulf War (1990–1) were aimed to locate and neutralize a handful of Iraqi mobile missile launchers in Iraq's Western Desert.

With the proliferation of weapons of mass destruction, the role of special operations in obtaining, guarding, and destroying individual weapon systems is likely to become more and more central.

(3) **People.** The killing, kidnapping, and rescuing of particular individuals could have political and strategic significance which outweighs even the destruction of entire military units or infrastructure facilities. For example, when in 1943 the Badoglio government imprisoned Benito Mussolini and began negotiating with the Allies, the fallen dictator was plucked from his secret prison on the top of Gran Sasso Mountain in a daring glider raid. Propped up by German power, he headed a puppet regime in central and northern Italy, securing the loyalty of significant segments of Italian society and easing German control of the country.[7]

Politicians and military commanders are not the only individuals possessing strategic importance. The rescue of Nils Bohr, a leading physicist, from Nazi-occupied Denmark contributed significantly to the progress of the Allied nuclear programme, while hampering the German one.[8] At the end of the Second World War the race between the Soviets and Americans to lay their hands on German missile scientists showed that both had grasped the far-reaching importance of such people. With the proliferation of weapons of mass destruction and increasing technologization of war, scientists are likely to become lucrative targets for special operations at least as much as politicians and generals.

(4) **Symbols.** In recent decades some of the most successful special operations have targeted people and objects possessing symbolic rather than material value. For instance, the massacre of the Israeli delegation at the Munich Olympics (1972) and the September 11 attacks (2001) were extremely successful

assaults on national symbols.[9] Whereas the material effects of these attacks were negligible, and they hardly harmed Israeli or American military power, their symbolic effects were immense.[10] In both cases, the success of the attacks gave a great boost to the attackers' morale and a corresponding shock to the Israelis and Americans. The impact of the attacks can be gauged from the fact that both Israel and America reacted by mounting a massive counterattack. The Israelis changed their intelligence-gathering priorities and invested many resources in combating Palestinian terror in Europe. The Americans reacted by proclaiming a global war on terror, which has so far resulted in the conquest of two sovereign states and a mounting wave of world-wide terrorism.

Special operations aimed at taking hostages and at releasing hostages and POWs can also be seen as operations whose targets possess a symbolic rather than material value. The rescue of a handful of kidnapped civilians or imprisoned soldiers cannot have any effect on the material balance of power, but it can be a great morale booster, proving both one's military abilities and one's largely symbolic commitment to do anything in one's power to save each and every citizen or soldier.[11] This latter commitment is of great symbolic value to modern states, and particularly to Western democracies, which is why kidnapping even a few of their citizens has become a worthwhile target for enemy special operations.[12]

✦

Part of the reason why special operations targeting symbols are potentially so successful is that in the late modern era special operations have enjoyed a privileged place in the media and in popular culture. Particularly after the First World War destroyed much of the aura of regular combat – replacing heroic images of gleaming bayonets and brave charges with tragic images of mud, blood, and barbed wire – the culture of war increasingly looked for glamour and heroism in the field of special operations. It was only there that the individualistic hero could still decide the fate of wars and nations.[13]

Special operations and special forces have consequently received enormous coverage in the media, and they loom even larger in (primarily male) popular culture. Whereas special operations comprise a fraction of all military operations, they are the subject of a huge percentage of popular military history books,[14] fictional war books, and war films. Even war films of the realistic and disillusioning genre, such as *Saving Private Ryan* and *Black Hawk Down*, focus on special operations (the rescuing of a private soldier for symbolic reasons in the first example, and the kidnapping of key enemy personnel in the second).

In the field of action films the dominance of special operations is even more pronounced. Special operation attacks on infrastructure facilities and weapon systems located deep in enemy territory form the main plot-line of everything from *Mission: Impossible* episodes and various *James Bond* films to *Raiders of the Lost Ark*, *Star Wars*, and the *Lord of the Rings* trilogy (if one accepts that the

'Lost Ark', the 'Death Star' and the 'Ring of Power' are weapon systems of mass destruction).

More popular yet are special operations targeting valuable persons. The *Terminator* trilogy revolves around the assassination and safeguarding of future leaders and present scientists, whereas one cannot imagine either political dramas or realistic action films without the assassination and rescue of threatened politicians, or fantasy action films without the rescue of kidnapped princesses. Special operations aimed at rescuing 'commoner' hostages and POWs are probably just as popular.[15] The prototype of the male action hero, and increasingly of the female action hero as well, is the special operation expert rather than the ordinary soldier or even the commander.[16]

Similarly in the field of computer and video games, for every game focusing on conventional warfare, there are probably a dozen in which the player impersonates a special operations expert trying to assassinate Hitler, blow up an enemy nuclear reactor, or rescue civilian hostages.

It is no wonder that real special forces such the British SAS, the American Green Berets, the Russian Alpha Force and Omon, or the Israeli Sayeret-Matkal, have been enjoying unprecedented public prestige. It has been argued with good reason that just as the ideal male hero of fiction culture is the special operations expert, so real special operation troops have come to personify the ideal of national manhood.[17] Consequently their members not only bask in the sunshine of popular admiration, but enjoy increasing influence in military and political circles. An increasing percentage of senior military officers have a background in special forces. For example, the commander of the British forces in the Gulf War, General Peter de la Billière, began his career in the SAS.

In Israel, not only do we find a long list of senior generals who are special forces veterans, but the three Prime Ministers that held office from 1996 to 2006 – Benjamin Netanyahu, Ehud Barak, and Ariel Sharon – have all owed at least part of their appeal to their special forces background.[18] It is not unfair to add to that list the current Governor of California, Arnold Schwarzenegger, who is probably best known to many of his voters for his assassination and counter-assassination missions on the silver screen.

The cultural attraction of special operations has magnified their potential impact on national morale. Since the national image, and particularly the national masculine image, is so invested in them, a successful operation boosts the national morale and an unsuccessful operation dampens it much more than a regular operation with equivalent results. Success in such operations will always seem more spectacular, and failure more humiliating, because the people who perform these missions are supposed to be the incarnation of the nation's manhood, and because the public is used to identifying with such operations from the movie theatres and computer game arcades.

✦

Parallel to the avalanche of popular writing on special operation themes, there has been increasing attention to special operations in academic circles as well, fanned by the September 11 attacks and the subsequent War on Terror. However, this attention focuses almost exclusively on the role of special operations in late twentieth-century, early twenty-first-century, and future conflicts.[19] This reflects a widespread assumption that prior to the Second World War, special operations occurred, if at all, only as part of partisan or guerrilla warfare.[20] Books dealing with the history of special operations usually go back only as far as the Second World War, and even the occasional exceptions rarely look earlier than the late eighteenth century.[21] It is characteristic that the only pre-eighteenth-century special operation in *From Troy to Entebbe: Special Operations in Ancient and Modern Times* is the mythical Trojan Horse story.[22] The earliest test case in William McRaven's influential study, *Spec Ops: Case Studies in Special Operations Warfare*, is the attack on Eban Emael in 1940. The only major exception to this rule, as far as I could ascertain, is Stephen Turnbull's *Ninja: The True Story of Japan's Secret Warrior Cult*, which studies the history of special operations and special forces in Japan, and focuses its attention on the medieval and early modern era.

It is also characteristic that in their efforts to locate antecedents to today's special forces, some studies confuse them with crack regular troops. For example, a chapter titled 'Commandos Through History' in James Dunnigan's *The Perfect Soldier: Special Operations, Commandos, and the Future of U.S. Warfare* treats as special forces such troops as the Immortals, the Persian royal guards; Alexander the Great's Companion cavalrymen; all medieval knights; English longbowmen of the Hundred Years War era; Mameluks and Janissaries; and early modern grenadiers and light cavalrymen.[23] Robin Neillands' *In the Combat Zone: Special Forces since 1945* finds antecedents to today's forces not only in the biblical King David, but also in Genghis Khan's units of irregular horsemen; in eighteenth- and nineteenth-century light infantry units such as the German Jägers and John Moore's Light Infantry forces; in the Spanish and Russian guerrillas of the Napoleonic Wars; in American Civil War cavalry forces; and in the First World War German stormtroopers.[24]

The lack of interest in pre-eighteenth century special operations is also reflected in studies dedicated to pre-modern warfare, which usually show only meagre interest in special operations. For example, studies of medieval and Renaissance warfare hardly ever discuss them. Though operations that can be classified as 'special' certainly appear in many narrative histories, analyses of medieval and Renaissance warfare do not treat them as a separate theme. Recent surveys of medieval and early modern war such as Jeremy Black's *European Warfare, 1494–1660*, John France's *Western Warfare in the Age of the Crusades*, or Helen Nicholson's *Medieval Warfare: Theory and Practice of War in Europe, 300–1500* do not contain any reference to special operations.

The present book tries to start filling the gap by examining inland special operations between 1100 and 1550. It first outlines the main characteristics of inland special operations in this era and the conditions which created these characteristics, and follows this by an in-depth description of a few chosen test cases. The aim is partly to provide a historical context for developments in the last century. More importantly, I believe that the study of medieval and Renaissance war can also benefit from a closer look at special operations.

The peculiar characteristics of special operations make them an excellent lens through which to understand the realities of war. Because the conduct of special operations involves a delicate balance between military ends and military means, they highlight the ends and means characteristic of warfare in any particular period. Thus medieval and Renaissance special operations draw some of the limits of both the desirable and the possible in medieval and Renaissance war.

In particular, special operations are an ideal testing ground for the relations between chivalry and military reality in the Middle Ages and the Renaissance. The debate about these relations has occupied a central place in the study of medieval and Renaissance warfare.[25] Some scholars, most famously Huizinga and Kilgour, have argued that chivalric culture was completely divorced from military reality, and its influence on the conduct of military operations was negligible. Princes and knights paid lip service to its ideals, and used it as a gloss over war's horrors, as a means to reconcile war-making with Christianity, and as a tool to inspire loyalty in their vassals. However, when it came to making war, the constraints of chivalric culture were laid aside whenever they interfered with the pursuit of victory.[26]

In recent decades most scholars have tended to emphasize the continuing relevance of chivalric culture. They have seen chivalry as a formative and influential factor which defined the proper values and norms of war long into the early modern age. Combatants often adhered to these norms even when it was inconvenient to do so, and tried to refrain from what chivalry defined as 'foul play'. Though the huge dividends of victory occasionally tempted combatants to bend or break these norms, the values behind them were rarely doubted.[27] In particular, the chivalric ideal of honour remained the central martial value and the main pillar of noble masculine identity throughout the Middle Ages and the Renaissance.[28]

Questions of chivalry and honour were particularly acute in the conduct of special operations. Whereas regular combat only occasionally involved the use of what chivalry considered 'foul play', special operations almost always necessitated it. They consequently tended to stretch the conventions of war to their limits. On the one hand, they seemed to breathe life into the exploits of the chivalric romances, enabling brave warriors to fight against overwhelming odds and win wars almost single-handedly (something which, despite the image perpetuated in films and popular military histories, was far from the reality of regular combat in the age of chivalry). On the other hand, these exploits often relied on deceit, treason, bribe, assassination, and other forms of foul play, which threatened to turn war into a dishonourable business and undermine the foundations of chivalric culture.

As the following pages demonstrate, the conduct of special operations in the age of chivalry was characterized by an unresolved and ever-present tension between the practical needs of winning wars and the ideals of chivalric fair play, which stressed that war was not a continuation of politics but rather a way of life, and that fighting honourably was more important than gaining victory.[29] This tension sanctioned the use of some types of special operations (such as rescuing one's lord), severely limited the use of others (such as assassinations), and influenced the overall effectiveness of all of them. These limitations certainly made sense from a broader perspective. Since war is always fought within the compass of a certain political culture, and since rulers derive both their identity and their power from that culture, fighting war in ways that undermine that culture can empty victory of its meaning by undermining the victor's own identity and authority.[30]

The Targets of Inland Special Operations in the Age of Chivalry

Despite their problematic place within chivalric culture, special operations were a central part of war in the age of chivalry, and they also enjoyed a unique cultural prestige similar to the one they have gained in late-modern martial culture. Indeed, it could well be argued that the present aura of special operations is to a large extent an inheritance of medieval martial culture. Whereas popular martial culture in much of the Classical world as well as in early modern and nineteenth-century Europe was dominated mainly by stories of regular warfare, medieval noble audiences were much fonder of the impossible escapades of small numbers of knights.[31]

For instance, the *Charroi de Nîmes*, one of the most popular *chansons de geste* of the twelfth century, focuses on a fictional special operation reminiscent of the Trojan Horse story. The chanson's hero, Count Guillaume of Orange, set out to capture the heavily fortified city of Nîmes from the Saracen King Otrant. In order to do so, he collected a thousand carts, placed a wooden barrel in each cart, and hid his men inside the barrels. He then dressed himself in foreign clothes, and pretended to be a rich English merchant on his way to the Nîmes market. The Saracens' greed was aroused by the sight of his caravan. Expecting to make a huge profit from tolls and presents, and beguiled by Guillaume's smooth tongue, King Otrant allowed the caravan past the gates. Once inside, Guillaume's men broke out of the barrels, and captured the city with fire and sword.[32]

Even more popular were small-unit rescue operations to save kidnapped princesses, which became the staple of chivalric entertainment. Henceforth such tales always remained in vogue, even if tales of regular combat were at times more popular. Chivalric special operation tales were perpetuated into late-modern cinemas through an unbroken chain of adaptations such as the sixteenth-century *Orlando Furioso* and *Amadis de Gaula*; the seventeenth-century works of Le Sage, La Calprenède, and Madeleine de Scudéry; the eighteenth-century adaptations of Courtilz de Sandras and the *Bibliothèque bleue*; and the nineteenth-century adaptations of Walter Scott and Victorian juvenile literature.

It is interesting to note that the basic plot of even futuristic special operations films such as the *Terminator* trilogy or *Twelve Monkeys* actually copies the plot of chivalric special operation romances. Thus the twelfth-century *Chanson du Chevalier du Cygne et de Godefroid de Bouillon* recounts how several years before the First Crusade, the mother of the Muslim ruler Corbaran (Kerbogah) – who was a powerful sorceress – foretold the events of the Crusade. She warned her son that a prince called Godfrey of Bouillon will come from the land of the Franks and conquer Nicea, Antioch, and Jerusalem. Corbaran's son and heir, Cornumaran, resolved to prevent this catastrophe. Taking with him a single companion, he disguised himself as a Christian pilgrim returning from the Holy Land, and set out to Europe to find Godfrey and kill him while he was still young. Cornumaran managed to cross the whole of Europe and reach Hainault without being detected, but there he was recognized by a real Christian pilgrim, and he consequently failed to change the future.[33]

In contrast to this cultural continuity between chivalric and late-modern special operations, the following overview demonstrates that the targets of special operations in the age of chivalry were often different than those of the late modern era.

Infrastructure (1): Capturing fortified places

The most important infrastructure facilities in the age of chivalry were fortified places such as towns and castles. Their fortifications represented a very large investment, and were the most expensive construction undertakings of most rulers.[34] They were the most important centres of military, economic, administrative, cultural, and religious activity.[35] Towns were furthermore the largest population centres, and housed a large portion of a country's wealth and skilled manpower.

Fortified places were important not only in themselves, but also as the hubs of communication, transport, and supply networks. All major ports and most of the important bridges were enclosed within the walls of a town or fortress. Similarly, all major roads, canals, and navigable rivers were dotted with strongpoints, which could effectively control the traffic passing along them by serving as a base for constant short-distance raids.

When a chain of fortified places guarded all the passages of a major river, these strongpoints could completely hinder the passage of enemy forces. Even when invading forces could bypass the strongpoints and ravage the countryside, it was impossible to secure lasting territorial gains without taking these strong-points.[36] In particular, an invading army could not hope to spend any length of time inside an enemy province without securing transport lines back to its supply bases. Should an army plunge forward recklessly and then get bogged down without secure supply lines behind it, the result could be its surrender or entire destruction, as happened to the French invasions of Flanders in 1197, of Egypt in 1250, and of Aragon in 1285.[37]

Thus when the French tried to invade and conquer Gascony in 1346, their huge field army, numbering up to 20,000 men,[38] had to rely on supply brought mainly along the rivers leading into Gascony. This forced the French – if they really wanted to conquer the land rather than merely pass through and ravage it – to take the various strongpoints controlling the river lines. In April 1346 the invading army settled down to besiege one of these strongpoints, namely the castle Aiguillon, which controlled the confluence of the Lot and Garonne rivers, two of the major French supply lines. Four months later they were still there. The 1,500 defenders of Aiguillon put up a very stout resistance, and the French could neither conquer the castle nor bypass it. They eventually gave up the siege and retreated north, after hearing of Edward III's invasion of the French heartland.[39]

The material and morale benefits of taking a strongpoint, and particularly a major town, could therefore be very big. Yet taking fortified places was easier said than done. The tactical superiority of defence over offence in siege war-fare meant that taking even a single strongpoint – provided it was resolutely defended – was a costly task which could take weeks and months, as the French learned at Aiguillon.[40] Entire campaigns, if not entire wars, often revolved around the siege of a single important town, as exemplified by the sieges of Nicea, Antioch, and Jerusalem during the First Crusade (1097–9); the siege of Damascus during the Second Crusade (1148); the siege of Acre during the Third Crusade (1189–91); the siege of Constantinople during the Fourth Crusade (1204); the siege of Damietta during the Fifth Crusade (1218–19); the sieges of Tournai (1340), Calais (1346–7), Rheims (1360), Rouen (1418–19), and Orleans (1429) during the Hundred Years War; the sieges of Gaeta (1503), Ravenna (1512), Pavia (1524–5), Florence (1530), Metz (1552), and Saint-Quentin (1557) during the Habsburg–Valois Wars; and the siege of Tenochtitlan (1521) during the Spanish conquest of Mexico. Many more wars were decided by sieges than by battles, and many major battles were waged in order to relieve a besieged strongpoint, for example Antioch (1098), Hattin (1187), Acre (1191), Muret (1213), Bannockburn (1314), Formigny (1450), Castillon (1453), Morat (1476), Ravenna (1512), Pavia (1525), and Saint-Quentin (1557).[41]

Though fortified places could sometimes hold out for months even in the face of overwhelming odds, they were surprisingly vulnerable to special opera-tions. The defenders' ability to resist regular assaults was based almost entirely on the tactical superiority they gained from their stone and wood fortifications.

If a special operation managed by ruse or treason to capture a gate or a section of the walls, the defenders' superiority was annulled, and the entire defence system could burst like a punctured bubble. A successful special operation of that kind could be a tremendous coup, costing very little in terms of blood, time, and money (certainly when compared to the cost of regular sieges), but having an impact similar to that of victory in a major field battle or in an entire campaign.

For example, in the early fourteenth century the city of Berwick was the largest and most prosperous city of Scotland, and one of its chief commercial centres. It controlled the crossing of the river Tweed and the main road connecting Scotland with England, and also possessed a fine harbour. Numerous campaigns were fought by the English and the Scots for its possession. In 1333 Edward III besieged it for three months. In order to save it, the Scots gathered a huge army and offered Edward battle at Hallidon Hill, though previously they had tended to avoid pitched battles. The battle ended in a decisive English victory, which turned Berwick into an English city and almost made Scotland itself into an English dependency.[42] In the following decades the pendulum of war swung back and forth, but Berwick remained in English hands. Edward spent huge sums to fortify and garrison the city, which served as a bastion for the defence of Northumberland and as a springboard for repeated English invasions of Scotland.

On 6 November 1355 a small body of perhaps 300 Scots landed in secrecy near Berwick. About midnight they left their concealed position, carrying scaling ladders with them. They sent three scouts ahead, who reported that the guard on the wall was negligent. At the break of dawn some of the Scots crossed the moat, placed their ladders near the Cow Gate, and climbed over the wall without being detected. They then captured the gate, and let in the rest of the raiders.

The garrison was overcome and the city taken with almost no resistance, but the citadel held out. Edward III was at the time leading a winter invasion of northern France. When he heard of Berwick's fall he cut short his campaign and quickly returned to England (though some sources say he terminated his campaign for other reasons, and did not hear of Berwick's fall till he landed in England). He then hurriedly marched north and reached Berwick in time to save the citadel and recapture the city itself. Though in the end the operation gained little for the Scots themselves, potentially it could have altered the balance of power on the Anglo-Scottish border. It also forced Edward to undertake a costly winter campaign that diverted resources from Aquitaine; according to some sources, it may well be credited with wrecking Edward's campaign in Picardy and thereby changing the strategic situation on the Continent.[43]

Another classic example was the seizure of Meulan in 1435 (see illus. 1). The main aim of French strategy in 1435 was to recapture Paris, which was then held by the English. Not having enough resources to directly invest or assault such a huge city, the French chose instead to cut off its supply lines and starve it into submission. Paris's most important lifeline was the river Seine, along which food was transported from English-held Normandy. On the night of 24 September 1435 a small French party stealthily approached the walls of Meulan, a small town west of Paris which not only straddled the Seine, but also enclosed within its walls a stone bridge that spanned the entire length of the river. Two of the French raiders, called Lacaigne and Ferrande, were fishermen by trade. They procured a fishing boat, hid a long ladder inside it, and then drifted on the river, pretending to ply their trade. At the appropriate moment they anchored their boat next to the bridge of Meulan, and quietly set up their ladder against the wall, perhaps aided by a traitor from within the garrison. They then scaled the walls and opened the way for their comrades to capture the town.[44]

In itself, Meulan was a small and insignificant place. Yet its control enabled the French to cut Paris off from Normandy and to traverse the Seine at their pleasure. Food prices in Paris sky-rocketed, whereas property prices plummeted. After several more nearby strongpoints fell — many of them through treachery and escalades[45] — the situation in the capital rapidly deteriorated. When the French laid siege to the city in February 1436 the population was eager to open the gates to them, and the English garrison — fearing treason and suffering from severe supply shortages — made only a lukewarm attempt to defend the place before surrendering.

Most special operations aiming to storm a stronghold followed the same pattern. A small force, consisting of from one to a few dozen persons, tried to seize part of the fortified perimeter by escalade, ruse, or treason. A much larger force followed closely on the heels of the advance party, ready to enter the stronghold through the captured section and defeat the defenders in regular combat. The special operation thereby constituted the initial and most essential part of a larger regular operation.

For example, in 1141 Earl Ranulf of Chester and Earl William of Roumare rebelled against King Stephen of England. They began the uprising by sending their wives to pay a friendly visit to Lincoln Castle, one of the most important royalist strongholds. The ladies were entertained for some time by the castellan's wife, until Earl Ranulf arrived with three of his knights to escort the ladies back home. They were unarmed, and were allowed inside without hindrance. Once inside, however, they suddenly snatched whatever weapons lay at hand, and took over the castle's gate. Earl William, who was waiting nearby in ambush with a large troop of men, quickly arrived to reinforce Ranulf, and Lincoln Castle together with the surrounding town passed into the rebels' hands.[46] Though Ranulf and his three knights could not have hoped to conquer and hold Lincoln castle all by themselves, their action enabled William's larger force to enter the castle and capture it with ease.

Sometime in the early 1380s the Bascot de Mauléon, a notorious freebooter captain, decided to seize the town of Thurie in the Auvergne. From an early reconnaissance he knew that the town's main spring was outside the walls, and that every morning the townswomen would exit the walls to fetch water from it. Leaving his base at the castle of Castelculier with about fifty of his men, Mauléon approached Thurie under cover of night. At midnight he placed the men in ambush near the town, while he and five others dressed up as women and, taking pitchers with them, hid themselves in a haystack just outside the gate.

When morning came, the gate was opened, and women began heading out to the spring. Mauléon and his five companions took their pitchers, filled them with water, and then started towards the town, covering their faces with kerchiefs as best they could. In his reminiscences, Mauléon recollected that the women coming towards them were surprised not by their physique, but by their diligence. 'Holy Virgin,' they exclaimed, 'how early you've got up!' Disguising their masculine voices and imitating the local accent, the brigands answered 'Yes, haven't we?' and slowly made their way to the gate. A lone cobbler was standing guard at the gate, mindful of no danger. Utilizing the cobbler's lack of attention, one of the brigands blew a horn to summon up the ambush. The cobbler was alarmed by the sound, but not perceiving where it came from, was persuaded by the 'women' that the horn had been blown by a priest going to chase hares. The rest of the brigands shortly arrived, and together they stormed into the town, meeting little resistance. Thurie was sacked, and then transformed into a new brigands nest.[47]

In March or April 1432 the city of Chartres was captured by a trick reminiscent of Count Guillaume of Orange's legendary exploit at Nîmes (see illus. 2). The Bastard of Orleans collected together a large army of about 4,000 men. He placed a force of about 50–100 foot in ambush a short distance from the Saint-Michel Gate, and another force of 200–300 cavalry was hidden further on, whereas the bulk of the army waited a few kilometres away. Two Chartres merchants named Jehan Ansel and Little Guillemin collaborated with Orleans. They undertook to lead into the city a convoy of wagons, laden with merchandise – in particular, with herrings for Lent. A few of Orleans's soldiers disguised themselves as wagoners, concealing weapons under their clothing. A friar who was the city's most popular preacher also collaborated with Orleans. On the morning of the planned operation he summoned the community for a special sermon, which was held on the opposite side of the city from the Saint-Michel Gate. Many of the leading burghers and garrison members came to hear the friar, and were not at hand when the attack was launched.

Ansel and Guillemin were well familiar to the gate-keepers, who opened the gate and allowed them, their wagons, and their wagoners inside. The merchants gave the gate-keepers some salted herrings for their trouble, and engaged them in conversation. Suddenly the wagoners drew their weapons and attacked the gate-keepers. According to some sources, they simultaneously killed the horses which drew the wagons, in order to block the gate and prevent the garrison from closing it. They also gave a pre-arranged sign, and the ambush sprang forward to their assistance. The French ambushers, followed by the main army, erupted into the city before the guards could overcome the wagoners and close the gate. The garrison at first tried to resist the invaders, but soon saw that all was lost, and fled along with many of the civilians. 'As for ravishment, violations, and other misdeeds,' writes Monstrelet, 'they were performed according to the customs of war, as happens in a conquered city.'[48]

Six years later, in February 1437, the English captured the town of Pontoise by a similar ploy (see illus. 3). The English commander, Talbot, had neither the men nor the resources to besiege that vital and well-fortified town, which controlled the Oise valley and the north-western approaches to Paris. Instead, he disguised a party of his men as French villagers, and sent them into the town carrying baskets and merchandise, as if they were going to the market. In the dead of night the English party gathered together and raised the war cry, shouting that the town was taken. Simultaneously, another small English force, dressed in white to camouflage it against the snowy countryside, stormed the town with ladders from outside. The French garrison, though it outnumbered the attackers, was convinced that the town had already fallen and fled without striking a blow. The capture of Pontoise was a key element in the English recovery of the late 1430s, and enabled the English to again threaten Paris.[49]

Many other strongholds fell to special operations aided by treachery from within. Classical and medieval military manuals regularly listed treachery as the most serious danger threatening besieged garrisons.[50] Besieged commanders normally kept only one eye on the enemy outside; with the other they were busy scanning for fifth columns within the walls.[51] Even the largest and best-fortified cities were not immune to this danger. For instance, in 1185 Thessalonica, the second city of the Byzantine Empire, fell to the Normans due to the treachery of a group of German mercenaries in Byzantine service.[52]

It should be stressed, though, that even when a willing traitor was found, a special operation usually had to be mounted in order to capture the stronghold, for it was not easy to betray a well-garrisoned city or fortress. For instance, in 1118 one Ascelin, due to a personal feud, informed King Louis VI of France that he would betray to him the castle and town of Andley (today Les Andelys), which at the time was part of the Norman patrimony of King Henry I of England. Louis sent Ascelin under cover of night 'some seasoned soldiers', whom Ascelin hid in his barn under the straw. When morning came, Louis with a large armed force approached Andley. The local population was alarmed, and many began fleeing into the fortified castle. At that moment the hidden French troops emerged from under the straw, and shouting out the royal English battle cry, mingled with the people who ran to the safety of the castle. Once inside, they threw off their disguise, and began shouting the French battle cry 'Montjoie!' They captured the castle's gate and opened it to the incoming French force, so that within a short while both town and castle were firmly in French hands.[53]

If the special operation was ill planned or badly executed, taking a town through treason could well end up in failure. For instance, on 3 February 1431 the great city of Rouen, capital of Normandy, was betrayed to the French by a Gascon serving in the English garrison. He allowed a party of 100–120 men into the city's castle, which was supposed to be shortly reinforced by another 500 men. However, when news of the successful surprise of the castle reached the commanders of the main army, instead of hurrying to take possession of the city, they began bickering amongst themselves over the expected spoil. This gave the English enough time to recuperate from the shock, launch a counterattack, and regain possession of the castle.[54]

Another case demonstrating the difficulties involved in such operations was the Imperialist attack on Turin, the capital of Piedmont, which was held by the French (1537). The Imperialist governor of nearby Volpiano, a Neapolitan called Cesare Maggi, contacted a Gascon corporal in the French garrison, who agreed to betray one of the city's outer bulwarks in exchange for a large sum of money. On the agreed night the Gascon undertook to mount guard on that bulwark, and chose two or three of the garrison's worst soldiers to accompany him. Maggi meanwhile left Volpiano with several hundred men and some ladders. At a sign from the Gascon they planted the ladders at the foot of the bulwark and quickly climbed up, while the Gascon's comrades – true to their reputation – fled without firing a shot. The bulwark was in fact an outlying fortification, and the main line of walls separated it from the city proper. A gate connected the bulwark to the city, but due to the darkness and perhaps to faulty intelligence, the Imperialists did not know that it was left open. Instead of rushing through the open gate, they laboriously drew their ladders up the bulwark and set them anew against the main walls. By then the alarm was sounded, the walls were manned, and the gate was shut right in the face of the advancing Imperialists. The Imperialists turned round the artillery pieces they captured in the bulwark, and their first shot burst open the gate, but they could not overcome the garrison's resistance. After losing perhaps 150 men the Imperialists abandoned the bulwark and retreated.

The Gascon traitor was captured by the French and questioned. He explained that he was acting with the knowledge and encouragement of the lord of Boutières, the garrison's commander, who planned the whole affair as a trap for the Imperialists. He was merely performing his loyal duty in inviting the Imperialists into the bulwark, but apparently Boutières forgot the date of the operation, and failed to perform his share of the plan! The French were not taken in by this story, and the Gascon was strangled to death.[55] Nevertheless, the Gascon's explanation was not completely far-fetched. One of the main difficulties of taking strongpoints through treason was that defenders quite often employed double agents to tempt attackers into carefully laid traps.

For example, in 1543 subordinates of the very same Boutières trapped three Imperialist forces by means of a single double agent. A merchant called Garunchin told the Imperialist commander of Fossano, Count Pietro Porto, that he would betray the fortress and town of Barge to him. The first Imperialist raiding party of forty men entered the fortress as planned, and was immediately captured. The French, however, pretended that the fortress had fallen. Its garrison hoisted the Imperial flag, took to wearing Imperialist badges, and cried out in Spanish, while another French force pretended to attack the fortress, though taking care to shoot high and harm nobody.

Count Porto then sent reinforcements to the 'hard-pressed' garrison. This new force was captured in its turn, though its commander showed some resistance and was killed. Porto now decided to come to Barge in person. He was, however, a very suspicious person. To assuage his remaining doubts, five or six women were sent into the fortress under the pretext of selling cakes, apples, and chestnuts, to discover whether it was really occupied by Imperialist forces. The French allowed the women to enter, putting up an elaborate show for their sake. French soldiers walked up and down the courtyard dressed with Imperialist badges, while Spanish-speaking French soldiers chatted amiably with the women in fluent Spanish. After the women reported their findings, Porto's doubts were quieted, and he arrived at Barge with a large force to take possession of the town and fortress. At the entrance to the fortress his suspicions again arose, and he refused to enter until he could speak with the commander of the reinforcements he had earlier sent. The French, knowing that the man was dead and buried, opened the gates and charged. The count was slain, and the force he brought with him barely extracted itself from the trap and fled back to Fossano.[56]

In 1193 the Armenian ruler of Cilicia captured Prince Bohemond IV of Antioch by a similar ruse. An Armenian double agent promised to betray the castle of Baghras to the prince, but in fact drew him into a well-laid trap.[57]

✦

When we take into account the importance of strongpoints both in themselves and as the keys to the communication and transport network; their ability to withstand regular assaults by vastly superior enemies; and their relative vulnerability to special operations, it is no wonder that the great majority of special operations in the age of chivalry were aimed to seize fortified places.

Conversely, one of the most widespread and important methods attackers relied upon to conquer strongpoints was special operations, and cities and fortresses lived in constant fear of conspiracy and surprise.[58] As I hope to demonstrate in chapters 2 and 5, siege warfare in the age of chivalry was usually a double contest, involving both a regular campaign of blockade, bombardment, and assault, and a simultaneous clandestine campaign of spies, traitors, and escalades. The latter type of campaign not infrequently proved to be more important.[59]

Infrastructure (2): Destroying infrastructure facilities

Whereas attempts to capture fortified places by special operations were legion, attempts to merely destroy infrastructure were rare. Theoretically, there could be situations in which it was impractical to seize and defend a strongpoint deep within enemy territory, yet it was still possible to infiltrate the place, destroy a bridge or a major workshop, and then retreat. Occasionally important infrastructure facilities were left unfortified, which should have made such destructive raids even more feasible. In fact, this was hardly ever attempted. The main reason for this was the absence of high explosives in the age of chivalry. As late as the sixteenth century, a raiding party that wanted to destroy a bridge, a dam, or a mill usually had to do so by means of fire or hard manual labour.

For example, in January 1544 a French force raided the strategically important Po bridge at Carignano, in the hope of destroying it and crippling the Imperialist transport network in the area. The raiders were provided with certain 'artifices of fire', which they were to attach to the bridge's posts. These gunpowder-based fireworks were supposed to ignite the bridge's posts and burn them down to the waterline. The raiders managed to surprise the guards and take the bridge. However, when the pioneers attached the fireworks to the bridge and lit them, they made a lot of noise and smoke but did no apparent damage. Luckily the French commanders, who were sceptical about these ingenious inventions, also brought with them several dozen workmen supplied with axes, hatchets, and saws. Even so it took them more than four hours to accomplish the mission, and it was daylight by the time the bridge was broken. If the nearby Imperialist forces had not been deterred by over-caution the French raiders would surely have been captured, or at least forced to flee for their lives, long before they had accomplished their mission.[60] If the bridge had been located within a town rather than outside it, no French raiding party could ever have hoped to destroy it, even if it somehow managed to infiltrate the fortifications.[61]

Similarly, in April 1347 the French attempted to relieve the besieged city of Calais by an ingenious method. One of the major supply lines of the besieging English army passed through the flatland of Bourbourg. The French hoped that if they could break the dam over the river Aa at Watten, the rushing water would flood the flatland and cut off the English from their supply bases in Flanders. A French raid managed to capture the dam without much difficulty, but destroying it proved a tougher task. The French brought with them a large workforce for this purpose, but before the labourers could accomplish their mission, rumours of a Flemish counter-attack and the threat to the raiders' line of retreat caused the French commander to sound the retreat.[62] When in 1438 Duke Philip the Good of Burgundy tried to swamp the entire city of Calais by breaching one of the nearby sea dykes, he again had to rely for the performance of this task on a large number of workmen rather than on a small troop of demolition experts. The mission ended in failure.[63]

In 1333, when Edward Balliol crossed the river Tweed to campaign in Scotland, Scottish troops under Andrew Murray sought to sneak behind Balliol's back, break down Kelso bridge, and thereby trap Balliol north of the river. However, the Scots took too long in destroying the bridge, giving Balliol's troops enough time not only to save the bridge, but also to defeat the Scots and capture Murray himself.[64]

The absence of explosives meant that most targets could be destroyed only if the attackers brought with them a very large working party, or if they spent a lot of time in the target area. In most cases this made operations impractical. The only targets which could be destroyed by a small party within a short time were highly inflammable ones.

For instance, in 1138 Count Geoffrey V of Anjou captured the town of Touques and attempted to utilize it as a base of operations against the nearby castle of Bonneville. The castellan sent back to the deserted town 'poor boys and common women', who according to his instructions kindled fires in forty-six different places all around town. The town was burned down, while the castle's garrison sallied out to pursue the fleeing Angevins.[65]

When in 1180 the ruler of Aleppo in northern Syria began attacking the territory of the Nizari sect, Nizari agents retaliated by infiltrating Aleppo in the night and burning down its market, which was the city's main source of wealth.[66] Their attack was successful because the market, crammed with inflammable merchandise, could swiftly be torched by a handful of individuals.

However, in the age of chivalry there were relatively few such inflammable facilities worth the effort. It was not easy to burn down whole towns, and stone fortifications could not be burned at all. As for economic infrastructure, even in relatively industrial areas such as Flanders, industrial production was done in large numbers of small workshops, where the main assets were skilled craftsmen and cheap labour rather than sophisticated and expensive equipment. Agricultural production was an even more dispersed enterprise, and relied even less on the existence of sophisticated equipment and infrastructure. Consequently, though armies systematically destroyed agricultural and industrial infrastructure in entire provinces in order to impoverish the enemy, this could not be done by special operations.

Big raids such as the Black Prince's *chevauchées* in 1355–6 could produce important strategic and political results by ravaging economic infrastructure, but such raids were full-scale military campaigns undertaken by large forces spread over large areas, and lasted for weeks and even months. Classifying such raids as 'special operations' would empty the concept of its analytical usefulness.

Smaller raids aimed to ravage agricultural and industrial infrastructure were a ubiquitous and almost ceaseless activity in medieval and early modern wars, but such individual raids could seldom produce important operational or strategic results, and hence they too do not fit the above definition of special operations. Only under unique circumstances could facilities such as the Aleppo market or the flour mill of Auriol become worthwhile targets for special operations (see chapter 7).

In particular, it should be emphasized that armies needed only limited quantities of weapons such as armour suits, swords, and helmets, and were seldom dependent for their supply on industrial production back home.[67] Arrows and crossbow bolts were needed in larger quantities. At times, princes bought or demanded hundreds of thousands of crossbow bolts. King John of England purchased 210,000 crossbow bolts in 1212,[68] and in 1272 James I of Aragon demanded 100,000 bolts from his dominions.[69] English armies operating in France during the Hundred Years War required even larger numbers of longbow arrows. For example, the English crown bought 425,000 arrows in 1421.[70]

Yet these quantities were still minuscule compared to the industrial requirements of late modern armies, and medieval rulers normally obtained the required numbers of bolts and arrows by manufacturing them on the spot, buying them from foreign merchants, or demanding small quotas of arrows from a large number of towns and villages.[71] James I's demand for 100,000 crossbow bolts in 1272 was parcelled out between several townships, so that Barcelona, for example, had to supply 15,000 bolts, and Huesca 4,000.[72] Even within each town and area, industrial production was performed in small workshops, where artisans manufactured individual items by hand, rather than in large assembly-line factories producing masses of identical items.[73]

Hence, even when armies relied on home industry for the supply of hundreds of thousands of bolts and arrows, these were produced by a large number of local craftsmen working in small workshops spread all over the country. Conducting a special operation to destroy a few such crossbow workshops in Barcelona, for instance, would have been a ludicrous idea, and it could have had absolutely no influence on Aragonese armies operating in Valencia or Southern Italy.

These industrial and strategic realities were not fundamentally changed by the gunpowder revolution, at least not by the sixteenth century. The amounts of gunpowder, cannonballs, and arquebus balls that armies required were certainly larger than the quantity of arrows and bolts needed by medieval armies. In 1513, 510 tons of gunpowder were shipped out of England for the invasion of France, and the 180 pieces of artillery at the siege of Tournai could consume up to 32 tons of gunpowder a day.[74] During the siege of Malta (1565) the Turks shot an estimated 130,000 cannon balls, and a far larger number of arquebus balls.[75] However, the methods of production were still medieval, there was still much reliance on buying gunpowder and arms from foreign merchants, and there were no huge armament factories to tempt special operations.[76]

Existing gunpowder stocks constituted a more attractive target, for technically it was very easy to destroy them,[77] and blowing up an army's gunpowder train, a fleet's gunpowder supply, or a town's gunpowder arsenal could be a devastating blow. For instance, at the battle of Gavere (1453) the Ghentenaar army panicked and fled when part of its gunpowder stock accidentally exploded due to a cannoneer's carelessness.[78] By the late fifteenth century, sieges often had to be lifted when the besiegers ran out of gunpowder, whereas besieged towns fell when their defenders faced similar difficulties.[79]

However, while gunpowder stocks sometimes exploded due to accidents, I could not find any occasion when such stocks were the target of a special operation.[80] The apparent neglect of this type of targets is perplexing. Perhaps it indicates that medieval conceptions of special operations continued to dominate military thinking and to obscure some of the new realities and opportunities of war in the wake of the gunpowder revolution.[81]

People

Political, military, and religious leaders were the other major target of special operations, for such leaders were often the sole thing that held together not only the enemy army, but the entire war effort. There were no standing armies and no permanent military hierarchies in the age of chivalry, so that it is impossible to speak of the medieval or Renaissance 'French Army' or 'Aragonese Army' as one speaks today of the US Army. There were only a varying number of 'French' and 'Aragonese' hosts, each of them an *ad hoc* conglomerate pieced together for a particular campaign out of feudal contingents, mercenary bands, town militias, allied auxiliaries, and individual drifters. At the end of the campaign the host dispersed back to its ingredients, and next year's host was invariably a different conglomerate.[82]

Loyalties were only slightly more enduring than armies. Though ties between individual men and their leaders could be extremely strong and long-lasting, armies as a whole were a different matter. Throughout the Middle Ages and the Renaissance armies were plagued by ill discipline, desertion, rebellion, and downright treason. Many armies were based on shifting alliances, and today's friend could well be tomorrow's enemy. Feudal loyalties, particularly in times of civil wars and wars of succession, were often fickle. Mercenary loyalties were even less certain, and soldiers, captains, and entire contingents sometimes mutinied or defected from one camp to the other in the middle of a campaign. If this was thought odious, it was the most natural thing in the world for a soldier, a captain, or a contingent to serve one prince in one campaigning season, and switch to his rival in the next.[83] In the sixteenth century whole armies seemed to be playing a giant game of musical chairs. With Swiss, Italian, and German contingents constantly switching their allegiances, roughly the same contingents that constituted the 'French' army in one battle, might well become the 'Habsburg' army in the next, and vice versa.

What caused soldiers to join (and leave) such armies was a variety of personal motives. Chief among these were usually loyalty to their feudal lord and to their particular friends; hope of regular pay, booty, and enrichment; hope for social status and advancement; desire to gain honour and to establish their masculine identity; and desire for adventure. Patriotic and religious feelings were normally of lesser importance.[84]

Armies composed and motivated in such a way were often held together only by the person of their commander. The loyalty of many units was to the commander rather than to any abstract ideal or political entity. To some he was their feudal lord, to some their friend or ally, to some their paymaster.[85] Thus the armies that Edward III led into northern France in 1339 and 1340 were comprised partly from vassals of the king of England, vassals of the duke of Aquitaine, and vassals of the count of Ponthieu (who, due to genealogical coincidence, were the same person); partly from mercenaries paid by the king of England; partly by vassals and mercenaries of various princes of the Holy Roman Empire, who allied themselves to Edward in his guise as Deputy of the Empire; and partly by Flemish forces and French malcontents who joined the flag of King Edward I of France in his war against the usurper Philip de Valois (by another genealogical coincidence, Edward I of France was of course Edward III of England).[86] The importance of the commander is evident from the many occasions when entire armies fell apart the moment he died. For example, when Emperor Frederick Barbarossa drowned on his way to the Holy Land (1190), the huge Crusader army he led quickly disintegrated, despite never having suffered any military setback.

Just as loyalty and motivation focused on the commander, so too whatever military hierarchy existed usually reflected the commander's social and family ties. Commanding a medieval or Renaissance army was not so much a matter of having tactical and strategic genius, as of having the right family connections and social skills. The various feudal and mercenary contingents comprising the army were loyal to different noblemen and mercenary captains. These men were not ideal subordinates. The noblemen in particular were usually autonomous territorial rulers who were not used to taking orders from anyone. They were frequently hostile to one another, and they were always very jealous of their honour. Commanders managed to make such hosts function militarily only because they commanded the familial or social obedience of these noblemen. This was the reason why military command was frequently entrusted to royal scions without any military experience or tactical skills in preference of seasoned and skilled veterans. This was also the reason why such royal scions not infrequently performed their role with relative success.[87]

Not only armies, but also kingdoms and empires were often held together only by the person of their ruler, for medieval politics were a family business. Large and often unlikely political constellations coalesced around rising dynasties. When a dynasty died out, these constellations either disintegrated back to

their smaller ingredients, or gravitated into the orbit of an even more powerful dynasty. Modern nations such as Britain, France, and Spain were united at
first by means of family alliances, and it took centuries for national identities
to replace the dynastic identities that conceived them. The different territories
comprising the Plantagenet 'empire' of the late twelfth century were welded
together only because they were the family possession of Henry II and Richard
I, inherited from different ancestors.[88] In the Middle East the Ayyubid Empire
was similarly the property of Saladin's family. In the fourteenth and fifteenth
centuries Burgundy became a major European power thanks to shrewd marriage alliances. Yet all of these family enterprises were dwarfed by that of the
Habsburgs. The Habsburgs began as minor Swiss landowners, but by the end
of the sixteenth century their patchwork of family possessions covered Europe
from the North Sea to Gibraltar, and sprawled the world from the Philippines
to Mexico.

Just as armies and empires were a family business, so too the aims of war
were often the personal or family aims of the commander. War was 'a continuation of litigation by other means',[89] fought by princes for dynastic interests and
rights of inheritance.[90] Except for the Crusades, all major conflicts of the eras
– such as the Aragonese–Angevin wars, the Hundred Years War, the Wars of
the Roses, and the Italian Wars – were to a large extent conflicts over dynastic
rights of inheritance. No European kingdom, duchy or county was spared its
wars of succession.

Since war depended to such an extent on the person of its leaders, a successful attack on the enemy leader could in some cases secure complete victory in
war without any need of battles, sieges, and campaigns. For instance, in 1127–8
the murder of Count Charles the Good of Flanders sparked a succession war
between William Clito and Thierry of Alsace, the two claimants to the county.
William decisively defeated Thierry at the battle of Axspoele (1128).[91] Flanders
succumbed to the victor, but, as William conducted a mopping-up operation
against the remnants of Thierry's supporters, a foot soldier in the garrison of
Aalst inflicted on him a minor flesh wound. William neglected to take proper
care of wound, it developed gangrene, and a few days later he was dead. This
ended the war, and the defeated Thierry was unanimously acclaimed count of
Flanders even by his erstwhile enemies.[92]

In other cases the death of a prince could lead to the disintegration of kingdoms and empires, especially if the succession was in dispute. For example,
when Saladin died in 1193 the Ayyubid Empire was quickly carved up between
a greedy host of sons, brothers, and nephews. The death of Duke Charles of
Burgundy at Nancy (1477) led to the even quicker disintegration of Burgundy.
Charles's great-grandson, Emperor Charles V, sought to avoid a similar fate by
abdicating in 1556 and dividing his vast empire between his son, Philip II of
Spain, and his brother, the Emperor Ferdinand I.

Even if the succession was not disputed, the transfer of power usually required much political reconfiguration, which could momentarily incapacitate kingdoms, or even doom them to long periods of turmoil – especially if the legitimate heir was a minor or a woman. The fall of the First Kingdom of Jerusalem resulted to a large extent from the succession crisis of the 1180s, whereas the chronic weakness of the resuscitated kingdom in the thirteenth century stemmed from the fact that it was ruled by a chain of minors, regents, and absentee lords, rather than by an adult male king. When a prince was held captive, it could have even worse consequences, since the prince himself could not wield effective power, whereas whoever was regent could never establish his power firmly. England during the captivity of Richard I, France during the captivity of Jean II, and Scotland during the captivity of David II all faced internal chaos and external disaster.

Enemy leaders were therefore prime military targets. In battle great efforts were made to locate the enemy leader and direct the attack against him, and equally great efforts were made to protect one's own leader. Gillingham in particular stresses that 'the surest way to win a battle was to kill or capture the opposing commander'.[93] The most famous demonstrations of this maxim are the killing of Harold at Hastings (1066), which decided not only the fate of the battle, but of Anglo-Saxon England as well; and the killing of Richard III at Bosworth (1485), which similarly decided the outcome of the Wars of the Roses.

At Conquereuil (992) and Elster (1085), the death of the victorious commanders turned their triumph into a defeat.[94] The deaths in battle of Gaston de Foix (1512), Charles duke of Bourbon (1527), and Maurice of Saxony (1553) are three famous examples for how the death of a general could, even in the sixteenth century, turn victory into something much closer to a defeat. In another celebrated incident, the French came close to defeat at the battle of Bouvines (1214) when a heavy attack directed against Philip August nearly killed him.[95] At Nicosia (1229) twenty-five knights were detailed to attack and kill the enemy commander.[96]

Accordingly, killing or kidnapping an enemy leader by a special operation could be an even more devastating blow than capturing a major strongpoint. Such a blow often deprived the enemy of the linchpin that held together the loyalties of the different soldiers and commanders, and could thereby lead to the breakdown of entire armies. Moreover, in the case of inheritance and succession wars, the killing or kidnapping of the enemy prince could eliminate the very reason for the war. Even if the war was not one of succession, in many cases such a blow could lead to either the momentary incapacitation of the enemy kingdom, or to its total disintegration.

The effectiveness of targeting enemy leaders was most clearly demonstrated by the Shi'ite Nizari sect, better known as the sect of the *Hashishin* or the Assassins. This small persecuted sect, which did not command any significant territorial, economic, demographic, or military resources, nevertheless managed to become an important power in the twelfth- and thirteenth-century Middle East thanks to its systematic use of subterfuge and assassination. The sect's trained and highly motivated assassins infiltrated princely households and penetrated princely bodyguards with disconcerting efficiency. It methodically eliminated and terrorized hostile enemy leaders, and ingratiated itself with potential allies by killing or terrorizing their particular enemies.

In the sect's heyday, kings and rulers throughout the Middle East and Europe sought to buy its goodwill by adopting a friendly attitude towards it, and perhaps by paying it protection money as well. Only the Military Orders of the Templars and Hospitallers felt safe from the Nizaris, and the latter had to pay tribute to the Military Orders rather than vice versa. The crusader memoirist, Jean de Joinville, explains this anomaly by the fact that the Nizaris' leader knew that 'if he had either the Master of the Temple or of the Hospital killed, another, equally good, would be put in his place; therefore he had nothing to gain by their death. Consequently, he had no wish to sacrifice his Assassins on a project that would bring him no advantage.'[97] That is to say, since the Orders were bureaucratic organizations rather than family enterprises, and since they were held together by means of hierarchical discipline rather than family and feudal ties, the removal of their leaders could not seriously disrupt their functioning.[98]

The rise of the centralized dynastic state at the end of the Middle Ages and through the Renaissance only increased the effectiveness of political murder, because it made the person of the ruler more important than ever. This fact was recognized by Machiavelli, whose *Prince* recommends murder and kidnapping as legitimate political tools. Similarly, in Thomas More's *Utopia* the Utopians' favourite means of waging war is to have the enemy leaders assassinated or kidnapped. More acknowledges that such a way of warfare is often considered mean and cruel, but, he writes, 'the Utopians are very proud of it. They say it is extremely sensible to dispose of major wars like this without fighting a single battle, and also most humane to save thousands of innocent lives at the cost of a few guilty ones.'[99]

In short, then, assassinating enemy leaders was probably the most cost-effective way of waging war in the age of chivalry. Since under the influence of chivalric culture politics were a matter of personal ties, and since the borders of kingdoms and empires were accordingly shaped by family inheritance laws, the carefully calculated murder of a handful of individuals could redraw the map of Europe far more effectively than any number of military campaigns.[100] One can hardly begin to estimate the consequences for European history if in 1152 Louis VII had sent an assassination squad to murder Eleanor of Aquitaine before she could marry Henry Plantagenet. Similarly, what would have happened if in 1498 French agents had poisoned Juana of Castile and Philip Habsburg, before the couple sired any offspring?

The advantages to be gained from killing or kidnapping enemy leaders were so huge that many were consequently tempted to use methods that flew in the face of chivalric conventions. For instance, during his siege of Bari (1068–71) Robert Guiscard had the Byzantine governor assassinated. The Byzantines themselves, less encumbered by chivalric traditions, were equally unscrupulous, and tried to have Guiscard assassinated in his turn. According to William of Apulia, a Byzantine hit-man managed to get inside Guiscard's tent and was about to kill him, but the Norman leader ducked his head under a table to spit just as the assassin threw a poisoned javelin at him. Guiscard then built a stone house for himself, so that he might feel more secure at night.[101]

On 19 May 1106 Count Geoffrey Martel of Anjou besieged the castle of Candé. When the garrison leaders saw that all hope was lost, they went out to parley with the count. However, as Geoffrey came nearer to speak with them, a marksman from the walls killed him with a well-aimed crossbow bolt, perhaps with the connivance of his treacherous superiors.[102] In 1119 Henry I of England besieged the citadel of Breteuil, held against him by Juliana, his own natural daughter. According to Orderic Vitalis, Juliana asked her father to meet with her and discuss terms of surrender. When the king approached, Juliana herself shot at him with a crossbow, but missed. When the citadel was captured, Henry spared his daughter's life, but forced her to leap half-naked from the battlements into the icy waters of the moat below.[103]

In 1127 Flanders was shocked by the murder of Count Charles the Good (see illus. 4). The conspirators, a group of disaffected noblemen, not only murdered their feudal lord, but they did so in church, during Lent, while the count was praying and giving alms to the poor.[104] In 1228 Frederick II broke all the rules of hospitality when he took prisoner the leaders of the Ibelin family and the king of Cyprus during a feast which they held in his honour.[105] At the following siege of Kantara (1230) a sharpshooter tracked down the commander of the garrison and killed him with a crossbow bolt, leading to the surrender of the disheartened garrison.[106]

In 1333 Edward Balliol, the claimant to the Scottish throne, nearly overran the whole of Scotland. His enemies sued for a truce, and numerous noblemen who had previously opposed him now flocked to offer him homage. However, some of these turned out to be traitors who helped a small force under Archibald Douglas to surprise Balliol's camp in a dawn attack. Balliol's only brother and many others of his followers were killed, while the claimant himself barely escaped with his life, fleeing half naked and wearing only one boot. His position in Scotland quickly crumbled.[107]

In 1353 King Charles the Bad of Navarre had Charles of Spain, the French Constable, murdered.[108] In 1356 he apparently conspired to kidnap or assassinate King Jean II of France along with the French crown prince.[109] Shortly afterwards the crown prince invited Charles the Bad to a reconciliation banquet at the castle of Rouen. During the banquet a troop of French soldiers led by King Jean in person seized the king of Navarre and many of his followers.[110]

In 1369 King Peter I of Cyprus was murdered by a group of discontented noblemen. In 1386 King Charles of Naples and Hungary was assassinated at Buda Castle by agents of the dowager Queen Elizabeth.[111] In 1389, on the eve of the fateful battle of Kossovo, a Serbian nobleman gained an audience with Sultan Murad I on the pretext that he wished to join his cause. He used the opportunity to assassinate the sultan, which could have saved Serbia from catastrophe, if Murad's son – Bajazet I – had not seized the moment and asserted his authority in a decisive manner.

In 1392 the duke of Brittany attempted to assassinate in a night ambush his arch-enemy, the Constable of France, Olivier de Clisson. In 1419 Duke Jean the Fearless was murdered on the bridge at Montereau during a summit meeting with the Dauphine. Half a century later Jean's grandson took King Louis XI captive at Peronne (1468), when the later made an uncharacteristic mistake and paid him a diplomatic visit without taking the necessary precautions.

Particularly telling was the life story of King James I of Scotland. In 1406 his elder brother was murdered by his uncle, the duke of Albany. James was sent to France for safety, but was captured *en route* by the English, and remained in English captivity for eighteen years. He was eventually released for a large ransom and promises of good behaviour, and was also provided with an English wife. Upon his return the king waged a civil war against Albany and his relations. On 20 February 1437 James was visiting the Blackfriars monastery in Perth. At about 1 a.m. the Earl of Atholl – brother of the duke of Albany – and thirty companions surprised the monastery, entered the king's chamber, and murdered him.[112] James's son, King James II, waged an equally bitter war against the Douglas family, who were his guardians during his early years. In 1439 James invited the Earl of Douglas and his brother to dinner in Edinburgh castle, and then had them murdered. Several years later, he invited the new Earl of Douglas to a reconciliation dinner at Stirling castle. Though he gave Douglas all the safe-conducts he requested, in the middle of dinner James stabbed Douglas to death with his own hands.

Even the princes of the church were not safe from such dangers. In 1075 Pope Gregory VII was abducted from the church of Santa Maria Maggiore in Rome while saying mass. In 1170 Archbishop Thomas Becket was murdered at Canterbury by agents of King Henry II. In 1208 the papal legate to Languedoc, Peter of Castlenau, was assassinated by a Cathar sympathizer, sparking the Albigensian Crusade. In 1225 Archbishop Engelbert II of Cologne was assassinated by disaffected noblemen. In 1242 the Church's Chief Inquisitor in Languedoc, responsible for the brutal persecution of the Cathars there, was trapped by Cathar raiders and killed together with his aides. In 1303 Pope Boniface VIII was abducted from the papal palace at Anagni; this apparently caused his death shortly thereafter.

In the sixteenth century assassination and abduction were used even more extensively in Europe, especially during the wars of religion. For example, during the French Wars of Religion Duke François and Duke Henry of Guise, leaders of the Catholic faction, were assassinated in 1563 and 1588 respectively; the Admiral Coligny and most other Huguenot leaders were assassinated in the famous St Bartholomew's Day Massacre (1572), after several earlier attempts on the Admiral's life failed; King Henry III was assassinated in 1589, and his heir Henry IV in 1610. In the Netherlands William the Silent, the Protestant leader, was assassinated in 1584.

The higher military echelons were targeted almost as often as the so-called political echelons. For instance, during the Schmalkaldic War of 1546 the Catholic generals tried to arrange the assassination of Sebastian Schertlin von Burtenbach, the Protestant commander-in-chief. On 29 September 1546 they hired Banthaleon von Lindau to infiltrate the Protestant camp near Donauwörth and kill Schertlin, promising to pay him 3,000 florins for his pains. (Lindau had hitherto been a common soldier, earning only 1 florin a day.) The assassin, who had served in Schertlin's own regiment on a previous campaign, found it very easy to infiltrate the Protestant camp. He disguised himself as a servant, and entered Schertlin's tent about 2 o'clock at night. Schertlin, who did not sleep well, woke up and asked Lindau – whom he mistook for a servant – what he was doing there with a drawn weapon. Lindau charged him, and his first blow injured Schertlin in his foot. Schertlin groped for his sword, but Lindau struck again, missing the throat by a few inches, and hitting the general's right shoulder instead. Lindau then repeatedly tried to stab Schertlin to death, while the latter defended himself with his two fists, and tried to keep the tent's main post between himself and his assailant. Eventually Schertlin managed to flee the tent, with Lindau hard on his heels. Only then did Schertlin's son and several of his attendants wake up, fall upon Lindau, and capture him. He was beheaded soon after.[113]

Outside Europe, too, early modern Europeans frequently relied on such underhand methods. During the conquest of Mexico (1519–21) Hernando Cortés quickly realized that his few hundred Spaniards could not hope to conquer the Mexican Empire by themselves. They faced tens of thousands of Mexican warriors, and the empire's subjected people were so afraid of their overlords that few of them dared to offer the Spaniards any help. Cortés therefore based his initial strategy on the hope of capturing the person of Emperor Montezuma II. Setting the precedent for aliens in Hollywood science-fiction films, from the moment Cortés set foot in the New World he pretended to be a diplomatic envoy, and repeatedly asked the natives he met to take him to their leader. Montezuma was rightly apprehensive of the Spaniard's intentions, and tried to delay the requested interview by polite excuses as well as by armed force. He eventually agreed to meet Cortés inside the imperial palace at Tenochtitlan. Though Montezuma had tens of thousands of warriors in the city, and hundreds of palace guards, Cortés relied on the overwhelming superiority that steel weapons gave the conquistadors in hand-to-hand fighting to capture the emperor during one of their diplomatic interviews (14 November 1519).[114] The centralistic Mexican Empire was paralysed for months, and though the Mexicans eventually repudiated the captive Montezuma, by the time they attacked Cortés their prestige and power suffered a crippling blow, and Cortés was able to establish a vast native coalition against them.

When Francisco Pizarro invaded the Inca Empire in 1531/2, he consciously imitated Cortés's strategy. He too pretended that his puny expeditionary force – 168 men and a handful of horses – was a diplomatic embassy, and asked for an interview with the Inca Atahuallpa. Atahuallpa, heading a force of at least 50,000 men, felt he had little need to fear Pizarro. On the morning of 16 November 1532 he came to meet Pizarro at the main square of Cajamarca, accompanied by thousands of armed men. However, the Inca warriors were no match in close combat for the Spaniards' horses and steel weapons, and Atahuallpa was captured, which enabled the tiny conquistador band to make the first decisive steps towards the subjugation of the Inca Empire. The ransom extracted from Atahuallpa amounted to 1.5 million ducats, an almost incredible sum in sixteenth-century Spain. Charles V's yearly income from the Kingdom of Castile amounted in 1539 to about 1 million ducats, which was also equivalent to the entire cost of the emperor's great expedition against Tunis in 1535.[115]

✦

The main drawback of the use of assassination and abduction was that these were dishonourable ways to fight, and while they fully utilized the weaknesses created by the dominant political culture, they weakened this culture as a whole. It was a classic case of the 'Prisoner's Dilemma'. The first to use such methods systematically was likely to gain immense rewards, but soon everyone would be forced to follow, and the political order would have to be changed, to the detriment of all rulers. It is telling, for example, that the medieval Middle East and Renaissance Italy were characterized both by far more recourse to assassination as a military tool and by far less stable dynasties and territorial entities than western Europe.[116]

In western Europe, despite the widespread use of assassination and abduction against heretics and infidels, and despite their occasional use against fellow Christians, these practices remained taboo, which contributed to the relative stability of feudal politics. Except for some Italian princelings and despots, no major political or military power in medieval or Renaissance Europe tried to imitate the Nizaris and the Utopians by making assassination a standard political or military tool, or by training special assassin forces. Even when assassination was practised as a military tool, it was acknowledged as a dirty and shameful method of warfare, rather than a humane and rational one.

The cultural taboo on assassinations and abductions meant that even when such operations were successful, they could still be costly in terms of prestige, whereas failure was always sure to be a propaganda disaster, unlike failure on the battlefield, which was often seen as honourable.[117] The fate of the Nizaris themselves is also indicative. When the Mongols conquered the Middle East their great Khan, fearful that he himself would sooner or later fall victim to their daggers and resentful that his invincible conventional armies could not protect him from such a threat, gave orders to totally wipe the sect off the face of the earth. All the Nizaris' efforts to placate the Mongols were doomed, and the majority of Nizari followers in Persia, the sect's main centre, were methodically killed by the fearful Mongols. This genocide was largely lauded by many of the Nizaris' Muslim neighbours, who were glad to be relieved of this menace.[118]

It is also telling that, even with the alleged rationalization of war from the eighteenth century onwards, kidnapping and assassination have remained a military taboo, a remnant of the chivalric martial ethos that sacrifices victory on the altar of honour and caste interest, and protects world leaders from the long hand of their enemies.[119] In his 1983 article on special operations David Thomas argues that chivalric considerations of honour have hampered special operations long into the twentieth century, for career officers commonly held such operations to be 'incompatible with the military code of honour'.[120] Yet Thomas himself, though he attempts to present a comprehensive overview of the recent history and future potential of special operations, avoids discussion of the conduct and usefulness of assassination.

Anyone who is inclined to dismiss the 'fair play' rules of chivalry as mere fantasy and to believe that in war any and every means is used to secure victory, need only think of the present-day controversies and limitations placed over the practice of targeted killings and political assassinations. Even at the height of the Cold War, Presidents, Chairmen, and Marshals who laid calculated plans for the complete destruction of the human race still looked askance at the assassination of their fellow leaders. For instance, in 1976 US President Gerald Ford issued Executive Order 11905 which outlawed employees of the US Government from conspiring political assassinations, an order upheld by President Reagan's Executive Order 12333 and by every subsequent US president.[121]

✦

In contrast to assassinating enemy leaders, rescuing one's own captive leaders was usually a legitimate and laudable – as well as highly profitable – enterprise. In economic terms, it could save much money, for the ransom of a captive prince was often larger than a kingdom's yearly income.[122] The political and military benefits were potentially even greater, for it could save armies and kingdoms from paralysis and disintegration. For instance, in 1142 King Stephen trapped Empress Matilda in Oxford Castle and closely besieged her. Had he captured her, Matilda's cause would probably have collapsed and the civil war ended. However, the Empress managed to escape the castle and make her way

unobserved through Stephen's camp, perhaps with the help of some loyal sup-
porter in the besieging host.[123]

In 1357 King Charles the Bad of Navarre was languishing as a prisoner in the
fortress of Arleux. One of his most loyal followers, Jean de Picquigny, attacked
the fortress in the early morning of 9 November, with about thirty men. They
scaled the walls in secrecy and snatched Charles away safely. His release dramatically changed the balance of power in France. Charles assumed the leading
role in the opposition to the tottering Valois dynasty, and nearly engineered its
collapse.[124]

Rescue operations could nonetheless involve the use of foul methods, such
as bribery and deceit. In particular, problems arose if the captive prince gave
his word of honour that he would not try to escape. For example, in 1346/7 the
sixteen-year-old count of Flanders, Louis de Mâle, was held prisoner by his
own subjects due to his pro-French inclinations. He was carefully watched day
and night by twenty guards, so that, according to Jean le Bel, 'he could hardly
piss in private'. In March 1347 Louis finally gave his word of honour not only
to be a dutiful ally of King Edward III, but also to marry Isabella, Edward's
daughter. He was consequently given more freedom of movement and better
living conditions. A week before the marriage ceremony Louis made use of this
newly acquired freedom to go hawking. By a pre-arranged scheme, he slipped
away from his escort while chasing a bird, put spurs to his horse, and made it
safely to France.[125]

Such conduct was highly problematic. It was common to guard captive
knights lightly, give them freedom of movement and comfortable living conditions, and even release them completely, if they gave their word of honour
to fulfil certain obligations. Count Louis's behaviour therefore threatened all
noblemen, and was dubious even in the eyes of the French court. Louis's overlord, King Jean II of France, behaved very differently when he became an English prisoner at the battle of Poitiers (1356). After giving his word of honour
to remain a prisoner, he discouraged French attempts to rescue him. Later
he was released from captivity upon certain conditions, including that some
members of the French royal family should be held at Calais as hostages to
the fulfilment of these conditions. When one of the hostages – Jean's second
son, Louis of Anjou – broke his parole, escaped from Calais, and refused to
return, King Jean was so outraged by this behaviour that he voluntarily surrendered himself back into English hands, becoming a prisoner yet again
(1364).[126]

✦

The late Middle Ages and the Renaissance also witnessed the beginning of the
Scientific Revolution. However, scientists and technicians never became targets for special operations. Though rulers and scientists alike began to dream of
developing new 'wonder' weapons as a means to gain military advantages, these

dreams were never realized. Technology certainly had an increasing influence on war, but this influence was largely due to the slow improvement of known weapon systems rather than to the sudden invention of new ones. The shady characters who introduced gunpowder to Europe and developed the first firearms in the early fourteenth century were no Nils Bohrs, and the immediate impact of their efforts on the military balance of power was negligible at best. Similarly, Leonardo da Vinci probably had far smaller military and political value than any number of Italian princelings and *condottieri*. The submarines, helicopters, and tanks he envisioned may enthral modern readers, but any Renaissance ruler who might have tried to build them would merely have wasted valuable time and money.[127]

Symbols

The most potent political and military symbols in the age of chivalry were princes and fortified places. Hence by killing a prince or storming a fortified place, a special operation simultaneously affected the material balance of power, and delivered a devastating symbolic blow.

By contrast, common people had no symbolic value in chivalric wars. Unlike modern democracies, medieval and early modern monarchies were not committed to do their utmost to safeguard the life of each and every subject. Hence, though civilians were frequently kidnapped and held for ransom in the Middle Ages and the Renaissance, it was mainly a means for combatants to get extra cash rather than a means to wage psychological warfare, and rulers made no serious efforts to rescue such civilians.[128]

While common people were therefore uninviting targets for special operations, there was a plethora of sacred objects which could tempt such operations. Relics in particular were considered important war trophies, and medieval chronicles abound with both true and fictitious stories of operations mounted specifically to steal or rescue a coveted relic. Perhaps the most famous such story was the Venetian theft of the body of St Mark the Evangelist. One of the most revered saints of Christendom, Mark was Bishop of Alexandria and was buried near the large Egyptian port. According to an unverifiable Venetian tradition, in 828 Venetian merchants stole St Mark's miraculously preserved corpse from its closely guarded tomb, replacing it, to avoid suspicion, with the corpse of another saint of lesser status. They then had several hair-raising adventures smuggling the holy corpse past the watchful harbour officials, at one point covering it with pieces of pork to repel the Muslim inquirers, and at another point hoisting it up to their ship's yard-arm. They ultimately brought it safely to Venice, whose patron saint St Mark now became. The possession of St Mark's body gave an important boost to the city's prestige and political standing. No city in Catholic Europe except Rome and Santiago de Compostela could boast such a sacred relic, and its possession buttressed the Venetians' claim for ecclesiastical autonomy.[129] This particular story may well be pure invention, but many other relics were certainly stolen and rescued during the Middle Ages.[130]

Some sacred objects such as St Mark's body gained great political significance, and became important national symbols. In theory, such objects in particular should have served as prime targets for special operations. Surprisingly, however, I could not trace any example of a special operation aimed to steal or destroy such a national symbol.

For instance, from 497 to the French Revolution the kings of France were anointed at their coronation with oil from the Holy Ampulla, which supposedly descended from heaven during Clovis's coronation, and which was preserved in Rheims Cathedral. This oil was of great political significance, proving the divine right of the kings of France. In 1429 Jeanne d'Arc chose to utilize her victory at Orleans by leading the French army in an attack on the city of Rheims. Though in purely military terms the choice of Rheims was hardly sound, politically Jeanne's success in capturing the place and then crowning Charles VII in the city's cathedral with the holy oil was a great public relations victory. The English reacted by crowning Henry VI of England as Henry II of France in 1431, but they had to crown him in Notre Dame Cathedral in Paris and without the holy oil, thereby depriving the coronation of much of its symbolic power, and actually demonstrating the declining fortune of the English. Theoretically, stealing the Holy Ampulla from Rheims, or torching Rheims Cathedral before Charles's coronation, could have been a worthwhile goal for a special operation, but as far as we know, it was never even debated.[131]

Another case in point is the Stone of Scone. Until 1292 generations of Scottish kings were crowned on this stone, which became a national Scottish symbol. In 1296, after conquering Scotland, Edward I hauled the Stone to London, where it was incorporated into a new coronation throne, which from 1308 until 1953 was used to crown the kings and queens of England, symbolizing their claim to overlordship over Scotland as well. One of the conditions of the 'Shameful Peace' imposed by King Robert Bruce of Scotland on the English in 1328 was the return of the Stone, but the English never complied. During Christmas 1950 four Scottish students stole the Stone from the coronation chair in Westminster Abbey, but it was found and brought back four months later. In 1996 the British government finally returned the Stone to Scotland, in response to growing demands from Scottish nationalists.[132] Unlike the 1950 students, no Scottish warriors of the Middle Ages or the Renaissance are known to have attempted to reclaim the Stone by force from Westminster.

Similarly, after losing their most cherished relic – a piece of the True Cross – at the battle of Hattin (1187), the Franks of Jerusalem repeatedly haggled to regain possession of it by diplomatic means. Whenever they negotiated or signed a treaty with Saladin and his heirs, they raised the issue of the True Cross, asking for its return. However, as far as we know, they never attempted to snatch it back by force.[133]

Weapon Systems

Whereas in the late-modern era weapon systems have been an important target for special operations, in the age of chivalry they were not as tempting. On land, the biggest and costliest medieval weapon systems were siege engines. During sieges, defenders frequently made raids targeting the besiegers' siege engines, which could become the objects of fierce combat.[134] However, their cost and their overall strategic impact were limited, and it was never worth while to mount a special operation simply in order to destroy a trebuchet.[135]

The introduction of firearms did not change the situation. Indeed, cannon were often cheaper and more numerous than the old mechanical siege artillery, which individually made them even less valuable as targets (though at least during the 1453 siege of Constantinople, a gunner was accused of blowing up the Byzantines' largest cannon after receiving a bribe from the Ottomans).[136]

This situation reflected the fundamental character of war in the age of chivalry. Even after the gunpowder revolution, technology played a relatively minor part in war, and individual men were far more valuable than individual weapons. It was only the accelerated technologization of war in the nineteenth and twentieth centuries that transformed weapon systems into valuable targets.

It should be noted that in the age of chivalry, weapons were of little importance not only as targets of special operations, but also as instruments of such operations. In the late modern era special forces often have at their disposal advanced and expensive technology that gives them an important edge when facing larger numbers of regular enemy troops. In some cases, innovative technology unknown to the enemy plays a crucial role in achieving surprise.[137] In contrast, special operations in the age of chivalry almost never relied on special technology. Fighting edge and surprise had to be achieved by different methods.

Special Forces?

Though special operations were an important part of war in the age of chivalry, special forces hardly existed, with the possible exception of the Nizari assassins. There were no medieval equivalents of the SAS or the SEALs. Whereas today it is emphasized that the only thing that makes special forces 'special' is their unique training,[138] in the age of chivalry no units were raised and trained specifically for the performance of special operations. Indeed, one of the characteristics of war in the age of chivalry is that there were few specialized or permanent military units of any kind.

With certain important exceptions such as the Templar, Hospitaller and Teuton Military Orders and the Spanish *tercios*,[139] most military units were *ad hoc* formations. There were no equivalents to the modern regiments and brigades with their peculiar identities, *esprit de corps*, habits, and loyalties, which sometimes endure for decades and centuries.[140] Similarly, there was little collective formal training. Individual warriors may have spent years training in riding or the use of sword, bow, and arquebus, but until the rise of standardized drill in the late sixteenth century, unit training was minimal at best.[141]

Individuals occasionally acquired considerable experience in such operations and became self-trained experts. For example, in 1443 the city of Luxembourg was stormed thanks to the efforts of two *eschelleurs*, i.e., experts in scaling walls, who first infiltrated it and scouted its fortifications, then led a raiding party to strike against its defences' weakest link. Olivier de la Marche, commander of Duke Charles of Burgundy's bodyguard, became an expert in kidnapping foreign princes (see chapter 6). Many freebooter captains, such as the Bascot de Mauléon, became experts in the storming of fortified places.

Yet though individuals who acquired special skills were to be found in most medieval and Renaissance armies, they were not grouped or trained together as special forces, and when a special operation was called for, commanders did not always turn to these self-made experts. Many special operations were performed by regular formations. Thus the Burgundian attempt to surprise the town of Huy in 1467 was entrusted to the regular company of the lord of Fiennes even though it was, according to one of Fiennes' men, an extraordinarily dangerous enterprise.[142] Not a few special operations were even performed by civilians, such as the fifty peasants who banded together in at attempt to assassinate Emperor Charles V at the village of Muy (1536).[143] In particular, the agents and double-agents used in treasonous plots were frequently civilians without prior military experience, such as the merchant Garunchin who trapped Count Pietro Porto in 1543.

Sometimes commanders at least took care to entrust such delicate missions to their best troops, as the Liégeois did in their attempt to kill Duke Charles of Burgundy (see chapter 6). But in many cases the choice seems to have been completely arbitrary. For example, the mission of raiding the Auriol mill (see chapter 7) was first offered to the commander of one regular formation. When he refused, it was offered to the commander of another regular formation, and was again refused. Eventually, a third officer volunteered to undertake it, and collected for that purpose a force of volunteers from different regular formations.

Despite the absence of specially trained forces, medieval and Renaissance regular troops were better equipped to undertake special operations than might at first be assumed. Let us take, for example, the company of the lord of Fiennes, which was entrusted with the 1467 raid on Huy, and in whose ranks served the memoirist Jean de Haynin. Its men, mostly noblemen from the region of Hainault, had ample individual training. Late medieval noblemen practised riding and the use of weapons since early childhood. Hunting forays, tournaments, and other chivalric sports further honed these skills as well as the men's physical fitness. Many of them had also served on previous campaigns. For instance, Haynin had served on a number of campaigns since the 1450s, including three different campaigns in 1465–7.[144]

It is commonly argued that collective skills are more important than individual skills, particularly in special operations. Military thinking since the Second World War – galvanized by studies such as S. L. A. Marshall's *Men against Fire*, Morris Janowitz and Edward A. Shils's 'Cohesion and Disintegration in the Wehrmacht in World War II', Martin Van Creveld's *Fighting Power*, and John A. Lynn's *Bayonets of the Republic* – has emphasized in particular the importance of small unit cohesion. This is seen as the prime factor in the success of regular operations, and even more so in the success of special operations.[145] Though it is true that Fiennes' company received little formal collective training, and was not a permanent standing unit, it nevertheless enjoyed an extraordinary amount of unit cohesion, which few modern formations could boast.

Though the company was formed anew for each campaign and disbanded at the end of the campaign, its personnel remained largely the same. Most of the company's men came from a small area in the County of Hainault, and knew each other well in civilian life. They were bonded by formal feudal and familial ties, as well as by less formal ties of friendship.[146] They were mostly Fiennes' own vassals, retainers, and family members, and each of them brought to the company his own little band of long-term followers.[147] Jean de Haynin, for example, was a vassal and friend of Fiennes. He served in the company together with his step-brother, Collart de Vendegies, and brought with him a retinue of between twelve and twenty soldiers and pages, whom Haynin raised from his own domains and whom he personally commanded on campaign.[148]

For Haynin and the other men in the company each campaign started when they assembled together in their home area, and they remained together throughout the campaign. They were bonded not only by the experiences of major battles such as Montlhéry (1465) and Brusthem (1467), in which they always fought together, but also by the more mundane experiences of life on campaign.[149] They normally lodged and foraged together, building up a strong company spirit *vis-à-vis* other formations in the army. For instance, Haynin tells how during the 1465 campaign they lodged at the village of Gerpinne, and that when the company of the lord of Neuville arrived at the village after midnight and tried to dislodge them, it almost led to a fight between the two companies.[150]

In mercenary forces, too, small-unit cohesion could be extremely strong. Though mercenary armies were very ephemeral affairs, the small mercenary bands that were the building blocks of these armies sometimes stayed together for years and decades. A successful mercenary captain such as the Bascot de Mauléon may have served one prince in one campaign, another prince on another campaign, and may have set up a private robbery and protection racket on other opportunities, yet his own band of followers stayed with him through all these changes of allegiance.[151]

In the Renaissance such long-lasting military bonds often took more formalized shape. Soldiers organized themselves in formal 'families' of comrades called *cameradas*, which contained half a dozen to a dozen men. Such groups existed among senior ranks too, and in most companies the captains had a *camerada* made up of attendants and accompanying gentlemen.[152] The *camerada* was the real centre of a soldier's life. It was very difficult to survive in an army outside such a group. While living in a *camerada*, soldiers often pooled their money and possessions. The *camerada* arranged food and lodging for its members, tended to the sick, and sometimes even took care of widows and orphans, and saw to the execution of wills. Comrades occasionally remained together even when the war was over.[153]

Hence despite the lack of standing armies and formalized collective training, many small 'regular' formations in medieval and Renaissance armies had both the individual skills and the group cohesion needed in order to execute special operations. Moreover, as the following chapters demonstrate, even groups of men with no formal training, limited individual skills, and limited group cohesion were occasionally able to perform successful and valuable special operations. The kidnapping of Emperor Montezuma II, an act of unequalled audacity and of even greater historical consequences, was performed by a gang of adventurers with no special skills, little military experience, no group training, and questionable group cohesion.

The kidnapping of Montezuma reveals another characteristic of special operations in the age of chivalry that distinguishes them from late modern special operations. Whereas in the late modern age special operations usually result from decisions taken by the highest military and political echelons,[154] in the Middle Ages and the Renaissance such operations, even when they were of great importance, were not infrequently conducted on the initiative of the men who performed them. Due to the difficulties and slowness of communication, and to the nature of special operations, such operations often had to be performed without authorization if they were to be performed at all. A unique opportunity to kidnap an enemy leader or infiltrate an enemy castle would have been lost if permission had to be sought from a distant commander or ruler.[155]

For instance, in 1174 King William the Lion of Scotland invaded England, while the English king, Henry II, was busy fighting against his own sons. William attempted to besiege Alnwick Castle with a small part of his forces, assuming that there were no English field forces nearby to oppose him. A small English contingent under Ralph of Glanvil, based at Newcastle, received information of William's action and of how lax his security measures were. Glanvil mounted a lightning strike against the Scottish camp, which surprised the Scots and captured their king (14 July 1174). Less than twenty-four hours passed from the moment Glanvil received the information until the king of Scotland was taken. If Glanvil had to ask for permission and instructions from King Henry II (then in Canterbury), the action would have been delayed for at least a week or two, and the opportunity would surely have been missed.[156]

Historiographical Considerations

Special operations in the age of chivalry are a particularly difficult subject for sound historical research. It is all too easy for the unwary reader to be deceived by the fanciful stories of medieval chroniclers and Renaissance propagandists, and take as gospel truth the figments of their imagination. On the other hand, it is almost as easy for the over-vigilant scholar to dismiss all of them as fables. This is a problem well known to medieval historical research, but it is particularly poignant in the case of special operations.

Due to the secret and controversial nature of many of these operations, little reliable information was disseminated about them, whereas propagandists of both sides deliberately spread unreliable and quite hysteric accounts. To make things worse, since these were usually sensational as well as controversial affairs, people were very eager to hear about them, and when not enough reliable information or even propaganda was forthcoming, completely imaginary tales tried to fill in the vacuum. In consequence, there is often a severe shortage of reliable accounts of such operations, made worse by the over-abundance of fictionalized accounts.[157]

Even more importantly, it is *ipso facto* hard to believe the stories of special operations. This does not result from literary conventions, but rather from hard military necessity. Special operations usually rely for their execution on the assumption that no one would consider them feasible. But the same rationale that had led, say, Prince Balak to keep only a light guard on Khartpert fortress in 1123, may also lead diligent historians to discredit the stories about how a group of Armenian soldiers sneaked into it to rescue the captive King Baldwin II of Jerusalem. And just as a military commander who wishes to execute special operations has to suspend his disbelief and trust that the impossible can be performed, so also the military historian who wishes to study such operations must not dismiss all resulting tales as impossible bravado or blatant propaganda. In the case of special operations, just because something sounds extremely fanciful does not mean it is not true.

Particularly noteworthy is the issue of poisoning plots. Allegations concerning these were very widespread in late medieval and Renaissance Europe. The nature of such plots was such, however, that one can almost never know for certain whether they were real or whether they were puffed-up propaganda ploys. Renaissance princes usually preferred to exercise personal caution, and took these stories very seriously. Duke Charles of Burgundy, for example, feared poisoning throughout his life, and instituted elaborate precautions in his kitchens and dining halls against this threat.[158] In contrast, modern historians – whose life is not at risk – almost always prefer to exercise scholarly caution, and discount these stories.

Here the activities of the Nizari sect may teach us an important historiographical lesson. Since the Nizaris usually killed their victims by stabbing them in a public place, many trustworthy accounts were written about their exploits, so that even the most doubtful scholars have been forced to accept some of them as true. Consider what would have happened had the Nizaris chosen to employ poison instead of daggers, which militarily would have been a sounder choice. In such an eventuality, scholars would probably have dismissed all the stories about them as pure fiction or propaganda, just as they habitually dismiss most poisoning stories emanating from Renaissance Europe.

The present book tries to steer a course between the two extremes. In the analytical section my aim has been to give an overview of the structural conditions that shaped special operations in the age of chivalry and that made these operations militarily important. In this part I have examined a large number of operations, and have analysed the potential position of special operations against the background of common trends in medieval and Renaissance war and politics. I consequently hope that even if I was duped here and there by the rich imagination of a medieval chronicler, it hardly detracts from the general conclusions.

In the test cases narrated below, my aim has been to present in-depth accounts of representative special operations, and to do so in both an informative and attractive way. I have done my best to carefully sift the remaining evidence, yet I would be surprised if the resulting narratives are wholly accurate. After 500 or 1,000 years, it is simply impossible to construct absolutely reliable tales of assassination plots and late-night infiltrations from a rather meagre diet of sources.

Whenever possible, I have allowed my doubts to show through, and left several options open. For instance, I allowed readers to decide for themselves whether King Louis XI really attempted to kidnap Charles of Burgundy in 1464, or whether Charles invented the whole thing. However, I could do so only a limited number of times. It is impossible to begin every sentence with a 'perhaps' or an 'either/or' and still retain a reader's interest. Hence, when reading the following narratives, I beg readers to remember that many of the narrated facts cannot be verified or vouched for, and that like medieval chroniclers, I often felt that my primary duty was to create an engaging story rather than to write down only what I could be certain of. I hope that the resulting narratives put flesh on the analytical discussion of the first part, and even if they are not absolutely reliable reconstructions of the events in question, they are nevertheless a plausible reconstruction of what a storming or assassination operation *could have* looked like.

✦

A final word is due on the spatio-temporal framework of the present study. The book examines special operations performed all over Europe and the Middle East, and occasionally mentions operations performed farther afield, as for example during the Spanish conquest of Mexico and Peru. The earliest test case examined in depth is the storming of Antioch in 1098, and the latest is the destruction of the mill of Auriol in 1536. War and warfare underwent many changes during the intervening centuries, not the least of which was the gunpowder revolution, and at any particular point in time there were great differences between warfare in different geographical areas.

Nevertheless, from a military viewpoint, in the field of special operations continuity far outweighed difference. Strategically and politically, the targets of special operations were largely the same in eleventh-century Syria and in sixteenth-century France. Similarly, since special operations always depended on ingenuity, surprise, and daring far more than on formal tactics, changes in technology and military organization, including those resulting from the gunpowder revolution, had little impact on them. Indeed, there was little fundamental change in either the targets or the methods of special operations between the Ancient World and the eighteenth century.[159] Only in the late-modern age did the Industrial Revolution, the technologization of war, and the appearance of weapons of mass destruction profoundly change some of the targets of special operations, as well as their methods of execution.

From a cultural perspective too, the gunpowder revolution and the rise of the modern state had only a limited impact on special operations. The norms and values of chivalry continued to exert a profound influence on Western warfare throughout the sixteenth century, and if they were often broken, they were broken almost as often in the eleventh and twelfth centuries. The book covers the period up to 1550 instead of stopping around the more conventional 1450 mainly in order to demonstrate that the gunpowder revolution did not constitute a watershed in the history of inland special operations.

NOTES

1   On the definition of special operations, see McRaven, *Spec Ops*, pp. 1–23; Thomas, 'Importance of Commando Operations', p. 689.

2   Baker, *Chronicon*, pp. 45–6, 225–9; Le Bel, *Chronique*, 1:102–3; Lescot, *Chronique*, pp. 21–2; Sumption, *Hundred Years War*, 1:115–16. Civil wars between parents and children were not uncommon in the Middle Ages. In 1152 a civil war erupted in the Kingdom of Jerusalem between King Baldwin III and his mother, Queen Melisende, who insisted on retaining power as regent although her son was already 21. Melisende's sister, Princess Alice of Antioch, had an even more telling record. She fought several civil wars, first against her father and then against her daughter, in order to remain regent of Antioch. Henry II of England had to wage several wars against his sons, who were over-eager to

assume power. Béla IV of Hungary was similarly troubled in his last years by the rebellion of his son, the future István V. In the 1460s a civil war between the duke of Guelders and his impatient heir tore the duchy apart.

3 For discussions of medieval and early modern espionage, see 'Excerpts of Poly-aenus', section 7, ed. Krentz, 2:870–2; Leo VI, 'Stratagems', sections 8.1–2, ed. Krentz, 2:1030; Archer, *Sovereignty and Intelligence*; Dvornik, *Origins of Intelligence Services*; Haynes, *Invisible Power*; Sheldon, *Espionage*; Thomas, 'Franzö-sische Spionage'; Marshall, *Warfare*, pp. 262–7; Amitai, 'Mamluk Espionage'; Prestwich, *Armies*, pp. 211–17; Prestwich, 'Military Intelligence', pp. 2–15, 17, 19–28; Hewitt, *Organization of War*, pp. 4, 165–8; Allmand, 'Intelligence'; Crook, 'Confession of a Spy'; Alban and Allmand, 'Spies', pp. 73–101; Arthur-son, 'Espionage and Intelligence'; Contamine, *War in the Middle Ages*, p. 226.

4 Brundage, *Richard Lion Heart*, pp. 237–41; Gillingham, *Richard Cœur de Lion*, pp. 66–7; Gillingham, 'Unromantic Death', p. 155.

5 McRaven, *Spec Ops*, pp. 29–72.

6 Dahl, *Heavy Water*, pp. 169, 192–208, 225–33.

7 McRaven, *Spec Ops*, pp. 163–200.

8 Dam, *Niels Bohr*, p. 56.

9 Other recent examples include the attacks on the State Legislature of Jammu and Kashmir (1 October 2001), on the Indian Parliament (13 December 2001), and on the Askariya Mosque at Sammara (22 February 2006).

10 Braudy, *From Chivalry to Terrorism*, pp. 544–7; Klein, *Striking Back*.

11 For instance, the Israeli raid on Entebbe (1976), in which about 100 Israeli citizens were rescued from terrorists holding them hostage, gave an impor-tant boost to Israeli morale and to the political position of the government (McRaven, *Spec Ops*, pp. 333–80).

12 See also McRaven, *Spec Ops*, pp. 245–332; Thomas, 'Importance of Com-mando Operations', pp. 694–5, 701.

13 Dawson, *Soldier Heroes*, p. 190. See also Paris, *Warrior Nation*, pp. 138–57, 184–5, 257–8; Neillands, *In the Combat Zone*, p. 2. For an overview of the impact of the First World War on the image of war, see Harari, 'Martial Illusions', pp. 43–8.

14 It is telling that it was possible to publish an SAS encyclopedia! (Crawford, *SAS Encyclopedia*.)

15 See for example the films *Executive Decision* and *Proof of Life*.

16 It is interesting to note that the recent political satire *Wag the Dog* depicts a Clinton-like US President who, in order to divert public attention away from his latest sexual scandal, fabricates a war with Albania which takes place solely on TV, and whose only actions are bogus special operations aimed at securing control of a nuclear bomb, raiding a terrorist nest, and rescuing an American POW.

17 Newsinger, *Dangerous Men*, pp. 105–36. On the modern connection between soldiers and the image of national manhood, see Braudy, *From Chivalry to Terrorism*, pp. 338–555.

18 Sharon founded the 101st Unit, one of the first permanent Israeli special forces, which attained legendary status in the 1950s and spawned most subsequent Israeli special forces (Sharon and Chanoff, *Warrior*, pp. 83–91). Both Netanyahu and Barak were officers in the Sayeret-Matkal (an elite special force). Barak later became Chief of the General Staff, yet the operations he has been most associated with in the mind of the Israeli public are the rescuing of the Sabena plane hostages (1972), and Operation Spring of Youth, in which Barak, disguised as a woman, led a special operation to assassinate leading members of Palestinian terrorist organizations in Beirut (1973). It is telling that the strongest criticism of Barak's military record also relates to a special operation – namely, his behaviour during a training accident of a special force allegedly preparing for the assassination of Saddam Hussein.

19 See for example Barnett *et al.*, *Special Operations*; Bohrer, *America's Special Forces*; Dockery and Albrecht, *Special Forces in Action*; Dunnigan, *Perfect Soldier*; Harclerode, *Secret Soldiers*; Harclerode, *Fighting Dirty*; Kiras, *Special Operations*; Marquis, *Unconventional Warfare*; Neillands, *In the Combat Zone*; Sarkesian, *New Battlefield*; Taillon, *Evolution of Special Forces*; Vandenbroucke, *Perilous Options*; Waller, *Commandos*; White, *Swords of Lightning*.

20 Thomas, 'Importance of Commando Operations', pp. 689–90, 701.

21 See for example Weale, *Secret Warfare*. Books on American special operations occasionally trace their lineage back to Rogers' Rangers, who operated during the American War of Independence (Landau, *U.S. Special Forces*, pp. 8–16; Dunnigan, *Perfect Soldier*, pp. 20, 34–44; Neillands, *In the Combat Zone*, pp. 9–11).

22 Arquilla, *From Troy to Entebbe*.

23 Dunnigan, *Perfect Soldier*, pp. 14–33.

24 Neillands, *In the Combat Zone*, pp. 1, 12–17.

25 For an overview of the debate, see Vale, *War and Chivalry*, pp. 1–10; Keen, *Chivalry*, pp. 1–3. See also Keen, 'Chivalry, Nobility'; Keen, 'Huizinga, Kilgour'; Strickland, *War and Chivalry*; Anglo, *Chivalry in the Renaissance*; Gillingham, 'War and Chivalry'; Ferguson, *Chivalric Tradition*; Hale, *War and Society*, pp. 37–8; Tallett, *War and Society*, pp. 17–18; Prestwich, *Armies*, p. 222.

26 This view has been stated most clearly in recent decades by Gillingham. See Gillingham, 'War and Chivalry', pp. 237–40.

27 Maurice Keen (particularly in *Chivalry*, in *Laws of War*, and in 'Chivalry, Nobility'), Malcolm Vale (in *War and Chivalry*) and Matthew Strickland (in *War and Chivalry*) emphasize the real importance of chivalry throughout the Middle Ages. For chivalry in the Renaissance, see Anglo, *Chivalry in the Renaissance*; Goodman, *Chivalry and Exploration*; Ferguson, *Chivalric Tradition*; Davis, *Chivalry and Romance*; Day, 'Losing One's Character'; Prestwich, *Armies*, p. 243; Vale, *War and Chivalry*, p. 174; Keen, 'Changing Scene', pp. 290–1. For a medieval discussion of this issue, see Pizan, *Book of Deeds*, pp. 163–4.

28 For honour and its centrality, see Vale, *War and Chivalry*, pp. 15–31, 166–7, 174, 249–51; Dewald, *Aristocratic Experience*, p. 45; Ruff, *Violence*, pp. 75–80; Groebner, *Defaced*, pp. 80–2; Keen, *Chivalry*, pp. 249–51; Kaeuper, *Chivalry and Violence*, pp. 153–5; Fallows, 'Knighthood', p. 130; Harari, *Renaissance Military Memoirs*, pp. 39–40, 98–103, 112–16, 128–9, 159–65, 170–8, 182–3, 194–5; Harari, 'Martial Illusions', pp. 70–2.

29 Keen, *Chivalry*, pp. 220, 228–37; Contamine, *War in the Middle Ages*, pp. 284–92; Prestwich, *Armies*, pp. 233–7; Strickland, *War and Chivalry*, pp. 124–31; Showalter, 'Caste, Skill, and Training', p. 417; Vale, *War and Chivalry*, p. 33; Gillingham, 'War and Chivalry', pp. 231–9.

30 Keegan, *History of Warfare*, pp. 1–12, 23–46.

31 Though in both Ancient Greece and nineteenth-century Europe, for example, war fiction normally focused on the deeds of individual heroes rather than on the movements of large formations, the heroes' deeds of valour were mostly performed in the midst of regular operations.

32 *Le Charroi de Nîmes*, sections 34–55, ed. Perrier, pp. 30–46. In his military manual, Emperor Leo VI recounts a similar trick, when the city of Babylon fell to a force of soldiers hidden inside baskets (Leo VI, 'Stratagems', section 2.2, ed. Krentz, 2:1014–15).

33 *Chanson du Chevalier au Cygne*, chs. 10–20, lines 2166–4221, ed. Hippeau, 2:79–153.

34 Contamine, *War in the Middle Ages*, pp. 110–11; Gillingham, 'Richard I and the Science of War', p. 224; Kagay, 'Shattered Circle', pp. 111–36; Davies, *Age of Conquest*, p. 358; Marshall, *Warfare*, pp. 94–8; Toch, 'Medieval German City', pp. 46–8; Wolfe, 'Siege Warfare', pp. 55–63; Pringle, 'Town Defences', pp. 98–9; Chevedden, 'Fortifications', pp. 39–42; DeVries, 'Impact of Gunpowder Weaponry', pp. 233–4.

35 On the non-military functions of castles, see Molin, 'Non-Military Functions'; Contamine, *War in the Middle Ages*, pp. 114–15; Ellenblum, 'Borders and Borderlines', pp. 112–18; Ellenblum, *Frankish Rural Settlement*, pp. 95–102, 205–9; Pounds, *Medieval Castle*, pp. 24–5, 96–101, 184, 201–7, 222–4; Strickland, *War and Chivalry*, pp. 204–5; France, *Western Warfare*, pp. 77–106; Davies, *Age of Conquest*, pp. 357–60; Marshall, *Warfare*, pp. 113–19, 122–6, 136–9.

36 Prestwich, *Armies*, pp. 206–11, 281–4; Strickland, 'Securing the North', p. 186; McGlynn, 'Myths', pp. 32–4; Gillingham, 'Richard I and the Science of War', pp. 216–17, 225–6; Harari, 'Strategy and Supply', pp. 331–3; Jones, 'Fortifications and Sieges', pp. 164–5; Smail, *Crusading Warfare*, pp. 60–2, 209, 214–15; Marshall, *Warfare*, pp. 93–4; Powers, 'Life on the Cutting Edge', pp. 17–26; Vann, 'Twelfth-Century Castile', pp. 22–6; Chase, *Firearms*, p. 61; Parrot, 'Strategy and Tactics', pp. 242–4; Parker, *Military Revolution*, pp. 57–60.

37 Harari, 'Strategy and Supply', pp. 305, 307–8, 310–11, 321, 324–33; Prestwich, *Armies*, pp. 206–11, 245, 251–2; Prestwich, *War, Politics, and Finance*, pp. 122–6; Bachrach, 'Logistics', pp. 57–78; Mott, 'Battle of Malta', pp. 167–8, 171; Morillo, *Warfare*, pp. 77–80, 124–31; France, *Western Warfare*, pp. 34–7;

Hewitt, 'Organisation of War', pp. 290–2; Hall, 'Changing Face of Siege War-fare', pp. 265–7; Gillingham, 'Richard I and the Science of War', pp. 219–24; Gillingham, 'William the Bastard', pp. 152–3; Gillingham, 'Up with Ortho-doxy!', p. 152; Warner, *Sieges*, pp. 32–4; Pounds, *Medieval Castle*, pp. 54–5, 152–63, 178–83; Marshall, *Warfare*, pp. 126–31.

38 Sumption, *Hundred Years War*, 1:485; Harari, 'Inter-Frontal Cooperation', pp. 383–4.

39 Sumption, *Hundred Years War*, 1:485–8, 496–7, 512–14, 519–20; Harari, 'Strategy and Supply', p. 331; Harari, 'Inter-Frontal Cooperation', pp. 383–4, 393.

40 Bachrach, 'Medieval Siege Warfare'; Prestwich, *Armies*, pp. 296–301; Con-tamine, *War in the Middle Ages*, pp. 101–6, 200–7; Gillingham, 'William the Bastard', pp. 150–3; Bradbury, *Medieval Siege*, pp. 78–88; Pounds, *Medieval Castle*, pp. 106–13; Strickland, *War and Chivalry*, pp. 206–8; Morillo, *Warfare*, pp. 136–43; Ayton, 'English Armies', p. 36; France, *Western Warfare*, pp. 108–27; Toch, 'Medieval German City', pp. 35, 45–8; Contamine, *War in the Middle Ages*, pp. 102–6, 193–207, 211–12, 240–1, 247–8; Marshall, *Warfare*, pp. 226–48; DeVries, 'Impact of Gunpowder Weaponry', pp. 238–44; DeVries, 'Cata-pults are not Atomic Bombs', pp. 466–7; Arnold, 'Fortifications'; Lynn, '*Trace italienne*'.

41 On the centrality of strongpoints and sieges in campaigns and wars: France, 'Recent Writing', pp. 456–8, 462–3; France, *Victory in the East*, pp. 26–7, 41; France, *Western Warfare*, pp. 153–4; Rogers, *Latin Siege Warfare*; Ellenblum, 'Borders and Borderlines', pp. 112–18; Ellenblum, 'Frankish and Muslim Siege Warfare'; Bachrach, 'Medieval Siege Warfare'; Pounds, *Medieval Castle*, pp. 44, 113–21, 152–63, 178–83; Strickland, *War and Chivalry*, pp. 204–8; Warner, *Sieges*, pp. 8–11; Morillo, *Warfare*, pp. 94–7; Toch, 'Medieval German City', pp. 37–40; Bradbury, *Medieval Siege*, p. 71; Jones, 'Fortifications and Sieges', pp. 164–5; Marshall, *Warfare*, pp. 210–12; Parker, *Military Revolution*, pp. 6–13; Eltis, *Military Revolution*, p. 29; Smail, *Crusading Warfare*, pp. 210–14; DeVries, 'Impact of Gunpowder Weaponry', pp. 241–4; Mallett, 'Siegecraft', pp. 247–55; Hall, 'Changing Face of Siege Warfare', pp. 258–64; Hall, *Weap-ons and Warfare*, pp. 158–63; Chase, *Firearms*, pp. 61–5; Arnold, 'Fortifica-tions'; Rogers, 'Vegetian "Science of Warfare"'; Morillo, 'Battle Seeking'.

42 Rogers, *War Cruel and Sharp*, pp. 48–76; Nicholson, *Scotland*, pp. 128–30.

43 Brown *et al.*, *History of the King's Works*, vols. 1–2: *The Middle Ages*, 1:563–8; *Rotuli Scotiae*, 1:782–3; Bower, *Scotichronicon*, 7:278–87; Froissart, *Œuvres*, ed. Lettenhove, 5:323–39; Froissart, *Chroniques*, ed. Luce, 4:140–1, 151–2, 359–60, 369–70; Wyntoun, *Orygynale Chronykil*, 2:482–4; Fordun, *Chronica gentis Sco-torum*, 1:372–3; *Chronicon Angliae*, pp. 32–5; Walsingham, *Historia Anglicana*, 1:280–1; Le Bel, *Chronique*, 2:207–19; *Chronique Normande*, pp. 106–7; *Chro-nique des quatre premiers Valois*, pp. 31–2; Baker, *Chronicon*, pp. 126–7; Ven-ette, *Chronicle*, p. 58; Rogers, *War Cruel and Sharp*, p. 335; Nicholson, *Scotland*, pp. 160–1; Sumption, *Hundred Years War*, 2:173–4, 187–8. In 1378 another special operation took place at Berwick. This time the handful of Scottish

raiders managed to infiltrate and capture the citadel, but the city held on and the raiders were eventually defeated (Brown *et al.*, *History of the King's Works*, vols. 1–2: *The Middle Ages*, 1:568; Fordun, *Chronica gentis Scotorum*, 1:382; Bower, *Scotichronicon*, 7:379; Froissart, *Œuvres*, ed. Lettenhove, 9:26–44). In 1384 the Berwick citadel was yet again captured at night by scaling (Fordun, *Chronica gentis Scotorum*, 1:382).

44 Chartier, *Chronique*, 1:181; Monstrelet, *Chronique*, 5:187; Basin, *Histoire*, 1:119; *Journal d'un bourgeois de Paris*, p. 308; Gruel, *Chronique*, p. 106; Bully, *Charles VII*, pp. 207–9. Aubigny, however, says that Meulan was captured by a ruse, when traitors from within admitted French soldiers who pretended to be wounded Englishmen coming back from the siege of St Denis (Aubigny, *Traité*, p. 21).

45 For example, Chartier, *Chronique*, 1:178; Basin, *Histoire*, 1:119.

46 Vitalis, *Ecclesiastical History*, 6:538.

47 Froissart, *Voyage*, pp. 101–3. Compare Aubigny, *Traité*, pp. 20–1; Machiavelli, *Art of War*, 7.99, 101, ed. Lynch, p. 152. See also the capture of Evreux in 1356 (Froissart, *Chroniques*, ed. Luce, 5:87–93).

48 Monstrelet, *Chronique*, 5:21–5; Aubigny, *Traité*, p. 22; Chartier, *Chronique*, 1:141–3. The city of Pont-de-l'Arche fell to a similar trick in 1449. In 1432 Monstrelet reports an attempt to capture the Castel Sant'Angelo in Rome which copied Guillaume of Orange even more closely. Allegedly, a Benedictine monk asked permission to store his possessions inside the castle. When permission was granted, he prepared 12 large cases, and thought to place 12 soldiers inside them, and to disguise another 24 soldiers as porters, thereby sneaking 36 men into the castle and betraying it to the duke of Salerno. The plot, however, was uncovered, and the monk hanged (Monstrelet, *Chronique*, 5:47–8).

49 Chartier, *Chronique*, 1:233–5; Monstrelet, *Chronique*, 5:274; Burne, *Agincourt War*, pp. 282–4. For another such operation, see the surprise of Mantes on 7 April 1364 (Froissart, *Chroniques*, ed. Luce, 6:100–4, 311–12). For examples of cities and castles that were captured by escalade, see the surprise of Pont Saint-Esprit in 1360 (Froissart, *Chroniques*, ed. Luce, 6:71–3); the surprise of Oudenarde and of Marquel castle in 1382 (Froissart, *Œuvres*, ed. Lettenhove, 10:256–64); the surprise of Louviers in 1430 (Monstrelet, *Chronique*, 4:372–3); and the surprise of Domart-en-Ponthieu in 1432 (Monstrelet, *Chronique*, 5:16–17).

50 Aeneas Tacticus, 'Defence of Fortified Positions', sections x–xiv, xvii, xxii, xxix–xxxi, xxxix, ed. Illinois Greek Club, pp. 62–74, 88–92, 106–18, 148–74, 192–4; 'Excerpts of Polyaenus', sections 31.5, 40.1–3, 54.6–7, 54.9, 54.17, 56.2, ed. Krentz, 2:926, 950–2, 980–6; al-Ansarī, *Muslim Manual of War*, pp. 114–15, 120–2; *Three Byzantine Military Treatises*, pp. 120–5; Frontinus, *Stratagems*, book 3, ed. McElwain, pp. 205–66; Vegetius, *Epitome*, 4.24–30, ed. Milner, pp. 128–31; Pizan, *Book of Deeds*, pp. 112–14; Machiavelli, *Art of War*, 7.108, 115, ed. Lynch, pp. 153–4; Aubigny, *Traité*, pp. 17, 20–2. On the general importance

of stratagem manuals in classical antiquity, see Polyaenus, *Stratagems of War*, 1:vi–ix.

51 See for example Blaise de Monluc's account of his experiences as the commander of Siena during that city's siege in 1554–5 (Monluc, *Commentaires*, pp. 271–346). See also chapters 2 and 5.

52 Rogers, *Latin Siege Warfare*, p. 122.

53 Vitalis, *Ecclesiastical History*, 6:216–18. Compare the attempt to capture Amiens in 1358 (Froissart, *Chroniques*, ed. Luce, 5:127–31).

54 Monstrelet, *Chronique*, 5:12–15.

55 Du Bellay, *Mémoires*, 3:410–13. For the failure of other treacherous attempts, see for example Usāmah, *Kitāb al-I'tibār*, p. 112.

56 Monluc, *Commentaires*, pp. 109–18; Courteault, *Blaise de Monluc*, pp. 145–7; Miolo, *Cronaca*, 1:179.

57 Bar Hebraeus, *Chronography*, 1:343–4. For double agents, see also Vitalis, *Ecclesiastical History*, 6:80–2; 'Excerpts of Polyaenus', sections 41.1–5, 44.3, ed. Krentz, 2:952–6, 960–2; Leo VI, 'Stratagems', section 2.4, ed. Krentz, 2:1016.

58 For conspiracies to betray cities and fortresses, and for widespread fears of such conspiracies, see for example Vitalis, *Ecclesiastical History*, 6:192, 342–4; *Gesta Stephani*, pp. 5, 69; *Istore et Croniques de Flandres*, 2:53; Groebner, *Defaced*, pp. 58–62; Bradbury, *Medieval Siege*, p. 281; Marshall, *Warfare*, pp. 267–70.

59 It is notable that, despite the growing interest in medieval and early modern siege warfare, the clandestine side of sieges has received relatively little attention. For instance, Jim Bradbury's *The Medieval Siege*, Randall Rogers's *Latin Siege Warfare in the Twelfth Century* and Christopher Duffy's *Siege Warfare: The Fortress in the Early Modern World, 1494–1660* – three groundbreaking studies of medieval and early modern siege warfare – focus on regular siege warfare and tend to neglect the central role of betrayal, guile, and surprise (though see Bradbury, *Medieval Siege*, pp. 82, 281).

60 Monluc, *Commentaires*, pp. 133–6.

61 Throughout the sixteenth century demolition devices gradually became more effective. For example, on the night of 4/5 April 1585 the Mantuan engineer Federigo Giambelli, working in Dutch service, blew up the Spanish bridge blockading the entrance to besieged Antwerp by means of two boats laden with between 6,500 and 7,500 pounds of gunpowder. Not only was the bridge destroyed, but 800 Spanish soldiers were blown to pieces along with it (Duffy, *Siege Warfare*, pp. 76–8).

62 *Istore et Croniques de Flandres*, 2:64; Sumption, *Hundred Years War*, 1:567.

63 Vaughan, *Philip the Good*, p. 84.

64 Rogers, *War Cruel and Sharp*, p. 50.

65 Vitalis, *Ecclesiastical History*, 6:526–8. In 1118 Louis VI attacked the town of L'Aigle. An unknown person – perhaps a royal agent – started a blaze, which, due to fierce winds, spread and consumed the entire town, leading to its surrender (Vitalis, *Ecclesiastical History*, 6:198).

66 Lewis, *Assassins*, p. 117.

67 France, *Western Warfare*, pp. 30–4; Morillo, *Warfare*, pp. 79–80.

68 Bachrach, 'Origins of the Crossbow Industry', p. 87.

69 Burns, '100,000 Crossbow Bolts', p. 163. See also Bachrach, 'Origins of the Crossbow Industry', pp. 86–7; Pounds, *Medieval Castle*, p. 109.

70 Prestwich, *Armies*, pp. 140–1.

71 Bachrach, 'Origins of the Crossbow Industry', pp. 77–9, 81–6; Burns, '100,000 Crossbow Bolts', p. 162. In 1250 Louis IX bought horn and glue for making crossbows in the markets of Damascus, though he was at war with the Sultan of Damascus (Joinville, *Vie*, section 446, ed. Monfrin, pp. 218–20).

72 Burns, '100,000 Crossbow Bolts', pp. 160–1.

73 Bachrach, 'Origins of the Crossbow Industry', pp. 82–7.

74 Contamine, *War in the Middle Ages*, p. 149.

75 Bradbury, *Medieval Siege*, p. 293. For the amounts of gunpowder and shot required by armies in the sixteenth century, see Bradbury, *Medieval Siege*, pp. 290–5; Contamine, *War in the Middle Ages*, pp. 145–50; Prestwich, *Armies*, pp. 245–54; DeVries, 'Impact of Gunpowder Weaponry', p. 231; DeVries, 'Gunpowder and Early Gunpowder Weapons', pp. 127–30.

76 DeVries, 'Gunpowder and Early Gunpowder Weapons', pp. 125–30; DeVries, 'Gunpowder Weaponry', pp. 130–45.

77 For the storage of gunpowder, see DeVries, 'Gunpowder and Early Gunpowder Weapons', pp. 127–8.

78 DeVries, 'Gunpowder and Early Gunpowder Weapons', p. 122; Vaughan, *Philip the Good*, p. 331. For another case of an accidental explosion of gunpowder stocks, see Wavrin, *Recueil des croniques*, 5:529.

79 See for example DeVries, 'Gunpowder and Early Gunpowder Weapons', p. 130.

80 For a possible exception, see Vaughan, *Philip the Good*, p. 327.

81 See also DeVries, 'Gunpowder and Early Gunpowder Weapons', p. 123.

82 Prestwich, *Armies*, pp. 141, 147–57, 160, 178–81; Morillo, *Warfare*, pp. 51–6 , 60–73; France, *Western Warfare*, pp. 124, 135–6; Marshall, *Warfare*, pp. 51–6; Hale, *War and Society*, pp. 127–78; Showalter, 'Caste, Skill, and Training', pp. 411, 418, 422; Arnold, 'War in Sixteenth-Century Europe', p. 40; Smail, *Crusading Warfare*, pp. 97–9.

83 Fowler, *Medieval Mercenaries, passim*; Mallett, 'Mercenaries', pp. 209–29; Isaac, 'Problem with Mercenaries', pp. 101–10; Allmand, *Society at War*, pp. 157–9; Prestwich, *Armies*, pp. 147–57; Van Creveld, *Command in War*, pp. 49–50; Contamine, 'Compagnies d'aventure', pp. 365–96; Contamine, *War in the Middle Ages*, pp. 98–100; Marshall, *Warfare*, pp. 85–6; Hale, *War and Society*, pp. 127–78; Tallett, *War and Society*, pp. 116–17; Luard, *War in International Society*, p. 188; McCormack, *One Million Mercenaries*, pp. 39, 46, 109; Black, *European Warfare*, pp. 14–19; Glete, *War and the State*, p. 132; Parker, *Army of Flanders*, pp. 185–7, 198–9, 206, 216–18, 290–2; Smail, *Crusading Warfare*,

pp. 97–9. It should be noted that the difference between feudal and mercenary loyalties was rarely clear-cut. Feudal forces, especially towards the end
of the Middle Ages, usually received pay, whereas feudal loyalties frequently
affected mercenary soldiers to some extent.

84 Hale, *War and Society*, pp. 75–126; Contamine, *War in the Middle Ages*,
pp. 253–5; Black, *European Warfare*, pp. 10, 13–19; Black, *Why Wars Happen*,
pp. 61, 77; McCormack, *One Million Mercenaries*, pp. 21–2, 74, 79–81; Harari,
Renaissance Military Memoirs, pp. 237–66, 303–6; Tallett, *War and Society*,
pp. 94–104.

85 DeVries, *Infantry Warfare*, pp. 196–7; Strickland, *War and Chivalry*, p. 101;
France, *Western Warfare*, pp. 139–49; Van Creveld, *Command in War*,
pp. 49–50.

86 Note that, by this stage, vassals were very often paid soldiers, and the line
separating vassals from mercenaries became finer and finer.

87 Prestwich, *Armies*, pp. 160–7, 178–81; Strickland, *War and Chivalry*, pp. 113–
17; Morillo, *Warfare*, pp. 60–73; France, *Western Warfare*, pp. 139–49; Van
Creveld, *Command in War*, pp. 22–3, 34–5, 49–50; Black, *European Warfare*,
pp. 7–8; Showalter, 'Caste, Skill, and Training', p. 411; Eltis, *Military Revolution*, p. 28.

88 Gillingam, *Richard Cœur de Lion*, pp. 34–49.

89 Hale, *War and Society*, p. 29.

90 Hale, *War and Society*, pp. 15–16, 23–5, 29; Black, *Why Wars Happen*, pp. 15–
20, 24, 63, 69–70; Black, 'Introduction', pp. 9–10; Black, *European Warfare*,
pp. 5–6; Luard, *War in International Society*, pp. 24–6, 85–92, 135–44, 187;
Howard, *Causes of Wars*, passim; Howard, *Weapons and Peace*, pp. 7–22;
Gunn, 'French Wars', pp. 28–35; Tallett, *War and Society*, pp. 15–20; Wilson,
'European Warfare', passim; Glete, *War and the State*, passim.

91 Galbert de Bruges, Histoire du meurtre, pp. 162–5; Oman, *History of the Art
of War in the Middle Ages*, 1:443–5.

92 Galbert de Bruges, *Histoire du meurtre*, pp. 170–6; Oman, *History of the Art of
War in the Middle Ages*, 1:445; Vitalis, *Ecclesiastical History*, 6:376–8.

93 Gillingham, 'Up with Orthodoxy!', p. 154; Gillingham, 'Richard I and the
Science of War', p. 217; Gillingham, 'William the Bastard', pp. 148–9. See also
Strickland, *War and Chivalry*, pp. 101, 103–4, 122.

94 France, *Victory in the East*, p. 27.

95 See also Vitalis, *Ecclesiastical History*, 6:48, 81–2, 238.

96 Novare, 'Estoire de la guerre', section 145, ed. Raynaud, p. 59.

97 Joinville, *Vie*, sections 451–6, ed. Monfrin, pp. 222–4. See also Bartlett, *Assassins*, pp. 190–2.

98 On the Assassins, see chapter 4. See also Lewis, *Assassins*, pp. 125–34; Bartlett,
Assassins, pp. xv, 48–9, 59, 64, 68–9, 74, 78, 90–1, 94, 97–8, 100–1, 107–11,
133–5.

99 More, *Utopia*, pp. 111–12.

100 See also chapter 6.

101 See note in Amatus of Montecassino, *History of the Normans*, V.xxvii, ed. Dunbar, p. 144.

102 Vitalis, *Ecclesiastical History*, 6:76.

103 Vitalis, *Ecclesiastical History*, 6:212–14.

104 Galbert de Bruges, *Histoire du meurtre*, pp. 20–8.

105 Novare, 'Estoire de la guerre', sections 127–8, ed. Raynaud, pp. 39–44.

106 Novare, 'Estoire de la guerre', section 152, ed. Raynaud, pp. 67–8.

107 Rogers, *War Cruel and Sharp*, p. 57.

108 Sumption, *Hundred Years War*, 2:124.

109 Sumption, *Hundred Years War*, 2:205.

110 Venette, *Chronicle*, pp. 57–9; *Chronique des quatre premiers Valois*, pp. 25–8; Froissart, *Œuvres*, ed. Lettenhove, 18:350–61; Sumption, *Hundred Years War*, 2:205–6.

111 Ford, *Political Murder*, p. 111.

112 Monstrelet, *Chronique*, 5:275–7.

113 Schertlin, *Leben und Thaten*, pp. 50–2.

114 Thomas, *Conquest of Mexico*, pp. 304–7.

115 Lockhart, *Men of Cajamarca*, pp. 6–13; Tracy, *Emperor Charles V*, p. 155. On Castile and Tunis, see Tracy, *Emperor Charles V*, pp. 66, 155.

116 For the use of assassinations in Renaissance Italian politics, see for example Simon, *Renaissance Tapestry*, pp. 20, 22–3, 37, 46; Ford, *Political Murder*, pp. 134–45.

117 Harari, Renaissance Military Memoirs, p. 162.

118 Bartlett, *Assassins*, pp. 176–7, 182–3; Juvaini, *History of the World-Conqueror*, 2:723–5.

119 It is true that in modern Western political culture, assassination is a less effective method of war than it was in the Middle Ages, because modern leaders are more akin to the replaceable bureaucratic leaders of the Military Orders than to medieval kings. However, its use still has immense potential, especially outside the West.

120 Thomas, 'Importance of Commando Operations', p. 689.

121 Ford's Executive Order 11905, of 18 February 1976, stipulates in section 5g that 'No employee of the United States Government shall engage in, or conspire to engage in, political assassination' (text from *Weekly Compilation of Presidential Documents*, vol. 12, no. 8, February 23, 1976). Reagan's Executive Order 12333, of 4 December 1981, stipulates in section 2.11 that 'No person employed by or acting on behalf of the United States Government shall engage in, or conspire to engage in, assassination.' The limitations that 'honour' placed on the use of assassination can also be compared with the limitations it placed on the use of espionage. See Alban, 'Spies', pp. 76–7.

122 Note not only the ransom paid for Inca Atahuallpa, but also the ransom of King Jean II of France, which amounted to the sum of 3 million gold *écus*. In comparison, Philip VI bought the entire province of Dauphiné for 400,000 *écus* (Rogers, *War Cruel and Sharp*, pp. 398–9).

123 *Gesta Stephani*, pp. 94–5; Prestwich, 'Military Intelligence', p. 16. For manuals advising leaders how to escape from a besieged town or from prison, see 'Excerpts of Polyaenus', sections 52.1–9, ed. Krentz, 2:976–8; Leo VI, 'Stratagems', sections 20.5–10, ed. Krentz, 2:1056–68.

124 Froissart, *Chroniques*, ed. Luce, 5:97–8; Venette, *Chronicle*, pp. 69, 226–7; Sumption, *Hundred Years War*, 2:295.

125 Le Bel, *Chronique*, 2:133–9; *Istore et Croniques de Flandres*, 2:50, 62–3; Rymer, *Foedera*, vol. 3, part 1, p. 8; Sumption, *Hundred Years War*, 1:563–4; Tuchman, *Distant Mirror*, pp. 89–90.

126 Tuchman, *Distant Mirror*, pp. 200–3; Neillands, *Hundred Years War*, p. 160.

127 DeVries, 'Gunpowder and Early Gunpowder Weapons', pp. 123–5; Hale, *War and Society*, p. 57.

128 See for example Fowler, *Medieval Mercenaries*, pp. 32, 95; Rogers, *Wars of Edward III*, p. 77.

129 Geary, *Furta Sacra*, pp. 88–94; Norwich, *Venice*, 1:52–4; Hodgson, *Early History of Venice*, pp. 81–5.

130 For numerous cases of relic theft, see Geary, *Furta Sacra*.

131 Beaune, *Birth of an Ideology*, pp. 57–62, 176, 331; Jackson, *Vive le Roi!*, pp. 13, 31–2, 37–8, 176–8, 188–9, 195–6; Schramm, *History*, p. 131. In 1793 the revolutionary government sent a special envoy to Rheims to ceremoniously destroy the Holy Ampulla. After the Bourbon Restoration it was claimed that only a fake was destroyed in 1793, and the 'original' was extracted from its hiding place.

132 Schramm, *History*, p. 13; Grant, *Independence and Nationhood*, p. 18; Webster, *Medieval Scotland*, pp. 45–6; Hamilton, *No Stone Unturned*.

133 Runciman, *History of the Crusades*, 3:53, 59, 68, 74, 161, 169–70; Murray, 'Mighty Against the Enemies of Christ'.

134 Pizan, *Book of Deeds*, p. 132. For a raid by a besieged garrison aimed at destroying the besiegers' siege engines, see for example Ambroise, *History*, lines 3656–94, ed. Ailes, 1:59.

135 Prestwich, *Armies*, pp. 287–91; Contamine, *War in the Middle Ages*, pp. 103–4, 194–6; DeVries, *Medieval Military Technology*, pp. 127–40; Pounds, *Medieval Castle*, pp. 109–12; Nicholson, *Medieval Warfare*, pp. 88–98; Warner, *Sieges*, pp. 25–32; Hall, *Weapons and Warfare*, pp. 20–2; Chevedden et al., 'Trebuchet', pp. 66–71; Chevedden, 'Fortifications', pp. 36–8; France, *Western Warfare*, pp. 119–24; Marshall, *Warfare*, pp. 212–14; Bradbury, *Medieval Siege*, pp. 241–70; Rogers, *Latin Siege Warfare*, pp. 243–8, 251–73; Bachrach, 'Military Administration of England'; France, *Victory in the East*, pp. 48–50.

136 Prestwich, *Armies*, pp. 292–3; DeVries, *Medieval Military Technology*, pp. 143–63; Pounds, *Medieval Castle*, pp. 252–5; Warner, *Sieges*, pp. 40–3; Contamine,

War in the Middle Ages, pp. 138–50, 196–200; Smith, 'Artillery', pp. 151–60; Bradbury, *Medieval Siege*, pp. 282–95; DeVries, 'Impact of Gunpowder Weaponry', pp. 227–33; DeVries, 'Use of Gunpowder Weaponry', pp. 2–6; DeVries, 'Gunpowder Weapons at the Siege of Constantinople', pp. 347–50, 354–62; DeVries, 'Gunpowder and Early Gunpowder Weapons', pp. 121–35; DeVries, 'Technology of Gunpowder Weaponry', pp. 285–93; Chase, *Firearms*, pp. 58–65. For Constantinople, see DeVries, 'Gunpowder Weapons at the Siege of Constantinople', p. 359; Hall, *Weapons and Warfare*, pp. 87–95, 135–46, 151–4.

137 McRaven, *Spec Ops*, pp. 13–14.

138 Neillands, *In the Combat Zone*, pp. 2, 4; McRaven, *Spec Ops*, pp. 2, 10, 15–16; Thomas, 'Importance of Commando Operations', pp. 689, 696.

139 *Regle du Temple*; Glete, *War and the State*, p. 128.

140 For regiments, see Keegan, *History of Warfare*, pp. 12–15.

141 Nicholson, *Medieval Warfare*, pp. 114–22; Prestwich, *Armies*, pp. 160, 178–81; Morillo, *Warfare*, pp. 88–91; Showalter, 'Caste, Skill, and Training', pp. 408–11. For drill in the late sixteenth century, see Wilson, 'European Warfare', p. 180; Eltis, *Military Revolution*, p. 19; Roberts, 'Military Revolution', pp. 14–16; Parker, *Military Revolution*, pp. 20–3; Parker, 'Military Revolution', pp. 40–1; Tallett, *War and Society*, p. 25; Parrott, *Richelieu's Army*, pp. 20–1; Lynn, *Giant of the Grand Siècle*, pp. 481–4, 515–25; Vaughan, *Charles the Bold*, pp. 209–10.

142 Haynin, *Mémoires*, 1:215–20.

143 See chapter 7.

144 Soldiers often served for much longer periods at a stretch. See for example Prestwich, *Armies*, pp. 8–9; Showalter, 'Caste, Skill, and Training', p. 416.

145 Marshall, *Men against Fire*; Janowitz and Shils, 'Cohesion and Disintegration'; Van Creveld, *Fighting Power*; Lynn, *Bayonets of the Republic*, pp. 21–40, 163–4; Strachan, 'Experience', pp. 371–2.

146 For the regional loyalties and close bonds within military retinues and other small units, see Prestwich, *Armies*, pp. 41–8; Showalter, 'Caste, Skill, and Training', pp. 409–10, 413, 416; Morris, *Welsh Wars*, pp. 92–3.

147 Again, it should be noted that, despite the importance of feudal obligations, all the men in Fiennes' company were paid for their military services.

148 Haynin, *Mémoires*, 1:149, 230–1, 2:100.

149 Haynin, *Mémoires*, 1:14, 59, 130–1, 162, 213, 221–30, 236, 2:100.

150 Haynin, *Mémoires*, 1:131.

151 See Froissart, *Voyage*, pp. 89–111. On cohesion in mercenary forces, see also Fowler, *Medieval Mercenaries*, *passim*; Showalter, 'Caste, Skill, and Training', pp. 418–19, 422, 425–30; Redlich, *German Military Enterpriser*, p. 14 and *passim*; McCormack, *One Million Mercenaries*, pp. 22, 74.

152 La Noue, *Discours*, pp. 341–7.

153 La Noue, *Discours*, pp. 343–5. For a fuller discussion, see Parker, *Army of Flanders*, p. 177; Harari, *Renaissance Military Memoirs*, pp. 139–41. For an example of a long-lasting *camerada*, see Guyon, *Mémoires*, pp. 90–1, 94, 106, 109, 135.

154 Thomas, 'Importance of Commando Operations', p. 706; McRaven, *Spec Ops*, pp. 2–3, 12, 29–33, 115–16, 163.

155 On the slowness of communication and its effect on military decision-making processes, see Van Creveld, *Command in War*, pp. 23–6; Arthurson, 'Espionage and Intelligence', p. 152; Harari, 'Inter-Frontal Cooperation', pp. 380–3.

156 Fantosme, 'Chronicle', lines 1702–1840; Prestwich, 'Military Intelligence', p. 20.

157 Consider what would happen to a historian in the year 2500 who tried to write a history of the Kennedy assassination based on a random sample of late twentieth-century accounts.

158 La Marche, *Mémoires*, 4:27. For the alleged poisoning of the Earl of Moray in 1332, see also Rogers, *War Cruel and Sharp*, p. 35. On poisoning as a military and political tool, see also Collard, 'Assassinant manqué'; Maleissye, *Histoire du poison*.

159 It is worth noting that Turnbull's *Ninja*, a study of special operations in medieval and early modern Japan, concludes that the main activities of *ninja* and *shinobi* were storming fortified places, assassination, espionage, attacking military camps, and disrupting the movement of armies.

1 **The surprise of Meulan, 1435,** from a 1484 manuscript of Martial d'Auvergne's *Vigiles de Charles VII* (Bibliothèque nationale de France, fonds français, 5054, fol. 85). French soldiers are shown approaching Meulan disguised as fishermen, then storming the wall with the help of a ladder. The main army awaits nearby to exploit their success.

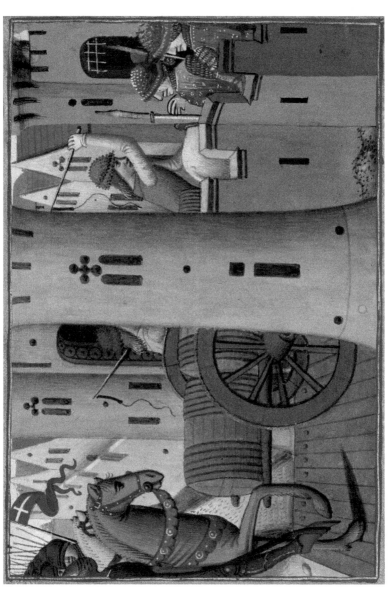

2 **The surprise of Chartres, 1432,** from a 1484 manuscript of Martial d'Auvergne's *Vigiles de Charles VII* (Bibliothèque nationale de France, fonds français, 5054, fol. 79v). The illustration shows the moment when a convoy of wagons enters Chartres, led by French soldiers disguised as wagoners. The soldiers block the gateway with their wagons, attack the gate-keepers, and allow the waiting French army to erupt into the city.

3 **The surprise of Pontoise, 1436,** from a 1484 manuscript of Martial d'Auvergne's *Vigiles de Charles VII* (Bibliothèque nationale de France, fonds français, 5054. fol. 91v). The illustration shows English soldiers disguised as peasants enter the town carrying merchandise for the market. At the bottom left corner the English ambush watches them expectantly.

4 **The assassination of Count Charles the Good of Flanders, 1127,** from a fourteenth-century manuscript of the *Grandes Chroniques de France* (Bibliothèque nationale de France, fonds français, 2813, fol. 206v). The illustration shows the assassins killing the count as he is kneeling in prayer at church. The assassination, performed in the holy season of Lent, resembled the contemporary exploits of the Nizaris, for it was calculated not merely to eliminate the count, but to do so publicly and in a holy space, thereby shocking and overawing public opinion.

5 A general view of Antioch from across the bridge gate (drawing by W. H. Bartlett, engraved by E. Smith, from John Carne, *Syria, the Holy Land, Asia Minor, &c., illustrated* (London, Fisher, Son & Co., 1836–8), between pp. 24–5; permission British Library, c2551-03). Though the illustration dates from the early nineteenth century, at that time Antioch's main features had changed little since 1098. The main bridge and the built area of the city, visible at the forefront, occupy the same place as they did in the eleventh century. The massive walls climbing up to Mount Silpius are largely the remains of the medieval walls.

6 The betrayal of Antioch, 1098, from a thirteenth-century manuscript of the *Historia* of William of Tyre (Bibliothèque nationale de France, fonds français, 9083, fol. 52). The illustration shows a Crusader climbing the ladder and accepted by Firuz into the tower of Two Sisters, while the other Crusaders watch apprehensively from below.

7 **The Nizaris in European imagination**, an illumination by the Master of the Mazarine, from an early fifteenth-century manuscript of Marco Polo's travels (Bibliothèque nationale de France, fonds français, 2810, fol. 17). Marco Polo's account, the most influential travel book of the Middle Ages, was responsible more than any other source for establishing the image of the Nizaris in Europe as 'the Order of the Assassins'. According to Marco Polo, the Order's Master, Alā al-Din Muhammad, trained his assassins in a secret garden of delights at Alamut castle, brainwashing them with the help of narcotics. The illustration shows the would-be assassins kneeling before the Master, who hands them a cup full of some drug.

8 The raid on Calais, 1350, an illumination by Loyset Liedet, from a fifteenth-century manuscript of Jehan Froissart's chronicles (Bibliothèque nationale de France, fonds français, 2643, fol. 188). The illustration shows the main French army waiting in the background, while Renti and his men are advancing to Aimeric's tower. Aimeric receives them on the drawbridge, and relieves them of the sack of coins. Within the gateway they are then surprised by the English ambush.

2

The Gateway to the Middle East: Antioch, 1098

IN 1095 Pope Urban II launched the First Crusade, one of the more successful and momentous military campaigns of the Middle Ages. It not only led to the foundation of four Crusader principalities in the Middle East, but also inspired numerous other crusades, which together wrought crucial cultural, political, and economic changes both in Europe and in the Middle East.

Yet in May 1098 the First Crusade – and the entire Crusader movement – was almost stillborn, despite the enormous material and cultural resources already invested in it. The so-called Peasants' Crusade, after cutting a swath of destruction through Central and Eastern Europe, massacring Jewish communities and pillaging Christian ones, was easily wiped out by the first armed enemy it encountered: the Seljuk Turks of Nicea (1096). The better organized and more heavily armed Princes' Crusade that crossed into Asia in the following year fared somewhat better. After helping the Byzantines capture Nicea, they defeated a Seljuk army at Dorylaeum (1097), and then marched across Asia Minor, meeting little opposition until they arrived before the walls of Antioch in October 1097. But there the crusade ground to a complete halt.

Antioch was one of the ancient metropolises of the Middle East. Founded as the capital of the Seleucid Empire, it later became the principal city of the Roman Levant, and one of the three original Christian patriarchates. The Muslims conquered it in 637. In 969 Christian soldiers in the service of the Muslim governor betrayed several towers in Antioch's wall to a small Byzantine force, which thereby reconquered the city. In 1085 Antioch withstood the assaults of the Seljuk leader Suleyman, but either Philaretos, its Armenian governor, or Philaretos's son, turned traitor. Under cover of night a Seljuk force was secretly admitted into the city, and at dawn of the following morning the citizens awoke to find themselves under Turkish rule.

The Seljuk Empire stretched at the time from Afghanistan to the Mediterranean, but upon the death of its great Sultan Malik-Shah (1092), the empire crumbled almost as quickly as it was formed. As Malik-Shah's sons struggled for the possession of Persia and Mesopotamia, the empire's fringes were divided between a host of greedy relatives, who soon fell to fighting amongst themselves, carving and recarving the empire until it was broken up into little shards. Antioch fell to the lot of Yaghisiyan, who was appointed governor of the city by Malik-Shah in 1086/7. In 1097 Yaghisiyan still owed his nominal allegiance to Ridwan of Aleppo, who owed allegiance to the Atabeg Kerbogah of Mosul, who was himself the nominal lieutenant of the distant Seljuk sultan, Berkyaruk. In practice, however, Yaghisiyan utilized the incessant succession struggles to build himself up as an independent power within the Middle Eastern kaleidoscope.

Antioch was potentially an excellent power base. Though by 1097 natural and man-made disasters had rendered it a shadow of its past grandeur, it was still a very formidable shadow. A fertile hinterland rich in wheat, barley, and olives supported a population more numerous than that of almost all other cities of eleventh-century Syria. Control of Syria's main river, the Orontes, as well as of the main roads connecting Syria and Asia Minor along the Mediterranean coast and through the passes of the Amanus Mountains made it an affluent commercial centre and a place of great strategic importance. In addition, it was a major religious centre for several Christian sects, which contributed both to its wealth and to the potential influence of its secular rulers. The Anonymous Syriac Chronicle rightly calls it 'the head of all Syria'.[1]

Antioch was also gifted with superb fortifications (see illus. 5). The Byzantines, at a time when they were the most accomplished fortifiers of Western Eurasia, built Antioch's defences in the sixth century. When they recaptured the city in the late tenth century they rebuilt its walls, and made Antioch their forward base in Syria and the most formidable stronghold on the Byzantine–Muslim frontier. Its fortifications suffered little in the ensuing decades, and were apparently repaired several times. In 1097 the city was surrounded by more than 10 kilometres of thick walls, about 12 metres high, and studded with numerous towers (360 or 450, according to some sources). The wall's north-western section hugged the wide Orontes river and its marshes, while its southern and south-eastern sections extended along the Casian Range, zigzagging up and down the steep slopes of Mount Iopolis, Mount Silpius, and Mount Stauris. The highest of these three, Mount Silpius, towered some 350 metres above the Orontes plain. It was crested by a massive citadel that dominated the city and offered a last line of defence. Both on the side of the mountains and on that of the river Antioch was virtually impregnable to a regular assault. The wall's northern and western sections, which were considerably shorter, ran through the Orontes plain. Here the fortifications partially rested on two smaller streams, the Phyrminus and the Onopnictes, and were made particularly strong, with a double wall protecting the most exposed sections. There were six large and heavily fortified gates in the walls, and a number of smaller postern gates, which presented difficult targets for any assailant, while making it easy for the defenders to receive supply and messengers, and to launch sorties.

It is no wonder that Antioch's fortifications stupefied the Crusaders, most of whom came from countries lacking major cities and dominated to a large extent by makeshift wooden castles. Fulcher of Chartres, for example, writes that it was so well fortified, that 'it could never be taken by enemies from without provided the inhabitants were supplied with food and were determined to defend it'.[2] The Crusader leader Stephen of Blois, in a letter written before the city fell, says that Antioch was 'fortified with incredible strength and almost impregnable'.[3]

The Crusaders' siegecraft was wholly inadequate to the task at hand. Indeed, already at Nicea it became evident that the Westerners' siegecraft could not overcome a city fortified in the Byzantine style. The Crusaders' attacks on the city were bloodily repulsed, and they were unable to cut the city's supply lines over the Ascanian lake. Nicea eventually surrendered to the Byzantines after the latter ingeniously transported a flotilla overland to seize control of the lake. Antioch's defences were even more formidable than those of Nicea, whereas the Crusaders' position there was considerably weaker. At Nicea the Crusader army was at the height of its numerical strength, received massive military, technical, and logistical assistance from the Byzantines, and campaigned a mere 100 kilometres from the friendly base of Constantinople. When the Crusaders reached Antioch their forces were already much depleted, Byzantine assistance dwindled to a trickle, and the they had to operate almost 1,000 kilometres away from Constantinople.

Of the 50,000 combatants who left Nicea according to the calculations of John France, many either died on the way or left the army. Others split off from the main army, and conquered various towns and castles in the areas surrounding Antioch. The remaining force still greatly outnumbered the 5,000-strong garrison of Antioch, but there was no question of mounting a frontal assault on the walls. Breaching or undermining the walls with siege engines and tunnels was equally beyond the Crusaders' abilities, and the few half-hearted attempts they made failed miserably.

Starving the city until it surrendered was hardly more feasible. It was well-stocked with food, and its walls encompassed an enormous area, which contained not only residential quarters but also mills, orchards, gardens, and pasture land. The size of the city hampered blockade in another way as well. Since the circumference of the wall was so huge, and since the Orontes river and the Cassian range made communication around the city extremely difficult, the Crusaders could not risk splitting their forces and investing the city from all sides. Instead they were forced to concentrate their forces on the northern side of the city, and maintained only a loose blockade of the other approaches, obstructing communications without ever severing them completely. As France convincingly argues in his superb study of the siege, since the Crusaders could hardly hope either to storm or starve the city, their policy was to stick out the siege as long as they could, harass Antioch to the best of their abilities, and hope that 'something would turn up'.[4]

Any number of things could 'turn up' to deliver Antioch into the Crusaders' hands, but special operations were probably at the top of the list. When a city could not be taken by direct assault, siege engines, tunnelling, or starvation, special operations were the most likely medieval alternative. Fulcher notes that from the start, the Crusaders hoped to take Antioch 'by force or stratagem'.[5]

Seizing a gate, a tower, or a section of the walls by surprise could succeed where both a full-scale attack and months of attrition could not. Sometimes this could be accomplished through mere luck and daring. Yet more often such operations could succeed only when helped from within.

As noted in chapter 1, medieval and classical manuals of war, whether Muslim, Byzantine, or Latin, regularly recommended the use of special operations during sieges, and viewed treason as one of the biggest threats to any stronghold. They enumerated a large number of methods that a besieger could use to induce treachery and seize a stronghold by surprise, and an equally large number of methods that a besieged commander could use to counter these threats. For instance, Frontinus's *Stratagems*, a first-century Roman war manual that was very popular in the Middle Ages, suggested to the besieged commander to have loyal troops pretend to turn traitors. These 'traitors' should conspire with the enemy, and lure him into traps. This not only harmed the enemy directly, but more importantly, it caused the enemy to distrust real traitors. Vegetius's manual, the most influential military manual of the Middle Ages, cautioned the besieged commanders against various stratagems that the besiegers might use, such as feigning retreat and then doubling back to the unsuspecting town and scaling it at night (a trick made famous, of course, by the *Iliad*, and suggested by many other classical, medieval, and early modern military thinkers, such as Polyaenus, Emperor Leo VI, Christine de Pizan, Niccolò Machiavelli, and the lord of Aubigny).

The fourteenth-century war manual of Umar al-Ansarī, recapitulating the wisdom of previous Muslim manuals, was adamant that treason was the best way to capture a stronghold, because it was the cheapest. He emphasized the need to make as much contact as possible with people inside the besieged stronghold, and recommended various stratagems and methods to induce treason amongst them. It would be particularly beneficial, he wrote, if one could attract one of the captains of the besieged garrison. As for the besieged commander, al-Ansarī wrote that the first thing he had to do was to secure the loyalty of his soldiers, promising them rich rewards and warning them against the enemy. He similarly had to possess the hearts of the common people through justice and beneficence.[6]

Even without reading such treatises, it was obvious to Yaghisiyan that the greatest danger Antioch faced was from special operations and internal treason. The precedent of 969, and even more so the precedent of 1085, must have weighed heavily upon his mind. He could also recollect how the nearby city of Aleppo fell to the Seljuk leader Tutush in 1086, when the warden of one of its towers let in the besiegers. Reports of recent events in Persia could only have increased Yaghisiyan's anxiety. In 1090 the impregnable mountain fastness of Alamut fell through treason into the hands of the Nizari sect, which began a campaign of sedition and terror against the Seljuk Empire. Within a few years the Nizaris, who were completely incapable of conducting any serious siege operations, captured a large number of fortresses throughout Persia by means of sedition and treason. By 1092 they had grown bold and strong enough to assassinate Nizam al-Mulk, their chief enemy and the empire's powerful grand vizier.[7]

Yaghisiyan was surrounded by potential traitors. He had ruled Antioch for little more than a decade, and was constantly engaged in treasonous plots against his own superiors and colleagues, playing the one against the other. Thus in 1095 Yaghisiyan attempted to assassinate vizier Janāh al-Dawla, the real power behind Ridwan of Aleppo. The plot failed, and in the following three years Yaghisiyan repeatedly switched his allegiance between Ridwan and Ridwan's brother and rival – Duqaq of Damascus. In such an atmosphere Yaghisiyan could not be completely sure even of his Turkish garrison members. He knew that the religious hostility between Muslims and Christians was not enough to secure the Turks' loyalty. When Antioch fell to the Seljuks in 1085, its staunchest defenders included a troop of Turkish mercenaries in Byzantine service, who continued to fight even after the city was betrayed.

The civilian population was an even bigger danger. Antioch was a populous and overwhelmingly Christian city. Though the Christians were divided into mutually hostile sects, and though many of these sects preferred the relatively tolerant rule of the infidel Seljuks to the more oppressive rule of the 'heretical' Byzantines, they still considered it as no more than the lesser of two evils. In addition to religion, barriers of race, culture, and language divided the Turks from the Antiochene population.

When the Crusaders approached Antioch local Christians revolted in several nearby forts and towns, killing or expelling their Turkish garrisons and opening their gates to the Crusaders. Within Antioch, Yaghisiyan took measures to prevent such rebellions, expelling or imprisoning the least trustworthy Christians, including the Orthodox Patriarch, forbidding most of the remaining Christians to bear arms, and ordering them not to leave their homes or gather in public places except at certain hours. According to Fulcher, during the siege he occasionally killed those of the Christian inhabitants he suspected of treason, hurling their heads over the walls with his mechanical artillery.[8] Ibn al-Athīr gives a different version, saying that the suspicious Yaghisiyan expelled many of the Christian men from Antioch, keeping their families inside the city as hostages, but taking great care that no harm would come to them. Nevertheless, like many other Muslim rulers of his time, Yaghisiyan – who was hard-pressed for men – retained in his service some Eastern Christian soldiers, particularly from amongst the warlike Armenians. Either way, enough potential traitors were left in Antioch to fuel Yaghisiyan's suspicions.

The vastness of the city, which prevented the Crusaders from blockading it effectively, also increased its vulnerability to treason and special operations. With a 10-kilometre wall encompassing an area of more than 6 square kilometres and inhabited by tens of thousands of indifferent or hostile people, it was impossible for Yaghisiyan to keep a close eye on all parts of the city or even on all sections of the wall. It was relatively easy for any disaffected civilian or soldier to communicate with the besiegers without being observed. Even worse, if a section of the wall was betrayed to the enemy, the city's size meant that before an effective counterattack could be mounted, the besiegers were likely to gain a firm foothold within, and then their overwhelming numerical superiority would tell. Unlike twentieth-century fortresses that relied on an in-depth defence system, and also unlike the typical medieval castle, Antioch was a strong but hollow shell, immune to regular assaults but extremely vulnerable to pin-prick special operations.

Hence, alongside the conventional warfare over supply routes and tacti-cal vantage points, the siege of Antioch also witnessed a constant clandestine struggle. Both Yaghisiyan and the Crusader leaders were ceaselessly trying to locate the weak links in the city's human defences, the former in order to neut-ralize them, the latter in order to utilize them.

This clandestine struggle was fuelled by the ease and volume of communi-cation between besiegers and besieged. People, merchandise, and information flowed in and out of the city throughout the long siege. The Crusaders never managed to block all the exits. The Turks, who depended on the incoming cur-rent of supply, could not supervise the traffic efficiently. As late as March 1098 Armenian and Syrian peasants and merchants were regularly bringing in from the mountains provisions for sale in Antioch, while refugees and deserters, as well as double agents and spies, constantly left Antioch to join the Crusaders outside. Consequently, Crusaders and Turks could easily spy on one another, and there were ample opportunities for the besiegers to try and secure inside help, and for the besieged to try and draw besiegers into traps.

As France notes, Yaghisiyan probably hoped to minimize the dangers of desertion and treason by fomenting religious and racial hatred between besieged and besiegers. He deliberately had several prisoners tortured to death in plain view of the Crusader army. In this Yaghisiyan was unwittingly helped by the Crusaders, who occasionally behaved no less cruelly towards their own prisoners, and several times shot the severed heads of dead Turks into the city.

Yaghisiyan also used some of the methods mentioned in contemporary military manuals to lessen the dangers of betrayal. According to Anselm of Ribemont, sometime in April or May 1098 Turkish double agents promised to deliver Antioch into the hands of the Crusaders. When a Crusader advance party entered the city, they were ambushed and wiped out. Walo of Chaumont-en-Vexin, the constable of the king of France, who apparently led this party, was among the dead.[9]

There seem also to have been genuine traitors and collaborators. In February 1098 the Crusaders captured in a skirmish the son of some important Turkish family. When they learnt that his family served as wardens for one of the wall's towers, the Crusaders displayed their captive in full view of that tower, and informed the distressed family that they could have their son back only if they secretly betrayed the tower. The family openly offered an enormous sum as ransom, but when their offer was refused, they entered into clandestine negotiations with the Crusaders to betray the city. Luckily for Yaghisiyan, his son – Shams ad-Daulah – was informed of these negotiations. Yaghisiyan quickly deprived the family of its tower, and the Crusaders' scheme was thereby foiled. The Crusaders retaliated by having their prisoner tortured to death in front of the walls.[10]

✦ ✦ ✦

AMONGST the Crusader leaders, one in particular had high hopes of the clandestine struggle. This was Bohemond de Hauteville. Bohemond, who was named by his father after a legendary giant, was scion to a conquering family. His forefathers sailed from Scandinavia to conquer what became Normandy; his father – the famed Robert Guiscard – began his career as a brigand and ended it as ruler of Sicily and South Italy. For several years Bohemond campaigned with his father against the Byzantines in an unsuccessful attempt to conquer the Balkans and perhaps Constantinople itself. When Guiscard died, his eldest son from his second marriage, Roger Borsa, seized the patrimony, depriving his older half-brother Bohemond of the inheritance. Several rebellions led by Bohemond failed to secure him more than a meagre footing at the heel of the Italian boot. Hemmed in at home, he gladly joined the First Crusade, inspired less by pious motives than by the dazzling new fields of conquest opened up by this enterprise.

Bohemond's ruthlessness and craftiness were demonstrated by the manner in which he took up the cross. In the summer of 1096 his half-brother Roger, with whom he was temporarily at peace, laid siege to the important port of Amalfi. Bohemond had already made up his mind to join the crusade, but he kept his intentions secret, and at first helped his brother gather a huge army. When the army settled down to besiege Amalfi, Bohemond proclaimed his intention of setting out for the east, and was enthusiastically joined by as many as half the soldiers. Thus Bohemond obtained a ready-made army for his expedition, whereas Roger had to raise the siege. Roger was probably so pleased to be rid of his brother that he forgave him his duplicity.

Throughout the march to Antioch, and during the long siege that followed, Bohemond established himself as the foremost Crusader commander. Yet though he acquired the respect of friends and foes alike, he also aroused deep suspicions. The Byzantine emperor in particular, who had fought against him in the past, mistrusted his intentions, rightly assuming that Bohemond was seeking to establish another Hauteville principality to replace the one robbed from him. The emperor's daughter, Princess Anna Comnena, had left her impression of Bohemond for posterity. That red-headed giant, wrote Anna, 'was an habitual rogue, quick to react to fleeting circumstance; he far surpassed all the

Latins who passed through Constantinople at that time in rascality and courage, but he was equally inferior in wealth and resources. He was the supreme
mischief-maker.' With the help of hindsight, she concluded that Bohemond left
Italy ostensibly to worship at the Holy Sepulchre, 'but in reality to win power
for himself'.[11]

Antioch presented Bohemond with both a target for his ambitions and a
challenge for his ingenuity. Bohemond was probably more keenly aware than
any of the other Crusader commanders that the easiest way into a strongpoint
of Antioch's calibre passed through a treacherous heart. In their campaigns
in South Italy and the Balkans the Normans habitually relied on treason and
special operations to conquer strongpoints, as in the case of Capua (1022),
Naples (1028), Melfi (1041), Montepeloso (1068), and Salerno (1077). In 1068
Robert Guiscard laid siege to the city of Bari, the Byzantine capital of Apulia.
For three years it withstood the Normans' attacks, until finally a local leader
betrayed to them one of the wall's towers (1071).

For Bohemond an even more obvious model was the siege of Durazzo, in
which he personally took part. Durazzo, the main port and the capital of Byzantine Illyria, was heavily fortified in the best Byzantine style. In 1081 Guiscard
and Bohemond together laid siege to the city. It held out for nine months, and
could have resisted far longer, if a Venetian resident had not betrayed it to the
Hautevilles (1082).

Thanks to his Italian and Balkan experience, Bohemond was not only more
likely to pin his hopes on the clandestine campaign than the other commanders, but he was also better prepared to wage such a campaign. South Italy and
Sicily contained a huge Greek population, and many soldiers of Greek descent
habitually served in the Norman armies. Sicily was a predominantly Muslim
country, and during its conquest the Hautevilles had formed alliances with
several Muslim powers, and recruited thousands of Muslim soldiers. Some of
the former Muslim rulers, such as Ibn Hamud, former prince of Enna, even
converted and became part of the Christian nobility. There is no evidence that
any Sicilian Muslims joined Bohemond's crusade, but it is not impossible. At
the very least, his Muslim and Greek subjects provided Bohemond with much
needed interpreters.[12]

Even with Turks Bohemond had some experience. During his campaigns
in the Balkans he had often confronted the Turkish mercenaries of the Byzantine emperor, who were recruited in Asia Minor and were the close relatives of
the Antiochene Turks. His experience in the Balkans proved to Bohemond not
only that Turks might well serve Christian princes, but also that they might be
convinced to desert. Both individual Turkish combatants and entire contingents deserted to the Normans during the campaigns of the early 1180s.

Lastly, it should be noted that Bohemond not only had more experience
in employing Eastern Christian and Muslim soldiers than any other major
Crusader leader, but he was arguably the least influenced by Crusader ideology

and religious biases. He therefore had a great practical and conceptual edge over the other leaders in the matter of making contact with the Turks and Eastern Christians inside Antioch. The idea of subverting Turkish soldiers probably came more readily to his mind than to that, say, of Godfrey of Bouillon, and he had at his disposal both the interpreters and cultural knowledge necessary to communicate with potential traitors.

We know of at least one success Bohemond had in his clandestine efforts quite early in the siege. By one means or the other he persuaded a capable and energetic Turkish soldier to desert and join his service. This man was baptized by Bohemond in person, and adopted the name of his new godfather. This 'Bohemond the Turk', according to Albert of Aachen, became the most useful agent of Bohemond de Hauteville, who used him both for spying and in attempts to subvert other members of the garrison.[13]

Other leaders may also have dabbled in such efforts, but though the Crusaders benefited from them in various ways, by May 1098 all such schemes had still failed to engineer the fall of Antioch. While they were thus making little headway in the clandestine struggle, the Crusaders seemed to be losing the conventional one. Although they managed to beat two relieving armies sent to raise the siege by Ridwan of Aleppo and Duqaq of Damascus, throughout the siege they were never able to make a dent in the city's defences. And though the protracted siege slowly emptied the city's storehouses, bled its garrison white, and sapped its morale, the besieging force was being eaten away at a faster rate by starvation and despair. By Christmas 1097 the Crusaders had consumed all the food from the nearby countryside, and from then on they were kept going only by supply received from long-distance raids, from the port of St Symeon, and from friendly towns such as Edessa. However, the supply received from these sources was never enough, and defending the long supply lines heavily taxed the Crusaders' dwindling forces. When detachments were sent to protect the supply lines they were frequently defeated, whereas the weakened army left before the walls of Antioch often had difficulties protecting itself from sorties.

During the winter the Crusaders' position deteriorated to such an extent that fewer than a thousand knights still had horses to mount, and many of the foot soldiers and camp followers were dying of hunger and cold. According to Fulcher they subsisted on a diet of wild herbs, thistles, horses, asses, camels, dogs, rats, leather skins, and grains found in manure.[14] According to another source, the poorest even ate the flesh of dead Muslims.[15] The commander of the small Byzantine contingent, Tatikios, took his soldiers and left Antioch in February, ostensibly to go summon help from the emperor. He never returned. Several of the Crusader leaders also fled, and the rank and file followed suit, deserting in ever growing numbers.

When any sane mercenary or roving warrior horde would have given up the siege long ago, the Crusaders somehow held on, buying time at the price of their lives. Their tenacity was such that perhaps, given a few more months of attrition warfare, Antioch might yet have fallen to them, like a big tree choked to death by some parasite shrub. In March and April 1098 their prospects indeed brightened a bit, especially after they defeated a relief army sent from Aleppo and tightened the blockade of Antioch.

But in May 1098 their time ran out. The Atabeg Kerbogah of Mosul finally answered Yaghisiyan's pleas, and having gathered a huge army from Mesopotamia and Syria, he was marching to succour Antioch. The Crusaders seemed to be doomed. Kerbogah's army was far larger than any they had encountered so far. If they waited for it passively, they would be crushed between that hammer and the anvil of Antioch's impregnable walls. If they tried to attack it on its way, they would either have to split their already meagre forces, or to abandon the siege of Antioch.

The Crusaders were given a short respite when Kerbogah chose to delay and lay siege to Edessa, instead of marching directly on Antioch. His decision was motivated partly by the need to wait for forces arriving from Syria and Asia Minor, and partly by the need to secure his communication routes back to Mosul. But it was also motivated by self-interest. It is unlikely that in 1098 Kerbogah or his overlord, the Seljuk sultan, viewed the Crusaders as a serious menace to Islam that should be countered by a united Muslim front. So far, the Crusaders had proved to be a limited threat, and several Muslim powers, in particular the Fatimid sultans of Egypt, were even willing to ally themselves with them. Rather, Kerbogah was marching to Antioch because he saw the Crusaders' incursion as a golden opportunity to reimpose his authority over the Empire's wild west. Faced by this new invasion, the independent-minded Syrian rulers might at last be willing to surrender to his authority.

Kerbogah accordingly did not rush to annihilate the Crusaders. Instead he camped near Edessa from 4 to 25 May, perhaps engaging in some half-hearted siege operations, but devoting most of his energy to consolidating his army and to negotiating with Yaghisiyan and the other Syrian princes. In exchange for his help Kerbogah demanded that Yaghisiyan completely submit to his authority. Until such time as Yaghisiyan submitted, Kerbogah was not going to lift a finger to help him. Yaghisiyan procrastinated, but eventually agreed. When the terms were settled, around 25 May, Kerbogah raised the siege of Edessa and resumed his march towards Antioch. He was apparently in no hurry, but even at a leisurely pace he was expected to reach Antioch no later than 5 June.

Kerbogah's approach struck terror into the hearts of the Crusaders, but it played into the hands of Bohemond de Hauteville. For some time now, Bohemond believed he had the key to the city in his pocket. His trusted agent, Bohemond the Turk, had contacted one of the garrison's captains, a man named Firuz, sometime in the winter or spring of 1098. Firuz was the warden of a section of the wall containing a tower called Two Sisters (or Kashkaruf), and perhaps two adjacent towers as well. Interestingly, Two Sisters was located at roughly the same area as the towers that were betrayed to the Byzantines in 969. Firuz showed some willingness to enter into secret negotiations with Bohemond. Bohemond the Turk and perhaps other trusted messengers went back and forth between the two, bearing seditious suggestions, promises, and pieces of information. According to Anna Comnena, Firuz and Bohemond at one time even conversed with one another directly, the former leaning over the parapet and the latter cajoling him from below, like the prsoverbial fox flattering the crow.

The story of these contacts is best told in a chronicle written shortly after the events by a Norman knight from South Italy who was one of Bohemond's followers, and who is known to modern scholars (like many of his fellow medieval chroniclers) as 'the Anonymous'. According to the Anonymous, Bohemond promised Firuz to have him christened and to bestow great riches and honours upon him, and eventually Firuz agreed. He assured Bohemond that in token of their friendship, and in exchange for the promised rewards, he would deliver Two Sisters to him and open the way into Antioch.

Modern scholars have not accepted the Anonymous's story at face value, and have tried hard to establish who Firuz really was and what motivated his actions. Back in 1098 Bohemond too was unable to know whether Firuz's story was true and what really stood behind the messages arriving from Antioch. Unlike modern scholars, however, Bohemond was betting his head on the answer. If he got things right, he could have Antioch on a plate. But if he got them wrong, as Constable Walo did, he would be delivering himself and his men into another Seljuk trap.

We cannot be sure how Bohemond – and Bohemond the Turk – checked up on Firuz, but the multitude of conflicting stories that survive in the sources indicate that the job was far from easy. The sources ascribe to Firuz different nationalities, different occupations, and even different names from the ones given him by the Anonymous. Thus some argue that he was an armourer, while others say he was a cuirass-maker, a secretary of Yaghisiyan, a wealthy Antiochene, or all of these combined. As for his motivation, though most ascribe his action to avarice, there are several other versions. One story explains that Bohemond had captured Firuz's son, and Firuz agreed to betray the city in exchange for his son's life. Other stories ascribe his actions to a divine vision he saw, or to a personal quarrel he had with Yaghisiyan. Those like William of Tyre who claim that Firuz was an Armenian, explain that he was motivated above all by a desire to free Antioch from the infidels and regain it for Christendom. William of Tyre adds another motive, unattested by any other source, namely that Firuz had discovered that his wife was betraying him with one of Yaghisiyan's chief lieutenants.

We cannot tell today which version was correct. In all probability, neither could Bohemond. But he decided to gamble and trust Firuz. In 1098 Bohemond was already in his late forties, having had too many disappointments in his life.

If he was going to match his ancestors and leave the name of a conqueror to posterity, this seemed to be his last opportunity, and he seized it with both hands.

Once he convinced himself of Firuz's trustworthiness, Bohemond summoned the other Crusader leaders to a conference, either in April or early May. Looking unusually happy and pleased with himself, he kept the good news to himself, and instead spoke of the desperate plight of the army. Then, still keeping the ace up his sleeve, he offered the other leaders a deal. Up to that moment different sections of the army had been commanded by their respective lords, with no single commander in supreme command. Given the desperate situation, they should now set up one of their number to be supreme commander, and if by any means he could manage to engineer the city's downfall, he should be rewarded with lordship over it.

Just as Kerbogah was unwilling to save Antioch just for some imaginary common good of Islam, so too Bohemond was unwilling to conquer Antioch for an equally imaginary common good of Christendom. However, the other leaders, still ignorant of Kerbogah's approach, and wary of Bohemond's craftiness and ambitions, flatly refused his offer. They may have surmised that he had found a traitor in the city, but they were not yet desperate. Even if Bohemond had indeed secured a traitor, nobody could be sure that it was not just another trap, and in any case, that was not a good enough reason to let him alone enjoy the fruits of such an arduous siege. Bohemond swallowed the bitter pill and kept his secret to himself. He had patience as well as guile.

This is how things stood when, around 10 May, news spread that Kerbogah was coming. The Crusader leaders hastily held another council, and just as Yaghisiyan eventually capitulated to Kerbogah's demands, so they too capitulated to Bohemond's.[16] If he could just take Antioch, they promised, the city would be his – provided only that the Byzantine emperor, who was its rightful lord, failed to show up and demand it.

According to Anna Comnena, during the council that gave Bohemond command of the army, the Norman still did not share his secret with the other leaders, but explained his suggested strategy in the following words: 'Not all victories are granted by God through the sword, nor are such results invariably achieved through battle. What the moil of war has not produced is often gladly given after negotiation … In my opinion it's wrong to waste our time to no purpose; we should hurry to invent some sensible and bold scheme to save ourselves before Kerbogah arrives. I suggest that each of us should try hard to win over the barbarian watching his particular section [of the wall].' Antioch would be the winner's prize.[17] The words are Anna's, but they may well reflect the spirit of Bohemond's suggested policy.[18]

According to Albert of Aachen and William of Tyre, at the decisive meeting Bohemond openly disclosed to the most important leaders that he had a trusted collaborator in the city, but that he was not going to do anything unless

Antioch was first promised to him. If they did not want to give him the city, they could try and find traitors of their own.

Having by one means or the other got what he wanted from his fellow commanders, Bohemond now found himself in a tight race with Kerbogah for the possession of Antioch. Bohemond had a slight lead, because at the time Yaghisiyan was still procrastinating, and Kerbogah was still beating his heels around Edessa. But time was obviously very short.

Bohemond began his tenure as supreme commander by halting all military actions. From mid-May till early June the Crusaders seemed to be paralysed. France suggests that an actual truce may have been arranged between the Crusaders and Yaghisiyan at this period. It is unclear whether such a truce had indeed been arranged, but it is certain that no desperate assaults were made on the city, no ingenious siege engines were constructed, and no special effort was mounted to seal off Antioch and prevent communication between the city and Kerbogah. Bohemond knew that it was too late for all that. The Crusaders' sole hope depended upon Firuz, and everything was geared to ensure optimum conditions for a *coup de main*. Halting all offensive movements, and perhaps negotiating a temporary truce, had two important advantages. First, it gave the impression that the Crusaders were demoralized, and caused the garrison to be off its guard. Second, it facilitated communications with the city, which were now of vital importance.

For it was now time for Bohemond to see whether Firuz would be as good as his word. His promise to betray Antioch was made well before the arrival of the news of Kerbogah's coming. Would he still keep his promise now that the city's relief was almost certain? While the rest of the army remained inactive, Bohemond sent daily messages to Firuz, piling flattery upon flattery and promise upon promise. At the very last moment, when Kerbogah was a mere three days' march away from Antioch, Firuz gave his consent. Still fearful of a trap, Bohemond requested some guarantee of Firuz's loyalty. Firuz's son was duly dispatched to Bohemond. If Firuz betrayed Bohemond, the son's life would be forfeit. Needless to say, though, in such an eventuality the entire Crusader army was also as good as lost.

The operation was set for the night of 2/3 June. The tower of Two Sisters was located on the south side of the city, on the slopes of Mount Silpius, roughly mid-way between the Gate of St George and the citadel (see map 1). It was thus on the opposite side from the Crusaders' main camp, in a mountainous and unpopulated area, accessible only on foot – and that too with difficulty. This meant that the Crusaders would find it problematic to reach the place, but it also meant that an attack from that quarter would not be expected. Taking a leaf from Homer as well as from Vegetius, Bohemond and Firuz together contrived the following plan. After weeks of inactivity, a large force would now bestir itself and pretend to leave Antioch towards the north, set on some important enterprise. The lookouts on Antioch's wall, and any advance scouts Kerbogah might have sent, would be able to see this movement and, hopefully, would guess that the Crusaders were either running away; using one last chance to plunder the countryside; or most likely, marching to confront Kerbogah.

Then, under cover of darkness, the force would double back, approaching Antioch from its southern side. As the main body waited, hidden in the mountainous terrain, a small body of troops, perhaps 700 strong, would silently sneak up Mount Silpius. These troops would divide into two parties. The bigger one, led by Bohemond, would take Two Sisters with Firuz's help. It would quickly spread out, taking as large a section of the wall as possible, and in particular securing at least one of the nearby postern gates. The smaller party, led by God-frey of Bouillon, would meanwhile climb higher up the mountain, and hide itself close by the citadel. Once Two Sisters was securely in Crusader hands, a horn would sound a signal, and Godfrey's party would then attempt to storm

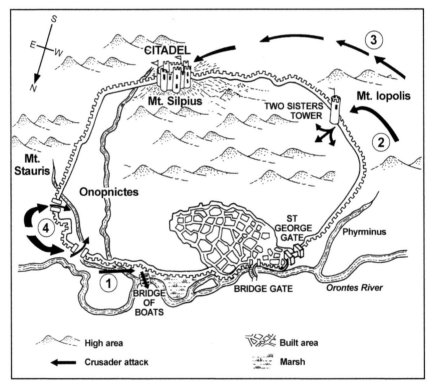

Map 1 The storming of Antioch, 2/3 June 1098. (1) The Crusader force leaves the main camp and crosses the Orontes by the bridge of boats. (2) Bohemond's advance party infiltrates Antioch through Two Sisters, and opens the way into the city. (3) Simultaneously, a small raiding party under Godfrey of Bouillon attempts to surprise the citadel. (4) The Crusaders in the main camp learn of the city's fall, and pour into Antioch from the nearby gates.

the citadel. At the same time the main army would also move forward, entering Antioch over the wall and, hopefully, through some captured gates.

Having made his plans, Bohemond shared them with a few of the other Crusader leaders and several of his most trusted men. The rest, including some leaders such as Tancred, were kept in ignorance for the time being.[19] One of Bohemond's followers, nicknamed Bad Crown, went around the camp and summoned the Crusaders to prepare themselves for an expedition against Kerbogah's approaching army. At the exhortation of Bishop Adhemar of Le Puy, who was privy to the secret, the Crusaders – many of whom had stopped shaving in the preceding weeks due to their weariness – shaved off their beards 'in the Franks' manner'.[20] This was done to enable the Crusaders to distinguish one another during the planned night attack, for the Turks and Eastern Christians alike were normally bearded.

According to plan, the Crusaders first pretended to march away from Antioch, then doubled back under cover of darkness. As the main body remained in hiding, some distance away from the walls, the two advance parties, commanded by Bohemond and Godfrey, made their way forward. Even those who still had horses now left them behind. The ground ahead was too difficult for riding, and in any case, the horses would have made too much noise.

Godfrey's companions, who were apparently informed in advance of their objective, began climbing Mount Silpius, going up and down valleys and sharp precipices. When they reached the foot of the citadel, they stopped in some concealed spot, making their final preparations and waiting for the sound of the horn from Two Sisters. Meanwhile, Bohemond's party was making its way towards Firuz's tower. The Anonymous, who was a member of this party, does not give any information on how they were chosen or what they had been told. By now they must have known their objective, especially as they were carrying a ladder with them. According to Albert of Aachen, they were led through the narrow paths by Bohemond the Turk, who had become familiar with the area from weeks or months of secretly sneaking in and out of Two Sisters. Firuz too did not sleep that night. Perched in his tower, he was scanning the ground below.

About 3 a.m. on Thursday 3 June the Crusaders were in place. The timing had to be exact, for Yaghisiyan had taken precautions. The prefect of the guard, accompanied by several trusted men, was making tours of the wall, checking that sentinels were neither asleep nor up to some treachery. Bohemond sent forward a Lombard interpreter from his household, who knew Greek well. The Lombard crept to the foot of Two Sisters, and found Firuz anxiously peering out of the tower's window. They exchanged a few words, Firuz informing the Lombard that they should remain hidden until they saw the prefect's lamp pass by, and then make all haste to climb the tower and secure the wall before he returned. The Lombard went back to inform Bohemond. After a while, they indeed saw a lamp approaching along the walls, passing through the tower, and continuing on its way. It was finally time to see whether Bohemond was justified in trusting Firuz. Bohemond addressed his men briefly. 'Go,' the Anonymous remembered him saying, 'strong in heart and with one mind, and scale the ladder into Antioch, which, if it pleases God, we shall have in our power in a trice.'[21]

The first wave of the assailants then crept forward to the base of the tower. A voice from above told them that all was clear, and that they should come up. With the help of ropes thrown from the tower, the ladder was hoisted up the wall and firmly secured to the battlements. A man named either Fulcher or Gouel was the first one up the wall. After him, one by one the Crusaders climbed up the rungs and disappeared into the tower (see illus. 6). Due to some miscalculation or the other, only one ladder was brought; the folly of this soon became evident. It was pitch dark, the wall was about 12 metres high, the Crusaders were encumbered with steel weapons, and extreme precaution had to be taken lest the sound of clinking metal alert the garrison. In addition, the men were still suspicious of treason, and apparently were not over-anxious to climb the ladder. Consequently, the operation proceeded with almost unbearable slowness, as a single file of men cautiously climbed up the rungs.

Bohemond himself remained below, perhaps suspecting a trap. After some long and agonizing minutes, when only about sixty Crusaders had ascended the ladder and occupied Two Sisters and the two adjacent towers, Firuz's nerves snapped. What kind of an operation was Bohemond conducting? Was he trying to get them all killed? Quiet as they tried to be, their presence was bound to be discovered soon. An unlucky soldier clanking his sword against a shield or a man losing his step in the dark could easily alert the neighbouring towers to what was happening. In any case, it would not be long before the prefect's next round came by. If they wanted to capture Antioch, they had to move faster.

Giving vent to his feelings, Firuz exclaimed – in Greek apparently – to the Crusaders already hiding in the tower: 'We have too few Franks with us! Where is that hero Bohemond? Where is that invincible hero?' One of the men scurried back down the ladder – holding up the operation still further – and ran to Bohemond, crying out under his breath: 'Why are you standing here, sir, if you have any sense? What did you come to get? Look! We have taken three towers already!' Stung by this rebuke, and appreciating its wisdom, Bohemond gathered his courage, commanded an all-out assault, and went up the ladder himself. His companions shouted their battle cry, 'Deus vult!' (God wills it!), and raced up the ladder after him. They spread out from Two Sisters, taking by surprise the nearby towers and killing all their occupants, including a brother of Firuz and perhaps the prefect of the guard as well. Just then, the ladder broke.[22]

The inexplicable lack of foresight in bringing only one ladder now threatened to wreck the entire operation. Luckily for the Crusaders, there was a postern gate not far from Firuz's tower. As the men spreading out from Two Sisters secured the area from within, their comrades who remained outside fumbled and poked about in the dark until they found the entrance. Together they broke open the heavy door. Most of the 700 men in the advance party were now able to enter Antioch, and they were soon followed by the main army, which was rushing to their help as fast as it could.

As dawn was breaking, the city woke up in terror. The Anonymous remembered how 'the shrieks of countless people arose, making an amazing noise throughout the city'.[23] The Crusaders were fast spreading through the city, butchering the garrison as well as many of the civilians. According to Albert of Aachen, some of Antioch's Christians joined the Crusaders, either spontaneously or by some pre-arrangement. The Crusaders nevertheless slaughtered far more civilian Christians than armed Turks – a total of 10,000 people according to Albert. Guibert excuses them by saying that in the dark, it was impossible to tell an Eastern Christian from a Turk, for they had the same clothing and were equally bearded (which hardly explains the slaughter of women and children). The shaving operation ordered by Bishop Adhemar proved itself by helping the frenzied Crusaders avoid slaughtering one another. The troops who stayed in the Crusaders' base camp woke up to the sounds of war, and were astounded to see Bohemond's blood-red banner planted upon the wall. They came running, and quickly joined in the fray. By noon the streets of the city were covered with corpses, and the stench of dead bodies, already putrefying in the Middle Eastern summer day, began poisoning the air.

Antioch was lost. But the Crusaders failed to secure the citadel. It was a touch-and-go affair from the start, and the delays at Two Sisters did not improve matters. Apparently, the horn was blown only after Bohemond's party secured the postern gate, and by then the citadel's guards were ready. They may have been alerted by the noises coming from Two Sisters, or they may simply have been doing their job well. They appear to have repelled Godfrey's initial attack with ease. Bohemond then gathered a larger force and made another attempt, but the defenders held their own, and Bohemond called off the attack after being himself wounded by an arrow.

Those of the garrison members who could, either fled to the citadel or escaped from the city. Yaghisiyan, wrongly thinking that the citadel too had fallen, belonged to the latter group. With a few of his men he rode south, until their horses were worn out. They took shelter in a village, but when the local population of Armenians and other Eastern Christians learned who they were, they captured their one-time lord, beheaded him, and sent the severed head as a present to Bohemond. According to another version, after riding for several miles, Yaghisiyan was so overcome by grief at the thought of the lost city and of the household and children he left behind, that he fell fainting to the ground, and remained there until a passing Armenian recognized him, cut off his head, and carried it in triumph to Bohemond. Either way, when Kerbogah arrived two days later, he found that he had lost the race.

Antioch's fall on the early morning of 3 June should not be considered as fortuitous or coincidental as some modern accounts make it to be. As the previous pages demonstrate, in contemporary warfare it was very common to capture strongholds by special operations, and mounting such operations was part and parcel of every siege effort, no less than building siege engines or enforcing a blockade. Of course, it was impossible to be certain of finding a traitor or some other weak link in the defence, but it was equally impossible to be certain that siege engines would manage to knock down the wall or that a blockade would manage to starve out the defenders.

◆ ◆ ◆

THE plight of the Crusaders did not end with the death of Yaghisiyan or with the capture of Antioch. Though their situation improved in some respects, the citadel was still holding out, and Kerbogah was undefeated. Unable to confront Kerbogah in the open, the Crusaders locked themselves up in Antioch, and from 5 to 28 June they found themselves besieged within it, fighting desperately both against Kerbogah's army outside and the citadel above. Only the great victory they gained over Kerbogah in the subsequent battle of Antioch finally saved the Crusaders, caused the citadel to surrender, and opened the way to Syria and the Holy Land. Antioch subsequently became the capital of a Norman principality, ruled over by Bohemond and his descendents. Two other Frankish principalities, Edessa and Tripoli, sprang up to the east and south of Antioch, whereas in the Holy Land the Crusaders established the Kingdom of Jerusalem, destined to endure, in one form or another, for almost two centuries.

Despite the failure to take the citadel, and though it took another great battle to save the Crusaders and open the way south, the operation that captured the city of Antioch was one of the most successful and most important special operations of the Middle Ages. If not for that operation, the Crusaders could not possibly have taken Antioch, and would have had to face Kerbogah in the open field, with an undefeated garrison at their back. Under such conditions their chances of defeating Kerbogah would have been considerably smaller, and it is very likely that the First – and last – Crusade would have ended in ignominious defeat under the walls of Antioch. It is equally likely that no more Crusades would have been mounted after such a colossal failure. When subsequent Crusades failed, contemporaries always had the example of the First Crusade to inspire them to new efforts. But had that initial expedition been wiped out without achieving anything, it is more than likely that eleventh-century Europeans would have concluded that they had made a mistake, and that God simply did not want it. The Crusades were a rather unlikely historical enterprise to begin with, and whereas there were no structural conditions that compelled the people of Europe to mount such expeditions, there were numerous structural conditions that hampered them.

Hence, if Firuz had not betrayed Antioch to Bohemond, and if the Crusaders had not emerged three weeks later from Antioch to defeat Kerbogah, it is likely that the Crusades to the Middle East would have concluded like the Viking forays to America: a curious historical anecdote, demonstrating nothing except the doomed irrational projects undertaken from time to time by medieval Europeans in defiance of objective reality.[24]

NOTES

1 'First and Second Crusades', p. 70.

2 Fulcher of Chartres, *Historia Hierosolymitana*, 1.15.2, ed. Hagenmeyer, p. 217.

3 *Stephani ... epistolae*, p. 888.

4 France, *Victory in the East*, p. 227.

5 Fulcher of Chartres, *Historia Hierosolymitana*, 1.15.5, ed. Hagenmeyer, p. 218.

6 al-Ansarī, *Muslim Manual of War*, pp. 114–15, 120–2; Frontinus, *Stratagems*, book 3, ed. McElwain, pp. 205–66; Vegetius, *Epitome*, 4.24–30, ed. Milner, pp. 128–31; 'Excerpts of Polyaenus', sections 31.6–7, 31.12, 33.2, 36.1, 36.6–7, 54.1, 54.3, 55.2, ed. Krentz, 2:928–30, 938–40, 944, 978–80, 986; Leo VI, 'Stratagems', sections 2.1–2.2, ed. Krentz, 2:1014–15; Pizan, *Book of Deeds*, p. 137; Machiavelli, *Art of War*, 7.92, 95, 105, 114, ed. Lynch, pp. 151–3; Aubigny, *Traité*, p. 22. See also ch. 1 n. 50.

7 Juvaini, *History of the World-Conqueror*, 2:674–8; Bartlett, *Assassins*, pp. 44, 56–9, 92.

8 Fulcher of Chartres, *Historia Hierosolymitana*, 1.15.10, ed. Hagenmeyer, p. 221.

9 *Anselmi ... epistola*, p. 892; Gilo of Paris, *Historia*, p. 750; Guibert of Nogent, *Dei Gesta per Francos*, 7.33, ed. Huygens, p. 332; *Historia Gotfridi*, pp. 472–3; *Balduini III ...*, p. 160; Robert the Monk, *Historia Iherosolimitana*, pp. 794–5. According to some of the accounts, however, the Turks arranged only for a temporary truce, and Walo was killed when the Turks treacherously broke the truce and attacked his party.

10 For this episode, see Albert of Aachen, *Historia Hierosolymitana*, p. 378. For a fictional scene in the twelfth-century chivalric romance *Roman de Thèbes* that is probably based on this episode, see Sanok, 'Almoravides at Thebes', p. 286. For other possible plots, see France, 'Fall of Antioch', p. 17; France, *Victory in the East*, p. 244.

11 Anna Comnena, *Alexiad*, 10.11, ed. Sewter, pp. 328–9.

12 See also Rogers, *Latin Siege Warfare*, pp. 100–2.

13 For Muslim converts and unconverted Muslims joining the Crusaders, see Kedar, *Crusade and Mission*, pp. 73–4; Kedar, 'Subjected Muslims'; Harari, 'Military Role', pp. 102–5.

14 Fulcher of Chartres, *Historia Hierosolymitana*, 1.16.2, ed. Hagenmeyer, pp. 225–6.

15 *Gesta Francorum expugnantium Iherusalem*, p. 498.

16 France has argued, on the basis of Albert of Aachen's testimony, that the Crusader leaders gave Bohemond the supreme command only on 29 May. The evidence is, however, inconclusive. As France rightly says, the Crusaders at Antioch were in close contact with Edessa, and since Kerbogah arrived near the latter city around 4 May, the Crusaders must have learned of his approach by 10 May. The Anonymous says that they immediately convened a war council which granted Bohemond his demands. If they actually waited until 29 May before submitting to Bohemond's demands, it is hard to explain the Crusaders' complete inaction during these crucial three weeks. The explanation given to this inaction in the following paragraphs presupposes that Bohemond was already acting as the supreme commander.

17 Anna Comnena, *Alexiad*, 11.4, ed. Sewter, p. 344.

18 According to Kamāl al-Dīn, Bohemond suggested to the other commanders that each should command the entire army for eight days in his turn, and whoever managed to capture Antioch during his allotted days would keep it.

19 At least according to Fulcher of Chartres, Stephen of Blois – a principal Crusader leader who was, on one occasion, chosen to act as commander-in-chief – actually fled the army on 2 June. If this is true, it means either that he was kept in ignorance of the plan, or completely distrusted it (Fulcher of Chartres, *Historia Hierosolymitana*, 1.16.7, ed. Hagenmeyer, p. 228).

20 Guibert of Nogent, *Dei Gesta per Francos*, 5.6, ed. Huygens, p. 206.

21 *Gesta Francorum et aliorum Hierosolymitanorum*, p. 46.

22 *Gesta Francorum et aliorum Hierosolymitanorum*, pp. 46–7. Some of the sources say that the ladder was made of ropes rather than of wood, and that it snapped rather than broke. If so, it is even less understandable why Bohemond brought with him just a single such ladder. Not only is it far easier to carry several rope ladders than a number of 12–metre-long wooden ones, but climbing up a dangling rope ladder is also trickier and takes more time than climbing up a wooden ladder.

23 *Gesta Francorum et aliorum Hierosolymitanorum*, p. 47.

24 The present chapter is based mainly on the following sources: *Gesta Francorum et aliorum Hierosolymitanorum*, pp. 28–48; Albert of Aachen, *Historia Hierosolymitana*, pp. 359–407; Fulcher of Chartres, *Historia Hierosolymitana*, 1.15–17, ed. Hagenmeyer, pp. 216–35; Fulcher of Chartres, *History of the Expedition*, pp. 92–103; Hagenmeyer, *Epistulae*, pp. 149–71; Ralph of Caen, *Gesta Tancredi*, pp. 651–66; Raymond of Aguilers, *Liber*, pp. 62–7; William of Tyre, *Historia*, 5.1–23, ed. RHC, 1:193–233; Ibn al-Athīr, *Min kitāb kāmil al-tawārīkh*, 1:191–6; Ibn al-Qalānisī, *Damascus Chronicle*, pp. 41–6; Matthew of Edessa, *Armenia and the Crusades*, pp. 166–71; Asbridge, *First Crusade*, pp. 153–211; France, *Victory in the East*, pp. 122–296; France, 'Fall of Antioch', pp. 13–20; Runciman, *History of the Crusades*, 1:213–35; Yewdale, *Bohemond I*, pp. 15–36; Rogers, *Latin Siege Warfare*, pp. 25–39. It is based to a lesser extent on: Abū'l-Fidā, *Muntahabāt min al-mukhtasar*, pp. 1–4; Anna Comnena, *Alexiad*, 11.3–6, ed. Sewter, pp. 342–52; 'First and Second Crusades', pp. 69–73; Baldry of

Dol, *Historia Jerosolimitana*, pp. 52–7, 79–81; *Balduini III...*, pp. 160–2; Bar Hebraeus, *Chronography*, 1:234–5; Cafarus, *Liberatione civitatum orientis*, pp. 49–53; Ekkehard of Aura, *Hierosolymita*, p. 22; *Gesta Francorum expugnantium Iherusalem*, pp. 497–500; Gilo of Paris, *Historia*, pp. 750–66; Guibert of Nogent, *Dei Gesta per Francos*, 4.3–5.28, ed. Huygens, pp. 169–232; Henry of Huntingdon, *De captione Antiochiae*, pp. 374–9; Kamāl al-Dīn, *Extraits de la Chronique d'Alep*, pp. 580–2; Vitalis, *Ecclesiastical History*, 5:84–94; *Primi Belli Sacri Narrationes Minores*, pp. 346–7, 354–7, 364, 371–2, 391–6; Robert the Monk, *Historia Iherosolimitana*, pp. 795–807; *Stephani ... epistolae*; *Anselmi ... epistola*; Peter Tudebode, *Historia de Hierosolymitano itinere*, pp. 53–5; Malaterra, *De rebus gestis Rogerii*; William of Apulia, *Geste de Robert Guiscard*; Amatus of Montecassino, *History of the Normans*; Asbridge, *Creation*, pp. 15–36; El-Azhari, *Saljūqs of Syria*, pp. 60–97; Bachrach, 'Siege of Antioch', pp. 127–46; Bouchier, *Short History of Antioch*, pp. 1–17, 213–33; Bradbury, *Medieval Siege*, pp. 93–114; Brown, *Norman Conquest*; Edgington, 'Albert of Aachen and the *Chansons de Geste*'; France, 'Anonymous *Gesta Francorum*'; France, 'Departure of Tatikios', pp. 131–47; Harari, 'Concept of "Decisive Battles"'; Loud, *Age of Robert Guiscard*; Nicholson, *Medieval Warfare*, pp. 13–20, 69–71, 135–42; Norwich, *Normans in the South*; Prawer, *History*, 1:120–2; Rice, *Seljuks in Asia Minor*, pp. 48–51; Riley-Smith, *First Crusade and the Idea of Crusading*, pp. 65–7; Riley-Smith, *First Crusaders*, pp. 88, 214; Riley-Smith, 'Casualties', pp. 13–28; Riley-Smith, 'Raymond IV of St Gilles'.

3

Saving King Baldwin: Khartpert, 1123

IN the two decades following the First Crusade the three Crusader principalities of Antioch, Tripoli, and Jerusalem gradually expanded and conquered almost the entire Levantine coast from the Taurus range to the Sinai peninsula. The fourth principality – the County of Edessa – meanwhile thrust eastwards across the Euphrates river, cutting off Muslim Syria from Asia Minor and Mesopotamia (see map 2).

In 1119 the Franks of Outremer – as the settlers came to be known – hit upon more difficult times. A new Turkoman dynasty, the Artuqids of the tribe of Döger, took upon itself to halt the invaders' progress and roll them back into the sea. At the battle of the Field of Blood in 1119 Il-Ghazi ibn Artuq – head of the Artuqid clan – wiped out the army of the Principality of Antioch, along with most of the Norman nobility and Prince Roger of Antioch himself. In 1121, as King Baldwin II of Jerusalem was striving to rescue Antioch and halt the Artuqid offensive, Count Pons of Tripoli rebelled against the king's authority, and only when Baldwin marched on Tripoli at the head of the royal army did Pons submit. In 1122 it was Edessa's turn. One of Il-Ghazi's nephews, Prince Balak, took captive Count Joscelin of Edessa, Count Galeran of Birejik, and sixty other Edessan knights.

King Baldwin II was thus forced to act as regent for both Antioch and Edessa, since the heirs of Prince Roger and Count Joscelin were ten-year-old boys, while simultaneously ruling Jerusalem and keeping a watchful eye on the unreliable Pons of Tripoli. Baldwin felt that his most urgent task was to succour Edessa and stabilize the Franks' north-eastern flank. However, as he was touring Edessa's threatened frontiers, disaster struck.

On the morning of 18 April 1123, as the Frankish royal army was just waking up and preparing for the day's march, King Baldwin decided to enjoy himself. He went ahead of the main body with only a small escort, in order to hunt with a falcon. As the king crossed a tributary of the Euphrates over the bridge of Shenchrig, Prince Balak swept down on his unsuspecting prey. Apparently the Artuqid prince had been stalking the royal army for some time, waiting for just such an opportunity. Baldwin was isolated, his escort was small, and the main army was disorganized and heavy with sleep. The Franks showed little resistance. Those who could, saved their lives by flight. Many were massacred, and the king himself was captured, along with his nephew. They were bound in chains, and sent to join Count Joscelin and Count Galeran in the dungeons of Khartpert fortress, the capital of Balak's domains.[1] Balak would not hear of ransoming them, except in exchange for huge territorial concessions. He was

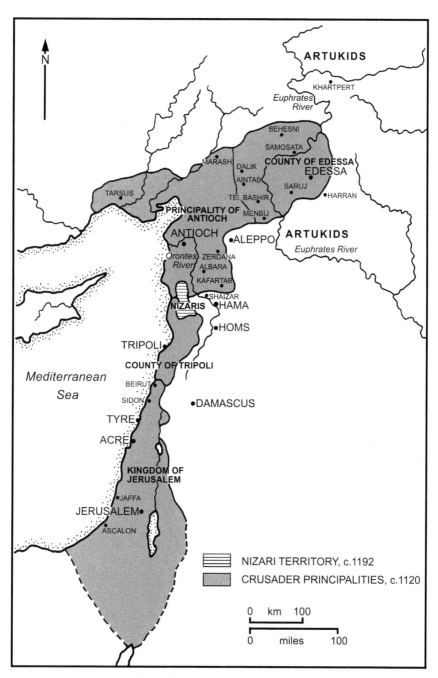

Map 2 The Middle East in the era of the Crusades

bent on utilizing his successes to make himself leader of Muslim Syria and to reconquer the Levant for Islam, rather than merely to enrich his coffers.

Thus in late April 1123 the Franks in the Levant found themselves completely leaderless. The king of Jerusalem and the count of Edessa were captives, the prince of Antioch was dead, and the count of Tripoli was a malcontent rebel who inspired little trust. The legal heirs of Antioch and Edessa were both minors, whereas King Baldwin had four daughters but neither sons nor sons-in-law. The Artuqids were poised to utilize their recent successes and overrun Antioch and Edessa. To make things worse, when news of Baldwin's captivity reached Egypt, the Egyptians felt they too could gain something from Balak's success, and their army invaded the Kingdom of Jerusalem, laying siege to the port of Jaffa.

The prelates and noblemen of the Kingdom of Jerusalem gathered for an emergency meeting in Acre. In it they unanimously elected Eustace Grenier, lord of Caesarea and Sidon, to act as regent. Eustace amply justified the trust put in him by defeating the Egyptian army at Jaffa and putting it to flight. Yet the situation remained difficult. The Egyptians were repulsed but not broken, and their fleet gathered at Ascalon in preparation for another invasion. Moreover, though Grenier proved to be a capable leader, he was only a regent, whose authority could never be as secure as that of a crowned king. It did not improve matters that he suddenly died, a fortnight after his victory at Jaffa.

If Jerusalem was in a plight, Antioch and Edessa were in a far worse condition. Apart from losing their princes, they were also bled white by the recent reverses, and most of their noblemen of fighting age were either dead or taken prisoner. Despair was rife, and they seemed to be at Balak's mercy. Balak by now became the virtual chief of the Artuqid clan. Il-Ghazi had died in November 1122, and his patrimony was divided between his sons, Suleiman and Timurtash, and his nephews, Badr and Balak. Though Balak received the smallest portion of the inheritance, a mountainous area surrounding the fortress of Khartpert, he was the ablest leader, and his recent successes in capturing Joscelin and Baldwin emboldened him and gave him immense prestige. After locking up Baldwin in Khartpert, Balak swiftly moved south in May 1123 and captured the town of Harran from his cousin Badr. He then marched against Aleppo, Badr's capital and the major Muslim city of Northern Syria. After a short siege, Badr lost heart and surrendered (29 June). Together with Aleppo, Balak took the mantle of Islam's chief leader in the fight against the infidels.

Now Balak was ready to turn against the Franks. After spending no more than a few days in Aleppo, he marched northwards toward Edessa, invading the area of Dalik and Tel Bashir (Turbessel), which previously escaped ruin. He ravaged the countryside, sending plunder and slaves back to Aleppo, and burning whatever could not be carried away. He could then strike either northeastwards towards the city of Edessa itself, or westwards toward the Principality of Antioch. He chose to ignore Edessa for the meantime and focus first on the fatter prize. If Antioch fell, Edessa too was bound to follow. In mid-July he invaded Antioch at the head of a large army, and soon captured the town of Albara. In early August he laid siege to the important fortress of Kafartab, which seemed destined to fall too, given that the military resources of both Antioch and Edessa were severely depleted, that morale in both principalities was at rock bottom, and that no help was forthcoming from either Tripoli or Jerusalem.

Meanwhile, Baldwin, Joscelin, Galeran, and dozens of other Frankish prisoners were languishing in the dungeons of Khartpert. With the help of some Armenian residents of the nearby town, they managed to send pleas for help to Edessa, but chances of rescue seemed extremely remote. Khartpert was situated deep in Artuqid-controlled territory. It was about 150 kilometres as the crow flies from Edessa's northern frontiers, and was further separated from Edessa by the formidable Anti-Taurus range, rising to heights of over 2,500 metres, and by the Euphrates river, swollen from the melting winter snows. Even if the Edessans managed to scrap together an expeditionary force and somehow make it to Khartpert, they could hardly hope to storm its formidable defences.

The fortress of Khartpert was a mountain fastness. Built on a steep hill, it rose 350 metres above the plain of Khanzit, overlooking the Hazar lake to one side and the Euphrates valley to the other. Its strategic location and natural strength had made it a place of importance throughout the centuries, and forts were continually maintained on that site since the days of the Urartu kingdom, in the early first millennium BC. Balak had ruled Khartpert since around 1113. He made it the capital of his domains, and since he housed there not only his most important prisoners, but also his harem and his treasury, he naturally fortified it to the best of his abilities. It was virtually immune to a head-on storming operation. Settling down to a regular siege was even more unthinkable for the Franks, for the lines of communication back to Edessa were long and exposed, and in any case, it would have given Balak ample time to hurry back home and wipe out the intruders.

Still, the captive princes sent their pleas to Edessa and prayed for a miracle. Their prayers were answered by a group of Armenian troops from the garrison of Behesni. Behesni was the Frankish fort closest to Khartpert, situated on the northern frontier of the County of Edessa. A group of between fifteen and fifty Armenian combatants (accounts differ as to their number) decided that, despite the enormous hazards, they would march to Khartpert and try to liberate the prisoners. The Turkomans had only recently settled in the area, and were mostly just a thin layer of warrior aristocracy. The peasants and towns-people were of different backgrounds, and around Khartpert in particular the civilian population was largely Armenian. Hence the Armenians from Behesni assumed they could infiltrate the area with relative ease and blend in with the local population. Once there, they could both reconnoitre the place and try to gain some local help for their enterprise. If no such help was forthcoming, and if the fortress proved to be too heavily guarded, they could always make their way back to Behesni.

It is not entirely clear whether the Armenians from Behesni embarked on this adventure on their own initiative, or whether they were talked into it by the Franco-Armenian leadership. (The Anonymous Syriac Chronicle attributes the initiative to Morphia, the Armenian wife of King Baldwin, and to the *de facto* regent of Edessa, Godfrey Almuin.) In either case, they had much to gain if they succeeded in their mission. Personally, they could expect great rewards in terms of both honour and wealth. It is probable that they were also motivated by personal loyalty to Joscelin. As count of Edessa, Joscelin was the Armenians' lord, and though relations between Franks and Armenians were not always congenial, Joscelin himself was quite popular with his Armenian subjects. Even before he became count of Edessa, as one of the county's leading magnates, he took care to establish good relations with the Armenian population, and married an Armenian princess.

The Armenians also had national interests at stake. Though the Franks were unpopular, the Armenians had at least as much to lose from a Turkoman victory as the Franks. The Franks were newcomers to the Middle East, and still had families, friends, and sometimes even lands back in Europe. In case of a total Muslim victory, their homelands and ancestral domains were secure. Hence defeat could never mean a familial or national holocaust, and whoever survived the defeat could simply return to where they came from. For instance, the noble Montlhéry clan, to which both King Baldwin and Count Joscelin belonged, was firmly planted in northern France, and no Turkoman victory could have uprooted or annihilated it. For the Armenians, on the other hand, there were no such easy outlets. They had been fighting for their religious, cultural, and political survival long before the Franks arrived, and defeat could mean an overwhelming national catastrophe for them – as it proved to be in the late 1140s.

Whatever motivated the Armenians of Behesni, and whoever set them on their adventurous course, it was entirely up to them to find a way to get to Khartpert, release the prisoners and make their way back in safety. They bonded themselves together formally, taking an oath of mutual loyalty and commitment. They then disguised themselves in civilian clothes, and set out for Khartpert sometimes in June or July 1123. Travelling in the height of the Middle Eastern scorching summer, they managed to cross both the Anti-Taurus range and the Euphrates river, reaching the vicinity of Khartpert without detection. There they apparently found sympathizers – perhaps even family members – who updated them on local conditions, and hid them while they acquainted themselves with the situation at the fortress and made their plans.

The Armenians soon discovered that the same factors that made Khartpert immune to a conventional assault made it potentially open to a clandestine operation. Given its massive fortifications, its distance from the nearest Frankish territory, the formidable natural barriers in between, and the state of Frankish military resources at the time, Balak thought with reason that it was completely beyond the capacity of the Franks to storm or lay siege to it. He therefore left there only a small garrison, and that garrison too was negligent, not expecting any immediate threat.

This was extremely good news for the Armenians from Behesni, but not all their problems were solved. Even though they were facing a negligent and comparatively small garrison, they could not simply scale the walls or walk in, especially as they were still outnumbered by the garrison and had with them only light weapons. Mining or breaching the walls was completely out of the question. Hence in order to get into the fortress, they had to find some further weakness in the defences. Luckily, they discovered that Khartpert was not only a military fortress, but also an administrative centre, and the commander of its garrison doubled as the governor of the nearby countryside. In this capacity, he was responsible for meting justice to the population, mediating disputes, and redressing wrongs.

Balak was careful to enforce law and order in his domains. Kamāl al-Dīn writes that once Balak took over the government of Aleppo, the highway robbers stopped their activities, and the gates of the city remained opened day and night without fear. Both the Anonymous Syriac Chronicle and Matthew of Edessa agree that he took particular care to protect his Christian subjects from harm and treated them well. He rooted out the brigands that infested the land, and it was said that he would impale a Turkoman for taking a bit of meat from a poor man. Here, thought the Armenians, lay the weakness of the defence, for if they could find some grievance to complain of, they could perhaps gain entry into the fortress.[2]

According to the Anonymous Syriac Chronicle, ten of the Armenians disguised themselves as poor villagers who came to Khartpert to complain of a wrong done to them by the village steward. Unarmed and carrying grapes, fruit, and fowls, they approached the fortress's gate, and told the officer on duty they wished for justice. The fortress had a double gate. An outer gate led into a small enclosed area, in which there was a guardroom. From this enclosure a second gate led into the fortress proper. The officer allowed the ten past the first gate, and told them to wait in the guardroom area while he sent somebody to ask his captain for directions.

The captain was just giving a banquet to the officers and other members of the guard; the wine was flowing freely, and everyone was merry. Only a few guards remained at the gate. While one of them went to inform the captain of the visitors' request, the 'villagers' dropped fruit and fowls, took hold of some weapons they found hanging in the guardroom, and charged the guards. They killed the officer and the few other men there, opened the gates, and called in their comrades who were hidden close by. Together they rushed on the diners, and massacred the entire garrison.

Fulcher of Chartres, a Frankish chronicler who was also an important official in the Kingdom of Jerusalem and was probably informed of the events at Khartpert by Joscelin himself, largely agrees with the above version. He writes that the Armenians approached the fortress in the guise of villagers selling merchandise, hiding daggers beneath their clothes. They were helped by a man from inside the fortress, who drew the captain of the fortress to the gate's guardroom, and engaged him there in a lively game of chess. The 'villagers' interrupted the game, wishing to inform the captain of some injustice done to them. As they surrounded the captain, loudly complaining and asking for his help, they suddenly drew the daggers and slew him. They then seized the weapons from the guardroom, killed the nearby guards, and charged into the fortress before the garrison could rally, killing about a hundred of its members.

William of Tyre offers a slightly different version. According to him, the Armenians disguised themselves as monks rather than villagers. Carrying daggers under their flowing clerical robes, they came to the fortress, declaring with tears in their eyes that they had suffered injury and violence, and that they wished to protest to the captain of the fortress about it, for he was responsible for maintaining order in that vicinity. Once they were admitted into the fortress, they drew their daggers, and killed the guards.

The Armenian chronicler Matthew of Edessa writes that the Armenians split into two groups, and approached the fortress quarrelling with each other, feigning the appearance of hostile plaintiffs seeking justice. The chronicler Michael the Syrian and the Jewish physician Gregory Abu'l Faraj Bar Hebraeus write that it was Armenian residents of the town of Khartpert who performed this deed. A few of them gathered together at the gate of the fortress, grumbling about their low pay and asking for the intervention of the captain. Once they were admitted within the gates, they seized some swords that were there, and killed the guards. Kamāl al-Dīn, the best informed Muslim chronicler, also sets the blame on certain residents of the town of Khartpert, including some of Balak's own troops.

All these versions largely agree with each other. Whatever pretext the Armenians of Behesni used, it is clear that they approached the fortress's gate in disguise, armed only with daggers – if at all – and enjoying the help and perhaps the active participation of certain local residents. They complained of some injury, and asked for justice from the fortress's captain. Having gained entrance into the guardroom under that pretext, they seized the weapons in the guardroom, overwhelmed the guards, and took over the fortress.[3] The Armenians then rushed to the prisoners' quarters, opened the gates of the prison, and with loud cries of joy broke their chains and gave them their liberty. It seems that they also sent word of their success to their friends in the town, and some local residents joined them in the fortress. Thus the first half of the plan was crowned with astounding success. With minimal expenditure of money and forces, and with no losses to speak of, King Baldwin, Count Joscelin and scores of other prisoners were rescued, and Balak's capital, treasure, and harem were theirs into the bargain.

Yet the biggest drawback of the Armenians' plan – or rather, lack of plan – became evident only now. Apparently, it had seemed to the Armenians of Behesni that the most difficult part of the operation would be getting into Khartpert, and that if God so favoured them that they succeeded in storming the fortress and saving the prisoners, they would also manage to get out by one means or another. Hence they had no clear plan of how they were going to return to Edessa. So now rescuers and rescued found themselves trapped together within the walls of the fortress, deep in enemy territory.

The dilemma facing them was not an easy one. On the one hand, Joscelin and Baldwin – who naturally took command of the situation – had at their disposal a force of at least several dozen combatants (the fifteen to fifty Armenians rescuers, a large number of Frankish prisoners captured by Balak in various battles, and perhaps some local sympathizers as well).[4] They also had at their command a fortress thought to be impregnable; full storehouses; Balak's treasure house; and a harem with Balak's wives and mistresses (eighty women altogether according to Matthew of Edessa). There were many sympathetic Armenians in the vicinity, the local Artuqid garrison was either killed or neutralized, and Balak was far away. (Kafartab was hundreds of kilometres south of Khartpert, and the two were separated not only by formidable natural barriers, but also by the County of Edessa.)

On the other hand, both space and time were on Balak's side. To leave the fortress *en masse* would have been suicidal. Now that the Turkomans were on the alert, it would have been absolutely impossible for dozens of combatants travelling together to cover the distance to Edessa without being detected on the way. In particular, the Euphrates was fordable in few places, and all were sure to be heavily guarded. And once the fugitives were detected, they stood no chance in open combat. Even if they armed themselves from the arsenal of Khartpert, seventy men could not defend themselves in the open against a horde of Turkoman cavalrymen.

They could of course stay in Khartpert and defend the fortress, but time was against them. The nearby Artuqid garrisons soon heard of the disaster, and quickly threw a cordon around the fortress to prevent the prisoners from escaping. Every day brought more Artuqid troops to the vicinity, and it made the chances of escape ever slimmer. And it was only a question of time before Balak himself would arrive on the scene with the main Artuqid army. And what then? Khartpert could not hold out forever.

Baldwin, Joscelin, Galeran, the leading Frankish knights, and the leaders of the Armenians came together to discuss the situation. For Baldwin and Joscelin, it was not the first time they found themselves together in such circumstances.

Indeed, they had a long and eventful history together. Baldwin – then known as Baldwin of Le Bourcq – had come to the East in the First Crusade, together with his distant cousins Baldwin of Boulogne and Godfrey of Bouillon. Godfrey became the first king of Jerusalem, whereas Baldwin of Boulogne captured Edessa and became its first Frankish count. When the childless Godfrey died, Baldwin of Boulogne left the County of Edessa to become King Baldwin I of Jerusalem, and appointed Baldwin of Le Bourcq as count in his stead.

It was then that Joscelin arrived on the scene. As a penniless younger son of the noble Montlhéry clan, at the age of around twenty he joined the ill-fated Crusade of 1101. Almost the entire crusader force perished on the way, but Joscelin was one of the lucky few who made it somehow to the Holy Land. There he was welcomed by Baldwin of Le Bourcq, who was his first cousin and was hard pressed to find European knights willing to settle in Edessa. Baldwin granted Joscelin a vast fief in the western part of Edessa, centred on the fortress of Tel Bashir, and made him his chief lieutenant. Together they went on various campaigns to expand the new principality, and after several victories, they were defeated at Harran and taken prisoner (1104).

They spent two years in captivity, while Edessa was governed by Bohemond and Tancred, the Norman princes of Antioch. The latter found the situation much to their liking, and refused to ransom Baldwin under various pretexts. Baldwin and Joscelin agreed that it would be best if Joscelin paid his own ransom first, and then utilized his freedom to effect the liberation of his lord. Joscelin accordingly paid the ransom and obtained his freedom, and then went around the Frankish Levant, beseeching help for the captive Baldwin and collecting money towards his ransom. His efforts bore fruit. In 1108 Jāwalī, the Muslim chief holding Baldwin, agreed to release him in exchange for a huge ransom and various other conditions. Joscelin brought the ransom money to Jāwalī, and turned himself in to serve as a hostage, guaranteeing that Baldwin would fulfil the terms imposed on him.

After Jāwalī released Joscelin, he and Baldwin governed Edessa together almost as co-rulers, until they fell out in 1112. Baldwin, writes Matthew of Edessa, was a modest, pure, and very devout man, but he was also mean and greedy. His insatiable love for money was matched only by his deep lack of generosity, and he was ingenious in devising means to seize the wealth of others. Joscelin's prosperous lands around Tel Bashir – originally given to him by Baldwin in an uncharacteristic act of generosity – now aroused Baldwin's greed, and, accusing Joscelin of disloyalty, he first imprisoned him, then expelled him from the county and confiscated his lands.

Joscelin, smouldering with rage and bitterness, left Edessa and went to Jerusalem. King Baldwin I, who recognized his merits, granted him the Galilee as a new fief, thus making him one of the foremost magnates of the Kingdom of Jerusalem. When Baldwin I died in 1118 without children, the leaders of the kingdom gathered to discuss the inheritance question. Some were in favour of summoning Count Eustace, the late king's brother, from Europe, to become the new king. Others supported the claims of Baldwin of Le Bourcq, the late king's cousin. At this critical position Joscelin set aside his feud with his cousin and former lord, and warmly pleaded Baldwin's case. His opinion carried the day, and Baldwin of Le Bourcq was made king. In return, Baldwin made Joscelin the new count of Edessa.

The situation at Khartpert was therefore uncannily familiar to Baldwin and Joscelin. They reached a similar decision to the one they made during their previous captivity. Though Joscelin, according to Kamāl al-Dīn, advised that they should all depart from the fortress as soon as possible and be content with saving their lives, King Baldwin refused. The king realized that they could not all travel together from Khartpert, and that if they split into small groups and made a run for it, most would surely be hunted down on the way. Perhaps he was also tempted by the opportunity that had fallen into his hands, and was disinclined to abandon the fortress of Khartpert and its treasures without a fight.

It was therefore decided that Baldwin would remain in Khartpert together with the bulk of their forces, draw the Artuqids' attention to himself, and hold out as long as was needed in the impregnable fortress. Joscelin would in the meantime stealthily slip out of Khartpert, break through the surrounding ring, and make his way to Edessa. Once there, he was to repeat his performance of 1108, tour the Frankish principalities, raise their morale, and plead Baldwin's cause. He should then come back to Khartpert at the head of an army.

Accordingly, one night shortly after the storming of Khartpert, if not on the very first night, while the Artuqid investment was still haphazard, Joscelin swore to Baldwin that he would neither rest, nor change his clothes, nor eat meat, nor drink wine (save during mass) until he returned to Khartpert at the head of an army. He then commended himself to God, and stole away from the fortress together with three other men. Two of them were Armenians who knew the area well and were to serve as his guides. The third was to be sent back to inform the king whether Joscelin had managed to break through the encircling Artuqid lines. Walking silently in the moonlight 'with as much fear as boldness', according to Fulcher of Charters, Joscelin and his companions passed through the Artuqid troops already encamped around the fortress. Once they cleared the encircling chain, Joscelin sent his companion back to the king along with his own ring, to show that he had indeed passed safely through the besiegers. He and his guides then made all haste to put some miles between themselves and Khartpert, marching hard throughout the night.

The Artuqids were apparently oblivious to Joscelin's escape, but the fugitives had to tread carefully. Night and day, Artuqid troops streamed from all sides to invest Khartpert and block all possible routes of escape. Proceeding mainly in the hours of darkness, Joscelin and his companions walked to the Euphrates. Joscelin's shoes were almost worn out by the time they reached the river, but greater hardships awaited him there. The fords of the Euphrates were heavily guarded, the Artuqids probably kept a close eye on any available boats, and Joscelin was too familiar a figure to escape notice. There was nothing to do but try and swim to the other side at some secluded spot. Unfortunately, the count of Edessa, despite all his other skills, did not know how to swim. He might easily have shared the fate of another illustrious Crusader, the Emperor Frederick Barbarossa, who drowned while having a bath in a Cilician river.

Joscelin's Armenian guides had a solution. The local inhabitants were used to crossing rivers and streams by hanging on to inflated leather skins. When they left Khartpert, the three took with them a few provisions, including two wine-skins. These they now inflated. They then placed Joscelin on top of the inflated skins and tied him to them with ropes. The Armenians – who were both excellent swimmers – swam on either side of the floating count, and together they navigated him safely to the opposite shore. Fulcher says that by the time Joscelin reached the southern bank he was excessively fatigued by his unusual journey, famished, and gasping for breath. Overcome by drowsiness, he dropped off to sleep under a nut tree, covering himself with brambles and brush in order not to be recognized if seen. Meanwhile he ordered one of his companions to beg or buy bread from some local inhabitant at any price.

In a nearby field a peasant was found, carrying dried figs and some grapes. He was brought before Joscelin, and recognizing the count, he fell at his feet saying, 'Hail, Joscelin!' The count was much alarmed at being recognized, and denied his identity, yet the peasant insisted that he knew him well. Then Joscelin frankly told the peasant of his plight and asked for his help, promising ample reward if he could contrive his escape. Whatever possessions he owned in those parts, Joscelin promised to give him more in his own domain of Tel Bashir. The peasant answered that he did not seek any rewards, and merely wished to help Joscelin, who had treated him kindly in the past. The peasant then went back to his house, and returned shortly after with many provisions, all his movable possessions and his family members. The count mounted the peasant's little donkey, and to make the disguise complete, was made to hold the peasant's little daughter (who, according to Fulcher, worried the count to death with her crying and weeping). Thus, disguised as a member of a peasant family on the move and carrying a crying child, Joscelin slowly made his way toward Edessa, and eventually reached his castle of Tel Bashir safely, about two to three weeks after leaving Khartpert.

Joscelin could not rest to recuperate from his travails. Anxious for the fate of his companions at Khartpert, and mindful of his oath, he gave orders to reimburse the loyal peasant, and then travelled with all haste to Antioch and from there to Jerusalem. His tale of the events at Khartpert electrified the Franks, and gave a great boost to their morale. He also reprimanded and shamed them for their previous inaction and their neglect of their king. If Joscelin really gave and kept the oath not to change his clothes before returning to Khartpert

– which is not impossible given the highly theatric nature of medieval noble culture – his mere presence must have spoken more eloquently than any words of the king's plight and his need for succour. As the leading nobleman of the Frankish Levant and as a representative of the besieged king, his entreaties to come to Baldwin's help may also have carried the force of commands.

One way or the other, the Egyptian threat was momentarily forgotten, and an expeditionary force was quickly organized to go to Baldwin's relief. Taking the True Cross with them, they marched north, gathering reinforcements along the way, until they reached Antioch. There they were joined by the Antiochene forces, and by early October the army entered Edessan territory and reached Tel Bashir.

Yet while Joscelin was making his escape and gathering the Frankish hosts, Balak was not idle. Balak learned of the fall of Khartpert within a few days of the event (according to Kamāl al-Dīn, he heard of it already on 7 August). Fulcher of Chartres and William of Tyre (who probably copied the story from Fulcher) write that the very night on which Khartpert fell, a terrible dream disturbed Balak's sleep, for he saw Joscelin blinding him. When he awoke in panic, he immediately dispatched messengers to Khartpert with orders to cut off Joscelin's head. These messengers arrived to find the fortress in Frankish hands, and hastily returned to inform Balak. Orderic Vitalis tells an equally fantastic tale, according to which three of Balak's wives hid themselves in a tower when the Franks captured Khartpert. From that tower, they dispatched a carrier pigeon with a message to Balak, who thereby learned of the fortress's fate with record speed.

By whatever means Balak learned of these events, when he heard that not only were the prisoners released, but that they held his capital, his treasure, his wives, and his mistresses, he went wild with rage. He immediately lifted the siege of Kafartab, and marched to Khartpert 'with the rapidity of an eagle', according to Matthew of Edessa. Within fifteen days Balak stood at the gates of Khartpert. Upon arrival he offered Baldwin generous terms, promising that if he handed the fortress and all that it contained intact, he and all his companions would be allowed to depart and assured safe conduct to Edessa. Orderic Vitalis says that Balak was particularly keen to get back his wives and mistresses safely, and offered Baldwin his freedom in exchange for them. His version is highly suspect, and no other source elaborates on the women's fate, either at the hands of the Franks, or later at Balak's hands.[5]

Whatever prompted Balak to make his generous offer, Baldwin rejected it, partly because he gave no credence to the promises, and partly because he felt confident in his ability to defend Khartpert until Joscelin's return. Balak swore that Baldwin would live to regret this rebuff. Fearing that a Frankish host may come to the relief of the castle, he made hasty preparations to storm the fortress by main force. On his side, Baldwin was busy strengthening the fortress's defences still further from the moment he was released.

Yet Balak knew something that Baldwin did not. For all its reputation of impregnability, Khartpert was really a giant with feet of clay. Though the fortress certainly had a magnificent location and formidable walls, the hill on which it was built was made of soft chalk, ideal for excavating tunnels. Balak set a large number of sappers to work, and within a fortnight, several tunnels were dug beneath Khartpert's walls, propped up by wooden planks. All the while, he bombarded the walls with hastily erected catapults and harassed the garrison day and night. Once the tunnels were ready, fire was set to the planks of one of them, and one of the fortress's towers came crushing down. Balak again offered Baldwin terms of surrender. Though by now Baldwin was apprehensive, he again refused, probably fearing more for the fate of his companions then for his own fate. As king, he guessed he was too valuable to be killed.

Balak now ordered the setting alight of another tunnel, which was dug right under the fortress's main tower. This tower, which commanded the fortress's water supply, duly collapsed with a loud noise. As smoke and dust rose from the debris, Baldwin realized the game was up. His empty hopes chilled him, writes Fulcher, and he at last lost his courage. He sent Count Galeran to ask for Balak's word of honour that the lives of all the garrison members would be spared. When Balak promised to spare their lives, the fortress surrendered (16 September 1123).

Balak kept his word only to a very limited degree. He spared the lives of King Baldwin, Count Galeran, and a nephew of the king who was with them. These three valuable prisoners were transferred to the city of Harran, where they were kept under close guard. The rest of the garrison, including the Armenians of Behesni, the Frankish prisoners they rescued, and whatever local inhabitants joined them, were left to face the full fury of Balak's vengeance. Breaking his word, Balak had them tortured in various ways. Some were flayed alive, others were sawn in half, and still others were buried alive. Some were handed over to Balak's men, to serve as targets in archery practice, and others were hurled down from the summit of the fortress to certain death.[6]

Hence when Joscelin's hastily assembled army arrived at Tel Bashir, there was no one left to succour. Baldwin and Galeran were incarcerated in Harran, and the rest of the Khartpert garrison members were dead. Not wishing to return empty handed, and desiring to get even with Balak somehow, the army turned upon the city of Aleppo. They ravaged the surrounding countryside, cut down gardens and trees, desecrated tombs and cemeteries, and destroyed some mosques that lay outside the city's walls. After avenging themselves on these plants and stones, the army returned south.

Joscelin himself stayed in the north. Though he failed to save the king, his own rescue was a huge boost to Frankish morale, and his presence was well felt throughout Northern Syria. He energized the Frankish forces, and throughout the winter of 1123/4 he led several destructive raids into Muslim territories.

In the spring of 1124 Balak renewed the offensive. He first made an incursion into Edessan territory, in order to punish the rebellious ruler of Menbij, a Muslim town which proclaimed its loyalty to the rescued count of Edessa. Balak easily captured the town itself, but the citadel resisted him. Joscelin meanwhile collected together the forces of Antioch and Edessa and came to Menbij's rescue. Balak left a small force before the citadel, and with the rest of the army met Joscelin in battle. The battle ended in a draw, as each side apparently annihilated one of its adversary flanks. The Franks suffered the worse of this exchange, for they could little afford this new loss of manpower. Joscelin had to retreat hastily back to Tel Bashir; Balak executed the prisoners who fell into his hands, then returned to besiege the citadel of Menbij.

Balak went in person to position the siege artillery. The day was hot, and he removed his coat of mail. At that very moment an archer on the wall shot an arrow which (depending on which version one accepts) hit either Balak's left shoulder or his buttocks. Wherever the arrow lodged, it proved to be a mortal wound. The archer, an Armenian Sun-Worshiper,[7] succeeded where all the Frankish armies and leaders had previously failed. The dying Balak summoned his cousin Timurtash to his death-bed and made him his heir (6 May 1124). When news of Balak's death spread, the Artuqid army panicked and retreated in great disorder. Many of Balak's subjects, including the Christians, deeply mourned his passing, for he dealt compassionately with them. For the Franks, however, Balak's death was a god-sent boon, and they reacted with great joy.

Success attended Frankish arms in the south too. A Venetian fleet came to the East, defeated the Egyptian fleet and lifted this menace. While Joscelin covered their north-eastern flank and kept Balak busy, the Venetians and the Franks of Jerusalem together besieged and captured the great port city of Tyre, which for twenty-five years had defiantly resisted all the Frankish efforts to capture it.

Upon the death of Balak, Timurtash inherited not only the dead man's territories, but also the captive Baldwin. Unlike Balak, Timurtash was more interested in comforts and good living than in conquest, and instead of utilizing Baldwin's captivity to wage all-out war against the Franks, he was more than willing to exchange him for money and security. The Muslim emir of Shaizar, who was on friendly terms with both the Artuqids and the Franks, soon brokered a deal. Timurtash agreed to release Baldwin for the grand sum of 80,000 gold dinars, as well as the fortresses and towns of Athareb, Zerdana, Azaz, Kafartab, and Jasr. This effectively meant delivering to Timurtash the entire line of fortresses along the border between Antioch and Aleppo, safeguarding the latter but opening the former to attack. Nevertheless, for the release of their king, the Franks seemed content to pay almost any price.

After receiving a down payment of 20,000 gold dinars, Timurtash released Baldwin. To make sure that the rest of the money and the fortresses were handed over, several important personages, including Baldwin's youngest daughter and Joscelin's son and heir, were given to the emir of Shaizar as hostages. Once freed, however, Baldwin refused to honour the agreement. He said that he would pay the money, but that he could not hand over the fortresses, because they belonged to the Principality of Antioch rather than to the Kingdom of Jerusalem, and he was only Antioch's regent, not its legal lord. Timurtash, eager to avoid war and to get the rest of the ransom money, accepted the explanation. The necessary sum of gold was eventually raised by the Muslims themselves. Baldwin won a great victory over a united Muslim army at Azaz (1125). The Frankish knights donated large portions of the ransoms they received from their prisoners to their king, who was then able to pay the amount still owed on his own ransom, and secure the release of the hostages.

Thus ended the affair of King Baldwin II's captivity. Though the storming of Khartpert failed to rescue him, and though the Armenians of Behesni certainly benefited little from it, it nevertheless exemplifies both the conduct of medieval special operations and their potential value. For almost no expense at all, the Franks nearly managed to get back their king, for whom they were later willing to pay an immense sum of money and give up a line of important fortresses.

Even as it was, the operation had important repercussions on the strategic situation in the Middle East. First, it immediately caused Balak to cancel his offensive and hasten back to Khartpert. Even after he recaptured the fortress, the lateness of the season and his exertions in the previous weeks meant that he made no further offensive moves in the campaigning season of 1123. Thus at the very least, the operation can be credited with rescuing the fortress of Kafartab, and delivering the Principality of Antioch and the County of Edessa from an extremely difficult situation. Secondly, the daring operation and the successful rescue of the count of Edessa seized the imagination of the Franks and gave an invaluable boost to their morale. After suffering a string of humiliating reverses, there was at last something to be proud of. Finally, the rescued count of Edessa was almost as valuable a person as the king of Jerusalem. His presence back amongst the Franks certainly galvanized the defence and lent new spirit to their operations in the winter of 1123 and in 1124.

Hence, though the tide ultimately turned thanks to the timely intervention of the Venetian fleet and of the Sun-Worshiper on the wall of Menbij, the storming of Khartpert fortress was more than just a daring escapade, and made a significant contribution to the revival of the Frankish fortunes in 1123/4.[8]

NOTES

1 There are various spellings to the fortress's name, including Kharpurt and Kharput. It was also known as Hisna Zayt, from the name of the Roman fort Castellum Zjata. The Franks pronounced its name Quart-Pierre, and its current Turkish name is Harput.

2 It is interesting to note that exactly that same year, 1123, Amaury IV of Montfort attempted to utilize a similar pretext in order to seize the town of Gisors.

Hearing that a certain Monday was fixed as a day for hearing lawsuits before the town's governor, Amaury sent several men to file a bogus suit, assassinate the unarmed governor during the legal hearing, and open the gates of the town in the ensuing confusion. The plan miscarried largely because the governor's wife delayed him to discuss private matters, and he was late for court (Vitalis, *Ecclesiastical History*, 6:342–4).

3 Only the Muslim chroniclers Ibn al-Athīr and Ibn al-Qalānisī and the Norman monk Orderic Vitalis offer substantially different versions. Ibn al-Athīr says that Khartpert was taken by a group of Frankish soldiers who gained entrance into the fortress by pretending to be part of Balak's own army. Ibn al-Qalānisī says that the prisoners freed themselves by means of some stratagem. The accounts of both these Muslim authors are not very reliable. Orderic gives a highly imaginative story. He too claims that the captives liberated themselves. He explains that they got the guards drunk during a banquet, and as the guards snored, the Franks took their arms, joined forces with some Armenian and Syrian Christian prisoners, and massacred the garrison. Orderic wrote his manuscript in the St Evroul en Ouce monastery in Normandy, never visiting the Middle East himself. Though he sometimes gained highly accurate information from pilgrims and knights passing through the monastery on their way back from the East, it is quite clear that his version of events in Khartpert is not to be trusted. It seems particularly likely that in this case, he felt uneasy about the idea that the helpless king of Jerusalem was rescued by a group of heretical Eastern Christians, and preferred to make the king and his Frankish companions the agents of their own liberation.

4 Matthew of Edessa writes that they had around 65 defenders all together. Bar Hebraeus gives the number of 70 defenders.

5 The presence of captive Western knights together with a harem of Oriental princesses in an Eastern fortress has been the stuff of romantic and colonial fables from the twelfth century onwards. The affair of Khartpert was quite fantastic to begin with, and it did not lose anything in the telling as it was circulated in the ports and taverns of the Mediterranean and Western Europe. By the time it reached Orderic's monastery, it must have already become a pretty impressive yarn. Sitting in his Norman cloister and fantasizing on these events in the exotic Orient, Orderic added a few touches of his own, concocting a lengthy story of the romantic relations that developed between some of the captured princesses and the Frankish knights. There is no other evidence of such relations, and I have generally discounted Orderic's version of events, but the fact that at least part of Balak's harem was captured at Khartpert is confirmed by independent sources, and it is likely that the Franks tried to use the captive women as bargaining chips. The kidnapping and ransoming of noble women was certainly common in the twelfth-century Middle East. For instance, during Baldwin's first imprisonment, his Muslim captors offered to release him in exchange for a large sum of money and the release of a Muslim noblewoman captured by the Norman princes of Antioch (Friedman, 'Women in Captivity', pp. 75–88).

6 Balak's cruelty is well attested not only by the hostile Frankish sources, but also by the Muslim sources and the Armenian and Syrian sources that otherwise praise his humane conduct. Michael the Syrian says that altogether seventy people were killed by Balak.

7 A pagan sect that still had adherents amongst a section of the Armenian population in the Middle Ages.

8 The present chapter is based mainly on the following sources: 'First and Second Crusades', pp. 89–95; Bar Hebraeus, *Chronography*, 1:248–53; Fulcher of Chartres, *Historia Hierosolymitana*, 3.14–26, ed. Hagenmeyer, pp. 651–93; Fulcher of Chartres, *History of the Expedition*, pp. 238–54; Ibn al-Athīr, *Min kitāb kāmil al-tawārīkh*, 1:349–56; Ibn al-Qalānisī, *Damascus Chronicle*, pp. 165–71; Kamāl al-Dīn, *Extraits de la Chronique d'Alep*, pp. 634–42; Matthew of Edessa, *Armenia and the Crusades*, pp. 228–36, 346–9; *Chronique de Michel le Syrien*, 3:210–12; William of Tyre, *Historia*, 12.17–21, ed. RHC, 1:536–45; Nicholson, *Joscelyn I*, pp. 52–74; Riley-Smith, *First Crusaders*, pp. 2–10, 169–75, 182–7, 244–6; Runciman, *History of the Crusades*, 2:143–74. It is based to a lesser extent on: Abū'l-Fidā, *Muntahabāt min al-mukhtasar*, pp. 14–16; *Balduini III...*, p. 184; *Guillaume de Tyr*, pp. 456–67; Vitalis, *Ecclesiastical History*, 5:108–29; Usāmah, *Kitāb al-I'tibār*, pp. 107–8, 150; Asbridge, *Creation*, pp. 82–6; Cahen, *Syrie du nord*, pp. 294–9; Ghazarian, *Armenian Kingdom*; Friedman, 'Women in Captivity', pp. 75–88; Friedman, *Encounter between Enemies*, pp. 33–186, 217–18; La Monte, *Feudal Monarchy*, pp. 8–11, 187–202; Mayer, *Crusades*, pp. 74–7; Payne, *Crusades*, pp. 129–32; Prawer, *History*, 1:209–18; Smail, *Crusading Warfare*, pp. 29–30, 46–53, 110, 178–81; Thomson, 'Crusaders through Armenian Eyes', pp. 71–82.

4

The Assassination of King Conrad: Tyre, 1192

M OST medieval special operations have long been forgotten, and have failed to leave a mark on either the popular or the academic image of medieval warfare. The sole exception is the operations conducted by the Nizari sect, made famous as the Order of the Assassins. The Nizaris not only bequeathed to posterity the memory of one of the most successful clandestine organizations in history, but have also enriched European languages with the word 'assassination' itself, denoting the use of premeditated murder of key individuals as a military and political tool. For *assassin* derives from the Arabic word *hashīshīn* – a pejorative term, meaning 'users of hashish' – by which hostile Muslim sources occasionally referred to the Nizari sect.[1]

The Nizaris were a radical millenarian sect that sprang up in northern Persia in the late eleventh century, a splinter of the Isma'ili sect, which was itself a radical splinter group of Shi'ite Islam. Nizari theology and practices ran counter to mainstream Sunni Islam, and were anathema even to most Shi'ites and Isma'ilis. The assassinations of which the Nizaris were proudest were those of two Sunni caliphs in 1135 and 1138. In 1164 the Nizaris even took the extreme step of proclaiming the *qiyāma*, or the end of time and of the Law. All prohibitions of Muslim Law were formally abolished, and the faithful were encouraged to ceremoniously break the Law by such gestures as drinking wine, eating pork, feasting on the month of Ramadan, and praying with their backs towards Mecca.

Their doctrines and practices roused the fears and hostility of Sunnis, Shi'ites, and moderate Isma'ilis, and of both the religious and secular powers. The Seljuk Empire strained itself to smother the fledgling movement in its cradle, whereas the Isma'ili Fatimid Empire, whose agents were the movement's initial leaders, soon began to perceive it as a deadly danger. A typical anti-Nizari tract argued that

> To kill them is more lawful than rainwater. It is the duty of sultans and kings to conquer and kill them, and cleanse the surface of the earth from their pollution. It is not right to associate or form friendships with them, nor to eat meat butchered by them, nor to enter into marriage with them. To shed the blood of a [Nizari] heretic is more meritorious than to kill seventy Greek infidels.[2]

In response, the movement's leader, Hasan i-Sabah, anticipated future revolutionaries by reverting to the use of special operations. Beginning around 1080 he orchestrated one of the most successful campaigns ever of assassination, subversion, and subterfuge. Within a few years i-Sabah liquidated some of his main critics and enemies, and took over a large number of fortresses and villages in the more remote and mountainous parts of Persia, including the famous Alamut, which became his headquarters. He realized that he was still too weak to venture into the plains and main population centres, so he established a loose-knit network of mountain theocracies, from which his followers set out on missions of proselytizing and subversion.

These theocracies were militarily weak, and a determined effort could have wiped them out. But the systematic assassination of hostile religious preachers and political leaders meant that few leaders had the stomach to suggest – let alone lead – an attack on the Nizari enclaves. As the Sunni historian Juvaini notes, merely to record the names of all those assassinated by the Nizaris would take too long.[3] i-Sabah then widened his sphere of action, sending missionaries far and wide. These missionaries attempted to copy the Persian example and establish independent Nizari enclaves in other parts of the Middle East. They strove to gain adherents by their missionary work, to seize fortresses by subversion, and to cow opponents by assassination.

In Syria their initial attempts to gain a foothold in or near the main cities such as Aleppo and Damascus failed. However, between 1132 and 1141 they managed to capture several castles in the Bahra mountains – a wild mountainous borderland between the Muslim and Frankish powers – where they established an independent Nizari principality (see map 2).[4] Perhaps 60,000 Nizaris lived there. From 1162 until 1193 the Syrian enclave was led by a charismatic leader called Rashīd al-Dīn Sinān, who became famous in the West as the Old Man of the Mountain. Hostile Muslim and Frankish sources were fascinated with Sinān, and most describe him in similar terms to Kamāl al-Dīn: 'an outstanding man, of secret devices, vast designs, and great jugglery, with power to incite and mislead hearts, to hide secrets, outwit enemy and to use the vile and the foolish for his evil purposes'.[5] Nizari sources give a similar picture of Sinān as an extremely capable man of unfathomable knowledge and the powers of a wizard, though they of course evaluate him in the most favourable terms.

The nature of Nizari activities sparked the imagination of medieval authors as well as modern ones, and gave rise to numerous tall tales. It is consequently very difficult to tell fact from fiction in Nizari history. In particular, almost every important assassination that took place throughout the Middle East and even Europe in the twelfth and thirteenth centuries was attributed to the Nizaris. They were an easy scapegoat for the real culprits, partly because they were indeed responsible for hundreds of assassinations, and partly because they had much to gain from their deadly reputation, and were therefore not unwilling to take credit for other people's handiwork.

Most of the Nizaris' victims were Sunni Muslims, and they were often on good or at least tolerable terms with their Christian and Frankish neighbours.

The only major Frankish leader assassinated by them before 1192 was Count Raymond II of Tripoli (1152), perhaps due to a border dispute with the Nizari Bahra principality.[6] Yet of all their various exploits, the one that left the deepest mark on Western historical consciousness was the murder of Conrad of Montferrat, a few days before he was crowned king of Jerusalem.

The Montferrats were one of the most important noble families of Northern Italy. They were related by blood to the Hohenstaufen emperors of Germany and to the Capetian kings of France, and were also closely allied to several of the imperial families of Byzantium. Conrad was the second son of William III, Marquis of Montferrat, and succeeded his father as marquis in 1190/1. After an impressive military career in Italy in the 1170s and 1180s, Conrad arrived in the Holy Land towards the end of July 1187, only to discover that a few weeks previously the Frankish field army had been annihilated at the battle of Hattin, and that the towns and fortresses of the Kingdom of Jerusalem were surrendering in droves to the victor, Saladin.

Docking at the important port city of Tyre, Conrad found it overflowing with refugees and ready to surrender at a moment's notice. Striking a defiant pose, he reassured the defenders that their situation was in fact far from hopeless, and offered to take charge of the defence himself, if in return they would accept him as their lord and commander. Tyre was part of the royal patrimony of the kings of Jerusalem, and the king, Guy de Lusignan, was alive. However, Guy was a prisoner of Saladin, and with the other native leaders either dead, captive, or in flight, Tyre's defenders accepted Conrad's offer with both hands.

Conrad quickly reinvigorated the defence, and while the rest of the kingdom was succumbing to Saladin, he worked ceaselessly to strengthen Tyre's fortifications and morale. When Saladin eventually arrived before Tyre in November 1187 he found the city ready for him. The siege ended in a decisive victory for Conrad on both land and sea. It was Saladin's first setback after Hattin, and in January 1188 his army lifted the siege. When the main armies of the Third Crusade began arriving at the Holy Land in 1189, Tyre provided them with a sorely needed bridge-head.

In the years 1189–92 the Holy Land witnessed two major struggles. Crusader armies that gathered from almost the entire continent of Europe, and were led by King Philip August of France and King Richard the Lion-Heart of England, strove to reverse the outcome of Hattin and re-establish the Kingdom of Jerusalem. Acre fell to them after a siege of two years, Saladin was defeated in several battles, and eventually a thin sliver of coastline was wrested from the Muslims and reconstituted as what historians term 'the Kingdom of Acre'.

Simultaneously, a fierce brawl took place for the possession of this rump kingdom. On the one side, after his successful defence of Tyre, Conrad of Montferrat began to see himself as the *de facto* king, or at least a potential king, by right of conquest. On the other side, there was King Guy, whom Saladin released from captivity in the summer of 1188 in the hope of fomenting discord amongst the Franks. Guy and Conrad did not disappoint Saladin's hopes, and quickly fell to fighting over the crown of the nonexistent kingdom. When the main Crusader armies arrived from Europe, the rivalry between Conrad and Guy was grafted unto a much weightier stock. King Philip August of France took up the cause of his kinsman Conrad, whereas King Richard the Lion-Heart of England supported Guy.

The legal ruler of the kingdom was actually neither Conrad nor Guy, but Guy's wife, Queen Sibylla. It was Sibylla who gave Guy the crown of Jerusalem by choosing him as her husband, against bitter protests of the Frankish nobility. In 1190 she and her two daughters died from an illness that struck the Crusader camp, thereby depriving Guy of any legal claims to the throne, whose rightful heir was now Sibylla's half-sister, Isabella. Under pressure from her mother and the Frankish nobility, Isabella was forced to divorce her weak husband, Humphrey of Toron, and marry Conrad instead (24 November 1190). Conrad thereby became the legal king of Jerusalem, as well as marquis of Montferrat (by which title many of the sources refer to him). Guy remained as no more than the late queen's widower.

Richard nevertheless continued to support Guy's claim against Conrad and Philip. When Philip went back to France and Richard remained behind to conduct his titanic duel with Saladin, Conrad distanced himself from the Crusader army to such an extent that many believed he had switched sides and reached some secret understanding with Saladin. However, in 1192 the deteriorating situation in England forced Richard to return home. Before leaving, he realized that he had to settle the dispute for the throne of Jerusalem. In early April he gathered at Ascalon a council of the leading men of the army and of the local Frankish noblemen to decide the issue. All present unanimously chose Conrad as king, and Richard reluctantly accepted their verdict.

On 20 April 1192 Count Henry of Champagne, Richard's nephew, arrived at Tyre at the head of an impressive retinue, and offered Conrad the long-desired crown. According to the *Itinerarium*, the delighted Conrad lifted his hands to heaven in exultation, and prayed: 'Lord God … I beg, Lord, that if You judge me worthy to govern Your kingdom, I will live to see myself crowned. But if You think differently about me, Lord, may You never consent to my being promoted to it.'[7] He then busily set about preparing for his coronation, which was to take place in Acre within a few days.

✦ ✦ ✦

In the last days of April 1192 Tyre was in a festive mood. Not only the destined king, but all his followers and the ordinary citizens made their preparations for the coming coronation. Money was borrowed and spent lavishly, clothes were sewn and mended, and weapons were polished, in order to make the best impression in the coronation ceremony and the following revelry.

Rashīd al-Dīn Sinān was also making preparations, but of a very different nature. Some time before, he had decided to eliminate the would-be king. Sinān's motives have been the subject of furious controversies ever since 1192. Many have claimed that the assassination was in fact Richard's doing, and that he convinced Sinān by some combination of bribery, threats, and promises to have the marquis of Montferrat killed. Others have placed the blame on Saladin, arguing that it was the sultan rather than the king of England who pressed Sinān to have Conrad murdered. It is worth noting that when Saladin subsequently concluded a peace treaty with Richard and the Franks, he insisted that the Nizaris too should be protected by it.

The fact that Conrad was murdered very shortly after the Ascalon conference may support either version. It could be that, after being rebuffed at Ascalon, Richard decided to remove Conrad by underhand methods. The conference provided Saladin too with a motivation he previously lacked. Before the conference Saladin benefited from the division within the Christians' ranks, and therefore had no incentive to kill Conrad. But once the marquis was unanimously acclaimed king, Saladin had much to fear from that capable and ruthless opponent, and much to gain from killing him and reopening the contest for the crown of Jerusalem.

If Saladin was indeed the culprit, it is interesting to note that the sultan of the Ayyubid Empire had to cajole the head of the tiny Nizari enclave in order to have Conrad assassinated, and did not command any suitable hit-men of his own. If, however, Richard was behind the murder, it is more understandable why he commissioned it from Sinān instead of entrusting the job to some of his own men. Richard must have been only too aware of the dangers of using one's own men to eliminate a Christian hero. He could well remember what happened to his father, Henry II, when the latter encouraged his household knights to free him from that ignoble priest, Archbishop Thomas Becket of Canterbury (1170).

Other sources argue that Sinān had his own motives to murder Conrad. According to one version Conrad had no one but himself to blame for his murder. When a ship belonging to Sinān anchored in Tyre, the marquis coveted its wealth, and ordered his men to seize it. Conrad twice refused Sinān's requests to return the captives and the stolen possessions, thereby sealing his own death warrant.[8] This story, however, has been questioned, and may well have been invented by Richard's supporters to exonerate him. It is not backed by any Muslim source.

It is impossible to be sure today what really motivated Sinān, and who was ultimately responsible for Conrad's murder. What is certain is that the Nizaris were neither puppets nor mercenaries. Just a few years earlier, when Saladin sent Sinān a threatening letter, the Nizari leader replied in the most insolent terms, writing to Saladin that 'it is astonishing to find a fly buzzing in an elephant's ear'.[9] Even if he was prompted to murder Conrad by either Richard or Saladin, Sinān would have consented to do so only if it served Nizari interests.

And whatever these interests were, by late April 1192, while Tyre was all hustle and bustle in preparation for the coronation, two Nizari assassins were walking its streets, stalking the marquis and awaiting their opportunity.

From a purely military viewpoint, the most interesting question regarding Nizari activities is how the *fidā'īs* – as the Nizari assassins called themselves – were trained and prepared for their mission. This question has taxed the imagination of writers from the Middle Ages till today, and gave rise to numerous legends and speculations. The most persistent of these legends concerns the term *hashīshīn*. Some Western authors have wrongly linked this pejorative term to the Nizaris' amazing skill in assassination, and concluded that Nizari assassins performed their deadly operations under the influence of narcotics, or were at least trained and brain-washed with the help of narcotics (see illus. 7). There is not a shred of truth in this story. Mainstream Muslim authors referred to the Nizaris as *hashīshīn* because the latter was a common pejorative in medieval Islamic culture, indicating libertinism and moral laxity. It was levelled against many sects suspected of unorthodox beliefs and behaviours, and had nothing to do with assassinations.[10]

Another common but baseless legend – initially spread by hostile Muslim authors – is that inside some of the Nizari strongholds there were secluded gardens of pleasure to which young recruits were secretly brought and told that they were in Paradise. There they indulged in sexual and other sensual pleasures until being removed from the garden. Fully convinced now of the existence of Paradise, and told that they could return and live there for all eternity if they sacrificed their lives for the cause, these recruits were henceforth willing to do anything asked of them, and gladly undertook even suicidal missions.

Though neither legend has any factual basis, they both highlight one of the main factors that contributed to the *fidā'īs'* successes, namely their unsurpassed motivation and willingness to sacrifice their lives. Their motivation was crucial for two reasons. First, as we shall see, *fidā'īs* were occasionally planted near enemy targets and remained there for months or years before being activated. Strong motivation was needed to keep them faithful during this long period of waiting. Secondly, once they were activated, their willingness to lose their life for the cause facilitated the accomplishment of assassination missions, for it is obviously far easier to plan and execute an assassination when you need not worry about escaping afterwards.

This strong motivation was, however, the product of religious conviction rather than of intoxication with drugs or sensual pleasures. During the Middle Ages as well as other periods, many sects and religions produced cohorts of martyrs who willingly underwent torture or killed themselves without the aid of drugs or sensual amusement parks. As Juvaini writes, the *fidā'īs* were largely prompted by 'misguided striving after bliss in the world to come'.[11]

Yet strong motivation in itself was not enough, for it does not necessarily turn people into effective fighters and assassins. The Nizari *fidā'īs* clearly possessed superb skills in the arts of infiltration and murder, which distinguished them from the run-of-the-mill medieval zealot, and transformed them into one of the most fearsome of medieval strategic weapons. How exactly did they acquire these skills, which obviously could only rarely be transmitted from one generation of *fidā'īs* to the next?

The Nizaris owed much of their covert skills to their experience as a persecuted missionary sect. Whereas many Muslim, Christian, and Jewish sects in the Middle Ages set a premium on a public profession of faith in the face of persecution, even at the cost of martyrdom, the Nizaris embraced and developed the Shi'ite doctrine of *taqiyya*, according to which the faithful were allowed and even encouraged to hide or repudiate their faith in order to avoid detection and persecution, and to spread their message. Even after establishing their mountain theocracies, Nizari missionaries were regularly sent into hostile territories to spread the faith, and often both these missionaries and their new converts had to live in secrecy and hide their true identities for long periods, thereby gaining ample experience in various clandestine arts.

For instance, Ibn al-Qalānisī writes that upon arrival in Syria, the Nizari missionary Bahrām 'lived in extreme concealment and secrecy, and continually disguised himself, so that he moved from city to city and castle to castle without anyone being aware of his identity', while gaining converts for the new faith.[12] According to Sinān's autobiography (parts of which were preserved by Kamāl al-Dīn and Juvaini), when Sinān was sent from Alamut to Syria he was given letters of introduction to Nizari agents in various towns along the route, who hid him and hired mounts for him, so that he was able to travel from Northern Persia to Aleppo in complete secrecy and relative ease. These clandestine networks of missionaries and converts produced people with excellent infiltration skills, and facilitated assassination missions.

Many sources, both Middle Eastern and European, also insist that the Nizaris groomed an elite corps of individuals who were particularly adept at these covert arts. According to these sources, Nizari leaders used to bring up in their strongholds a number of boys, whom they raised and schooled from a young age, teaching them in particular many languages and the manners of different races and people. These could then be sent on various covert missions to foreign lands, whether as missionaries or assassins. Farhad Daftary argues that this is just another baseless legend spread about the Nizaris, but there is much firmer evidence supporting this particular story. According to Sinān's own autobiography, he first arrived at Alamut as a penniless youth after fleeing his home, and was schooled there by Muhammad ibn Buzurgumīd, leader of the Nizari movement from 1138 to 1162. Muhammad had two sons, and Sinān recalled that Muhammad 'put me in school with them, and gave me exactly the same treatment as he gave them, in those things that are needful for the support, education, and clothing of children'.[13] His education complete, Sinān was sent as a missionary to Mesopotamia and Syria. According to other accounts preserved by Kamāl al-Dīn and to a Nizari biography of Sinān, once he arrived in Syria, Sinān worked for up to seven years as a schoolmaster for boys.

The linguistic skills of *fidā'īs* and their ability to merge into different cultural habitats were often commented upon not only by ignorant Europeans, but also by far better informed Middle Eastern authors and even by Nizari authors. Thus an apocryphal Nizari tale, which is a garbled account of Conrad's murder, and which was preserved in a Nizari biography of Sinān, tells how Sinān had 'a king of the Franks' assassinated at Acre. The tale stresses the importance of the *fidā'īs'* linguistic skills, explaining that the two *fidā'īs* who killed the Frankish king were taught by Sinān to speak the Frankish tongue, were dressed in Frankish customs and carried Frankish swords, and were thereby able to infiltrate the Frankish camp at night, enter the king's pavilion, and cut off his head.[14]

Moreover, the idea of bringing up children from a tender age in 'state-owned' boarding-schools, under the supervision of the head of state, and instructing them in various arts for future military and political usage, was certainly very common among contemporary Islamic powers. Many Islamic courts habitually raised such *Mameluks* and *Ghulams*. Some were educated in military arts to become elite fighting troops, while others were educated in civilian arts to become administrators. Though no source makes the comparison, it may well be that the Nizaris copied the practice, except that their *Mameluks* were trained primarily for covert operations rather than for regular combat or administration.[15]

The Nizaris' final asset was patience and foresight. Once they decided to eliminate a person, they often waited for months and years before making an attempt on his life. For example, the attempt on the life of Buri of Damascus, which is discussed below, took place almost two years after he massacred the city's Nizari community. This gave the *fidā'īs* time to plant themselves near the target and get to know him and his surroundings. At other times, it seems that the Nizaris planted *fidā'īs* in key locations as a matter of course, to be activated as and when a need arose. This was not always effective as a response to unforeseen short-term threats, but over decades it built up an enormously effective reputation of terror.

For example, Kamāl al-Dīn narrates that when Saladin attacked the Nizari enclave in the mid-1170s, Sinān sent a messenger to the sultan and ordered him to deliver his message only in private. Saladin, naturally fearful of an assassination attempt, had the messenger thoroughly searched, but even when he was found to be unarmed, Saladin refused to part with his bodyguard. The messenger insisted that his message must be delivered only in private. Saladin eventually consented to send away all his attendants and bodyguards, except for his two most faithful Mameluk guards. When the messenger insisted that they too be sent away, Saladin told him that 'I regard these as my own sons, and they and I are as one', and that he would not send them away. Then the messenger turned to the two Mameluks and said, 'If I ordered you in the name of my master to kill this sultan, would you do so?' The Mameluks unsheathed their swords, saying that they were at his command. The messenger then left, taking the two Mameluks with him. The awe-struck Saladin quickly made peace with Sinān.[16]

Though the Nizaris twice tried to assassinate Saladin, in December 1174 and May 1176, this particular tale is most probably fictitious.[17] It nevertheless highlights the methods by which the Nizaris sought to reach their closely guarded targets, and the awe inspired by these methods. The *fidā'īs* were not some Middle Eastern ninjas who overcame princely security measures by means of arcane martial arts. Rather, they usually reached their victims by dint of forethought, good education, and patience. In the multicultural society of the twelfth-century Middle East, where every polity was a patchwork of many races and faiths, and where the armed forces and administrative services of all rulers included mercenaries and recruits from various ethnic and religious origins, a well-educated foreign youth, especially one with good linguistic skills, could quite easily find employment in princely retinues or at least in close proximity to princely courts. Once he established himself near a potential target, and if he did not mind perishing along with his victim, it was only a question of time till a good opportunity for assassination presented itself. As Sinān once replied to Saladin's threats, 'I will defeat you from within your own ranks and take vengeance against you at your own place.'[18] The Crusader chronicler Ambroise concurs, writing that once the *fidā'īs* were given a target, 'they go away and spy out the great man and watch over him and become part of his household, being clever in their speech, until they manage to take his life'.[19]

For instance, in 1126 the grand-vizier of the Seljuk empire, Mu'in al-Din Kashi, launched an armed campaign against the Nizari enclaves in Persia. In revenge, two *fidā'īs* managed to enter his service as grooms, and then murdered him in March 1127. In 1129 Buri, upon becoming the ruler of Damascus, turned upon the Nizaris, who were his late father's allies. Setting the town militia as well as frenzied Sunni mobs upon the hated heretics, Buri was allegedly responsible for the death of between 6,000 and 20,000 Nizaris. From that day onwards Buri naturally went nowhere without a heavy suit of armour and a heavily armed bodyguard, but it availed him little. Two Turkoman soldiers he had accepted to his service turned out to be *fidā'īs*. They fell upon him and severely wounded him on 7 May 1131, and he died from his wounds after a year of agony. In 1138 the deposed Abbasid Caliph al-Rashid was killed by some of his servants who turned out to be *fidā'īs*.

In 1270 two *fidā'īs* came to Tyre dressed as regular Mameluk soldiers. They pretended to be deserters, and asked Philip of Montfort, the lord of Tyre and the most prominent Frankish leader in the Levant, to be baptized and to enrol in his service. Montfort did not suspect them. One took the name of Philip, after their new godfather, the other was named Julian. A short time later Philip of Montfort was warned that Sultan Baybars had sent *fidā'īs* to murder him.

Philip ordered his men to monitor closely all people who entered Tyre, but he did not suspect his two new retainers, and kept them in his own residence. On a certain Sunday one of the *fidā'īs* stabbed Philip to death as he went to his personal chapel for Mass, and almost succeeded in killing his son and heir as well. The latter saved himself only by hiding behind the altar. Simultaneously the other *fidā'ī* tried to murder the lord of Sidon, but he was uncovered and had to flee without accomplishing his mission.[20]

It is notable that on many occasions the *fidā'īs* disguised themselves as ascetics or monks, and often murdered their victims in or near mosques and other holy places. Thus the Nizaris' first famous victim – Nizam al-Mulk – was killed by a *fidā'ī* disguised as a *Sūfī* ascetic (1092).[21] When the Nizaris first arrived in Syria, one of their principal enemies was Janāh al-Dawla, the ruler of Homs. Fearful of an attack, Janāh al-Dawla left his citadel as little as possible, and when doing so, went about dressed in full armour and surrounded by a bodyguard. On Friday, 1 May 1103, he left the citadel and went to the town's main mosque to take part in the Friday prayers. As he was taking his customary place, three *fidā'īs* 'dressed in the garb of ascetics' charged him, and neither his armour nor his bodyguard saved him from their daggers. Aside from these three *fidā'īs*, ten other genuine *Sūfī* ascetics who were present at the mosque were immediately killed.[22] Similarly, in 1126 the Seljuk ruler of Mosul, Bursuqi, was assassinated in Mosul's main mosque by eight *fidā'īs* disguised as ascetics.

The advantages of posing as ascetics were manifold. First, it was unseemly to question yhem or bar their way too rudely. Secondly, ascetics were often unattached foreigners and wanderers, thus providing the best possible cover for a *fidā'ī*. Thirdly, ascetics were not infrequently learned people, whose linguistic and administrative skills were valued as much as their piety. Hence by posing as one, a learned foreigner could not only explain his good education and avoid too many questions about his past, but could also worm his way more easily into the households of targeted potentates.[23]

Even if the *fidā'īs* failed to find a place in the service of any potentate, their education and their experience in disguise could enable them to stay near the targets for weeks and months, until by one means or the other an opportunity for assault presented itself.

As for the actual means of assassination, it is not known whether the *fidā'īs* were given training in any martial art or the use of weapons. What is certain is that for two centuries, almost all of their hundreds of victims were killed with daggers in a public space. Clearly, on many occasions it would have been easier to poison princes than to stab them, especially when fearful targets began wearing armour at all times and surrounding themselves with guards. However, the *fidā'īs* stuck to their daggers, and apparently seldom or never attempted to poison their victims, or use bows or some other long-distance weapons. This was done for theatrical reasons. Like medieval kingship, medieval terror too was a show. Its effectiveness relied not merely on the elimination of one's enemies, but even more so on frightening other potential enemies and heartening comrades and potential friends. Poison was theatrically far less effective than daggers, because it was often impossible to ascertain whether a potentate's death was caused by poison, and if so, who the poisoner was.

In addition, death by poison usually occurred in the privacy of the palace. In contrast, the *fidā'īs* usually stabbed their victim to death in broad daylight, in a public place such as a street or a mosque, and while he was surrounded by guards and attendants. Even when the *fidā'īs* entered the service of their intended victim, they normally took care to stab him in public. By disdaining more subtle means and choosing to kill their victim in the most direct and visible manner, the Nizaris showed their contempt for their enemies' security measures, indicating that no such measures could hope to forestall them, and advertised their abilities and achievements both to other potential victims and to the general populace. Since they were revolutionary missionaries hoping to overthrow the established political and religious order, their assassinations should be understood not merely as political tools, but also as missionary propaganda. Tales of their amazing exploits and of the helplessness of the most powerful rulers were calculated to spread their message and draw new converts.

✦ ✦ ✦

CONRAD'S assassins actually arrived in Tyre well before April 1192. If the story of the ship is true, then Sinān waited a long time before exacting his revenge. If the murder was commissioned by Richard or by Saladin following the Ascalon conference, it means that Sinān had already taken care to plant some of his agents near the person of the marquis before he had any clear plans to eliminate him. As noted earlier, it may well have been standard Nizari practice to systematically plant *fidā'īs* in key locations and near potential targets.

'Imād al-Dīn and Ibn al-Athīr say that the *fidā'īs* arrived in Tyre around November 1191, pretending to be Christian monks or ascetics. By living a life of piety and asceticism, and frequenting churches, they acquired the confidence and entered the service of Balian II of Ibelin and Reginald of Sidon, two of Conrad's close associates. While accompanying these two noblemen, they often came into the presence of the marquis himself, who thus became familiar with them. According to the *Continuation* of William of Tyre, one of them entered the service of Balian, whereas the other entered Conrad's own service. According to Ambroise and the *Itinerarium*, both *fidā'īs* were accepted into Conrad's retinue, and served him faithfully for months before they found an opportunity to kill him.

When exactly Sinān decided to activate them cannot be known for sure. If Richard or Saladin persuaded him to have Conrad murdered following the Ascalon council, then Sinān's orders could not have reached his agents much sooner than 25 April (given that Richard's or Saladin's messengers had to travel to Sinān's stronghold in northern Syria and confer with him, and then Sinān had to send his own messengers to Tyre).

It does not seem that Conrad took any special precautions to safeguard his person, either before or after he heard the news from Ascalon. Other threatened rulers are known to have arranged elaborate security measures to counter the Nizari threat, besides the common use of body-armour and bodyguards. When in 1122 the Fatimid Caliph 'Al-Ma'mūn felt himself threatened by the Nizaris, he ordered the governor of Ascalon – then Egypt's eastern portal – to remove from office all men who were not known to the local population. Further, he was ordered to examine thoroughly all persons arriving in Ascalon, and to deny entry to all comers except those who were known and regular visitors, and whose identities were beyond doubt. He then had to send written reports to Cairo, stating the numbers of the arriving persons, their names, the names of their servants, the names of their camel-drivers, and a list of their merchandise. Upon arrival in Egypt, the caravans were cross-checked against these reports. In addition, the caliph ordered the governors of Cairo to register the names of all inhabitants, street by street, and not to permit anyone to change his abode without permission, so that any stranger coming to the city could be easily monitored. Finally, 'Al-Ma'mūn employed many spies and informers, and by all those means managed to unearth a number of Nizari agents.

Saladin, after the two attempts on his life in 1174 and 1176, began sleeping for a while in a wooden tower, and allowed no one whom he did not know personally to approach him. When in 1332 Philip VI of France contemplated a new crusade, a German priest called Brocardus who had spent some time in Armenia composed a treatise to advise the king on this project. Among other dangers, he warned the king against the 'Assasinis'. The only way to protect the king against them, wrote Brocardus, is 'that in all of the king's household, for whatever service, however mean or brief, no person should be admitted, save those whose country, place, lineage, condition and person are certainly, fully and clearly known'.[24]

These security measures could never ensure complete safety from the Nizari *fidā'īs*, and in any case, they were not easy to implement, especially by Conrad in 1192. Like most contemporary princes, Conrad lacked the bureaucratic institutions and skills possessed by 'Al-Ma'mūn, without which it was impossible to monitor visiting foreigners or even the members of one's own extended household. Moreover, he was himself a foreigner, and Tyre in 1192 was overflowing with refugees and Crusaders whom he could not have hoped to supervise effectively.

As for implementing tighter security measures, these would have availed Conrad little once the *fidā'īs* were accepted into his or his associates' service. Furthermore, such measures could have harmed his bid for the crown of Jerusalem. Since medieval princes were performers as much as functionaries, and medieval kingship was a matter of ceremony as much as of government, princes had to display themselves often and make themselves accessible and visible to their subjects. Consequently, if a prince barricaded himself behind walls, cordons of bodyguards, and tight security, and made himself inaccessible and invisible to his subjects, it would have constituted a very serious injury to his prestige and power. It would also have presented him as fearful and even cowardly. After all, medieval princes were regularly required to expose their persons to the dangers of battle. Such measures would have been particularly harmful when the prince in question was a foreigner making a contested bid for the throne.

The Crusader Jehan de Joinville recounts an incident which demonstrates the harmful effects of security measures. During Louis IX's Crusade (1250–4), the king once went riding near Sidon together with Joinville. In the course of their ride, they came upon a church in which mass was being celebrated, so they went inside to participate in the holy rite. Joinville noticed that the clerk who assisted at the service was 'a tall, dark, lean, and hairy fellow', and he immediately suspected him of being a Nizari assassin. When the clerk approached the king carrying the holy *pax* – a representation of the Crucifix that was customarily kissed by the priest and the congregation – Joinville intercepted him, took the *pax* from him, and brought it to Louis himself, not allowing the clerk to approach the king. Louis – whose fame and authority rested upon a carefully cultivated image of sainthood and humility – later complained of Joinville's action, for he believed it reflected badly on him, as if he were too proud to allow a simple clerk to approach his person. Even when Joinville explained his motive, Louis insisted that he acted wrongly.[25]

Whether due to lack of resources, lack of fear, or fear of alienating his subjects and harming his image, Conrad took no special steps to protect his person. Hence once the orders to assassinate him reached the two *fidā'īs*, they had only to wait for a proper opportunity. They apparently formed no elaborate plans, and merely kept their eyes and ears open. The events of the subsequent assassination prove that it could not have been preplanned, for Conrad's actions on the fateful day were extremely erratic, and did not follow any preconceived schedule.

The *fidā'īs'* opportunity presented itself on 28 April. On that day Queen Isabella, who was pregnant with Conrad's daughter, went to the baths and did not come back home in time for the meal. The marquis waited for her, but was told that she was taking her time and would not be arriving soon. He was hungry and did not wish to eat alone, and therefore decided to visit his friend, the bishop of Beauvais, and dine with him. Mounting his horse and taking only two knights with him, he rode to the bishop's residence, but discovered to his dismay that the bishop had already finished his meal. 'Sir Bishop,' said Conrad, 'I have come here to eat with you. But since you have already eaten, I will return to my place.'[26] The bishop said he would be happy to give the marquis something to eat, but Conrad decided it would be better to return home and dine there. He left the bishop's house, passed by the money-changers and the gate of the cathedral of Tyre, and then turned into a narrow lane. Two men in monks' robes were sitting on either side of the lane.

The two monks were none other than Sinān's *fidā'īs*. They may have watched Conrad's palace for some time, seen him heading for the bishop's house, and then posted themselves in an opportune place, waiting for his return. For people who had been in Tyre for perhaps six months, and knew both the city's geography and the marquis himself well, this should have presented no difficulty. Similarly, they were by then familiar figures in Tyre, and hence they could wait in full view without arousing any suspicion. Certainly seeing two monks sitting outside the cathedral was not a particularly suspicious sight.

The marquis paid no attention to them, and rode on. When he passed between them, they rose, and one of them approached Conrad with an outstretched arm, handing him a letter. As the marquis held out his hand to take the letter, the man suddenly drew a knife with his other hand and stabbed Conrad. While all attention focused on this assassin, his companion sprang from his place, jumped on the horse, and stabbed Conrad in the side. One *fidā'ī* was apparently killed on the spot by the two knights who accompanied Conrad, while the other fled into the nearby church.

According to one version of the story, Conrad was instantly killed, and fell dead from the horse. According to another version, he was only wounded, but was then carried into the same church into which the surviving *fidā'ī* fled. According to this version, no one perceived the *fidā'ī's* flight, and his robes enabled him to conceal himself inside. When he saw the marquis brought in and heard him speak, the *fidā'ī* realized that their mission was incomplete. He then assaulted Conrad again, and this time his blow proved fatal.

The *fidā'ī* was captured and questioned under torture. Before expiring, he confessed that he and his companion were sent on their mission at the instigation of the king of England. Even if these details are accurate, it proves little. Several sources explain that Sinān instructed the *fidā'īs* that if they were caught, they were to implicate Richard in the crime, in order to sow confusion in the Frankish camp. Moreover, the men who tortured and questioned the captured man were of Philip August's party. They may consequently have invented the confession themselves, or at least were only too ready to be persuaded by the *fidā'ī's* allegations.

✦ ✦ ✦

Conrad's murder at first caused great fear and consternation among the Franks of all camps. However, the immediate crisis was soon resolved. Count Henry of Champagne, the messenger who brought Conrad the news of his election to the throne, was unanimously recognized as the best candidate to succeed the marquis. He was related to both Richard and Philip August, and was popular amongst the local Frankish nobility and the Crusader army alike.

By 5 May 1192 – barely a week after Conrad's death – he was married to the pregnant Queen Isabella, to the embarrassment of the European chroniclers and to the utter disgust of the Muslim and Eastern Christian commentators. The couple was then crowned in Acre, so that at least the costly preparations for the ceremony were not wasted.

As for the long-term impact of the assassination, both medieval and modern authors disagree. Some assert that it was a great boon to the Muslims, for Conrad was a ruthless politician and an excellent soldier, the best man to fill Richard's shoes and continue the reconquest of the Holy Land. Others argue that his death actually benefited the Franks, because he had been a controversial and divisive figure, whereas the count of Champagne was popular with all camps. Richard and Philip were both pleased to see their relative on the throne of Jerusalem, and the various factions of the local Frankish nobility, including Guy's diehard supporters, could unite behind him. In addition, Henry soon proved himself to be a wise and capable ruler, who managed to consolidate the newly conquered territories during his brief reign, and lay firm foundations for the renascent Kingdom of Acre.

Whether the Franks won or lost by Conrad's death, Sinān and the Nizaris certainly profited from it. The fact that Conrad's death did not bring about the collapse of Frankish power did not disappoint Sinān, for he had no interest in the complete destruction of the Franks. The survival of his own small principality depended on keeping a balance between Franks and Orthodox Muslims. An overwhelming Muslim victory would have allowed Saladin to turn against the heretical Nizari enclave and extirpate it, as indeed happened in the late thirteenth century. Rather, the Nizaris' main gain from Conrad's death was psychological. Their deadly reputation among both Muslims and Christians received a timely boost. Henry of Champagne in particular learned from his predecessor's mistake, and treated the Nizaris with great respect and care throughout his reign. He certainly made no attempt to avenge his predecessor's murder.

In Europe wild rumours spread that greatly inflated the abilities of the Nizaris. Kings and chroniclers were gripped by baseless fears; not realizing that the Nizaris' main enemies were Sunni Muslims rather than the distant and relatively harmless European Catholics, they began believing that Nizari *fidā'īs* were infiltrating European courts and targeting European monarchs.[27]

Rulers started accusing one another of conspiring with the Old Man of the Mountain to have their rivals murdered, an allegation that would become a staple of European propaganda wars. The sect was consequently held in awe by Europeans throughout the thirteenth century and beyond, irrespective of the small number of Christian leaders it actually assassinated, and of its general disinterest in the affairs of Europe. Its methods, however, were never copied by either European or Middle Eastern powers. They were simply too successful, and threatened to undo the political fabric.[28]

NOTES

1 The name Assassins became known in Europe as early as the 1170s. Thus a German account of the Levant from 1175 describes the 'Heyssessini' (Arnold of Lubeck, *Chronica Slavorum*, 7.8, ed. Pertz, p. 274). The word began to denote hit-men in general towards the end of the Middle Ages. Before that time other terms were used to designate trained hit-men, such as 'sicarii' (see for example Vitalis, *Ecclesiastical History*, 6:342).

2 Quoted in Lewis, *Assassins*, pp. 47–8.

3 Juvaini, *History of the World-Conqueror*, 2:678.

4 Usāmah Ibn-Munqidh narrates how a single Nizari agent managed to capture the supposedly impregnable castle of al-Khirbah by himself (Usāmah, *Kitāb al-I'tibār*, pp. 107–8).

5 Lewis, 'Kamāl al-Dīn's Biography', pp. 230–1, 261.

6 William of Tyre, *Historia*, 17.19, ed. RHC, 1:791–2.

7 *Itinerarium peregrinorum*, 5.25, ed. Stubbs, pp. 337–8; Ambroise, *History*, lines 8718–24, ed. Ailes, 1:141.

8 See also Ralph of Diceto, *Opera Historica*, 2:127–8.

9 Lewis, 'Kamāl al-Dīn's Biography', pp. 234, 265.

10 On the bad reputation of hashish in medieval Islam, see Rosenthal, *Herb*, pp. 101–19, 137–62.

11 Juvaini, *History of the World-Conqueror*, 2:676. Compare Ambroise, *History*, lines 8822–3, ed. Ailes, 1:143.

12 Ibn al-Qalānisī, *Damascus Chronicle*, p. 179.

13 Lewis, 'Kamāl al-Dīn's Biography', pp. 231, 262.

14 Guyard, 'Grand Maître', pp. 463–6.

15 The idea of specially trained missionaries was certainly not unique to the Nizaris. Christian missionaries from the late classical period until today have often been prepared for their missions by learning as much as they could about the languages and customs of their intended flocks. On the raising of Mameluks, see in particular Pipes, *Slave Soldiers*.

16 Lewis, 'Kamāl al-Dīn's Biography', pp. 236–7, 266–7.

17 For a somewhat similar story, in which the frightened victim was the Seljuk Sultan Sanjar, see Juvaini, *History of the World-Conqueror*, 2:681–2.

18 Lewis, 'Kamāl al-Dīn's Biography', pp. 235, 265.

19 Ambroise, *History*, lines 8817–21, ed. Ailes, 1:143.

20 'Chronique du Templier de Tyr', section 374, ed. Raynaud, pp. 194–8; Harari, 'Military Role', p. 102.

21 Juvaini, *History of the World-Conqueror*, 2:677.

22 Ibn al-Qalānisī, *Damascus Chronicle*, pp. 57–8.

23 Christian agents were also quite fond of disguising themselves as monks. In 1118 King Louis VI and a troop of his men disguised themselves in the black habits of monks, thus infiltrating and capturing the town of Gasny (Vitalis,

Ecclesiastical History, 6:184). In 1451 the Burgundians tried to seize the town of Lunéville in Lorraine by smuggling into it troops disguised as pilgrims (Vaughan, *Philip the Good*, p. 101).

24 Brocardus, *Directorium*, pp. 496–7.

25 Joinville, *Vie*, sections 588–90, ed. Monfrin, pp. 292–4.

26 *Chronique d'Ernoul*, p. 290; William of Tyr, *Continuation*, ch. 137, ed. Morgan, pp. 140–1.

27 The only attempt to assassinate a European prince in the thirteenth century which can safely be attributed to the Nizaris is the attempt on the life of the future Edward I in 1270 (Langtoft, *Chronicle*, 2:156–60).

28 For the Third Crusade the present chapter relied mainly on: Bahā' al-Dīn, *Rare and Excellent History*; Bahā' al-Dīn, *Kitāb*; Edbury, *Conquest of Jerusalem*; William of Tyr, *Continuation*; *Chronique d'Ernoul*; Ambroise, *History*; *Itinerarium peregrinorum*; *Chronicle of the Third Crusade*; al-Kātib al-Isfahānī, *Conquête de la Syrie*; Ibn al-Athīr, *Min kitāb kāmil al-tawārīkh*, 1:712–44, 2:1–73; Johnston, *Crusade and Death*; Gillingham, *Richard I*; Bradbury, *Philip Augustus*, pp. 87–101; Nicholson, *Joscelyn III*, pp. 164–98; Runciman, *History of the Crusades*, 3:1–75; Mayer, *Crusades*, pp. 137–51; Richard, 'Philippe Auguste'; Prawer, *History*, 1:526–61, 2:3–92; Turner and Heiser, *Reign of Richard Lionheart*.

For the history of the Nizaris in general, the present chapter relied mainly on: Ibn al-Athīr, *Min kitāb kāmil al-tawārīkh*, 1:272, 291, 304–5, 384–5, 400, 438; Abū'l-Fidā, *Muntahabāt min al-mukhtasar*, pp. 6, 10, 12, 17–18, 21, 25, 147, 181; Guyard, 'Grand Maître'; Brocardus, *Directorium*, pp. 496–7; Ibn al-Qalānisī, *Damascus Chronicle*, pp. 57–8, 72–4, 115, 145–8, 163, 175–80, 187–95, 202–3, 263, 342; Juvaini, *History of the World-Conqueror*, 2:666–725; Joinville, *Vie*, sections 451–63, 588–90, ed. Monfrin, pp. 222–8, 292–4; Barber and Bate, *Templars*, pp. 73–7; Usāmah, *Kitāb al-I'tibār*, pp. 107–8, 146, 153–4, 190, 192–3; Arnold of Lubeck, *Chronica Slavorum*, 7.8, ed. Pertz, pp. 274–5; Lewis, 'Kamāl al-Dīn's Biography', pp. 225–67; William of Tyre, *Historia*, 14.20, 17.19, 20.29, 20.30, ed. RHC, 1:634, 791–2, 996, 999; Ambroise, *History*, lines 8797–8824, ed. Ailes, 1:142–3; Lewis, *Assassins*; Mirza, *Syrian Ismailism*, pp. 19–55; Daftary, *Assassin Legends*; Bartlett, *Assassins*; Ford, *Political Murder*, pp. 100–4; Wilson, 'Secrets of the Assassins'.

For Conrad's assassination the present chapter relied mainly on: Ambroise, *History*, lines 8694–8886, ed. Ailes, 2:141–4; *Chronique d'Ernoul*, pp. 289–91; Bahā' al-Dīn, *Rare and Excellent History*, pp. 200–1; Bahā' al-Dīn, *Kitāb*, pp. 202–3; al-Kātib al-Isfahānī, *Conquête de la Syrie*, pp. 376–8; Guyard, 'Grand Maître', pp. 463–6; Edbury, *Conquest of Jerusalem*, pp. 114–15; William of Tyr, *Continuation*, ch. 137, ed. Morgan, pp. 140–1; *Itinerarium peregrinorum*, 5.25–7, ed. Stubbs, pp. 337–42; *Chronicle of the Third Crusade*, 5.25–7, ed. Nicholson, pp. 304–8; Ibn al-Athīr, *Min kitāb kāmil al-tawārīkh*, 2:58–9; Gabrieli, *Arab Historians*, pp. 238–45; Ralph of Diceto, *Opera Historica*, 2:104, 127–8; Bartlett, *Assassins*, pp. 141–4, 188–9; Gillingham, *Richard I*, pp. 197–202; Runciman, *History of the Crusades*, 3:64–6.

Also relevant to Conrad's assassination are: Arnold of Lubeck, *Chronica Slavorum*, 4.16, ed. Pertz, pp. 145–6; Bar Hebraeus, *Chronography*, 2:339; *Chronique de Michel le Syrien*, 4:210; 'Chronique de Terre-Sainte', p. 14; Johnston, *Crusade and Death*, pp. 37–8; Roger of Howden, *Chronica*, 3:181; Walter of Coventry, *Memoriale*, 2:18–19; Ralph of Coggeshall, *Chronicon Anglicanum*, p. 35; Lewis, *Assassins*, pp. 4–5, 117–18, 133; Mirza, *Syrian Ismailism*, pp. 36–7; Daftary, *Assassin Legends*, pp. 72–3; Hindley, *Saladin*, pp. 176–7; Nicholson, *Joscelyn III*, pp. 195–7; Richard, *Crusades*, p. 230; Mayer, *Crusades*, p. 148. Note that the chronicle translated in Edbury's *Conquest of Jerusalem*, the chronicle edited by Morgan in her *Continuation de Guillaume de Tyr*, and the *Chronique d'Ernoul* are in fact different versions of the same text. The text known as the *Itinerarium* relied heavily upon Ambroise's *History*, but apparently utilized other sources as well, and should therefore be considered an independent source for at least some of the described events.

5

For a Sack-full of Gold Écus: Calais, 1350

Around midday 3 August 1347 a mournful procession emerged from the city of Calais. Six of its most distinguished citizens humbly walked out of the main gate, dressed only in their shirtsleeves, with nooses around their necks and the city's keys in their hands. Behind them men, women, and children were weeping bitterly and wringing their hands in despair. Outside the gate they were received by the wrathful King Edward III of England, by Edward's wife, Queen Philippa, and by tens of thousands of enemy soldiers. For eleven months Edward had besieged Calais in what turned out to be the biggest military undertaking of his reign and one of the costliest sieges of the Middle Ages. Roughly 32,000 men were shipped from England for the siege – the largest English army sent overseas in the Middle Ages. A fleet manned by another 15,000 sailors blockaded the city from the sea, while an allied Flemish field army of about 20,000 men supported the English on land. Edward's rival, King Philip VI of France, gathered a huge force to oppose Edward, numbering at least 20,000 men, and made every effort to hamper the siege.[1] Hunger eventually forced the city to capitulate, but only after it had successfully withstood all of Edward's devices and threats, and after the siege had drained the financial resources of both England and France to the breaking point. There was no longer any food left inside the starving city, and Philip's army could not risk a field battle so soon after the disaster it suffered at Crécy.

When the city agreed to surrender, Edward promised to spare the lives of the citizens and garrison members, but resolved to execute the six leading burghers, partly to appease his anger and partly to frighten other cities into surrendering more quickly. Sir Walter Mauny, one of Edward's foremost soldiers, tried to assuage the king's wrath and save the burghers, but Edward was adamant. Then his own wife, the pregnant Queen Philippa, went down on her knees and pleaded for their lives. With his keen theatrical sense, he allowed his anger to ebb, and gave the burghers their lives.

However, the thankful burghers and almost the entire civilian population of Calais were ordered to leave Calais, which Edward intended to repopulate with more loyal subjects and to turn into his main French beach-head. Hitherto, transporting armies from England to the Continent had been a difficult affair. Landing an army on a hostile beach was an extremely troublesome task, not because the beaches were defended, but rather because it made extreme demands on the logistical abilities of fourteenth-century kings. If an army of several thousand men wanted to land on a hostile beach, it meant that the entire army, together with thousands of horses and all the necessary camp equipment and supply, had to be transported and landed in one go. This required gathering together hundreds of ships and large amounts of supply and equipment. Things were far easier if the army could instead land and assemble in some friendly port. In such a case, a far more limited number of ships could accumulate over time the necessary amounts of equipment, supply, and even horses in the port of debarkation, then transport the rest of the horses and men either in a single concerted effort or in a few relays.

Up until 1347 Edward did not possess a good debarkation port in France. The friendly ports of Gascony were too far away, and whereas the few Breton ports held by him and his allies were closer at hand, their possession was not secure, and they were mostly backwaters that did not offer easy entry into France. For a time the ports of Flanders were opened to Edward by the rebellious faction that ruled the county in the 1340s. However, Flemish politics were extremely turbulent. Helping that rebellious faction stay in power exerted a constant drain on his resources, and it was quite evident that it would sooner or later fall, as indeed happened in 1349.

Calais was the answer to Edward's strategic difficulties. Ships could easily cross from Sandwich and Dover in a few hours, so by plying back and forth between the two ports, a modest fleet could in a relatively short time prepare a major invasion. Moreover, unlike the Breton ports, Calais gave easy access both to the plains of northern France and to the Low Countries.

After taking the city and expelling its former inhabitants, Edward repaired its defences and installed a strong garrison of about 1,200 men. He then returned to England, having signed a temporary truce with Philip in September 1347. It was too late in the year to embark on further campaigns, and in any case, there was not a penny left in Edward's treasury.

The truce expired in July 1348 and hostilities were resumed, but meanwhile a common enemy struck both France and England. The Black Death had arrived at France's Mediterranean coast already in December 1347. During the winter it progressed rather slowly up the Rhône and down the Garonne. In the spring of 1348 it gathered momentum, and just as the truce expired, it spread through France like wildfire. It reached Paris in August, killing at least a third of the population and sending the king and the leading magnates fleeing to the supposed safety of the countryside. Simultaneously, the plague accomplished what French armies had been unable to do in more than a decade of fighting. Boarding ship somewhere along the Atlantic coast, it landed in Dorset in July 1348. It then devastated victorious England even more rapaciously than it had ravaged defeated France, killing perhaps half the population within a year. In November 1348 the two kings agreed to renew the truce until May 1350.

Truce and plague combined were not enough, however, to put an end to the actual fighting. Throughout the terrible years of 1348 and 1349, when at times it seemed as if the entire human race was about to perish, the soldiers kept at it, while the kings turned a blind eye to their activities. In Brittany and Aquitaine in particular, mercenary gangs began to practise a form of warfare which would soon become the scourge of France. Professing nominal allegiance to one king or the other, gang leaders set themselves up as virtually independent rulers of petty fiefs, extorting protection money from the local populace and constantly fighting against the neighbouring gangs. Castles were the focal points of these territorial struggles, and since siege operations were largely beyond the gangs' ability, escalades and treason became the military staple.

Jean le Bel described the regular method used by these 'brigands'. They would first spy on the target stronghold for a day or two. Then a small force of perhaps thirty or forty men would approach it under cover of night. At the break of day they would strike, bursting in, setting fire to some dwelling and making as much noise as possible. The startled garrison and inhabitants would be so terrified, thinking that they must be attacked by a large force, that they would often flee, leaving the stronghold to be looted or held by the assailants. This, says Le Bel, is how the brigands captured Donsenac, Comborn, and many other strongholds.[2]

During 1348 and 1349 several towns and castles in Brittany and Aquitaine changed hands by such escalades, whereas several of the freebooter captains, such as Raoul de Caours, gave an indication of things to come by switching their allegiance and selling themselves to the highest bidder. In such an atmosphere it is not surprising that even respected knights and trusted royal commanders tried their hands at treason and escalade. In this as in many other things, it was the scope of ambition rather than the methods employed that distinguished kings from gangsters. Thus in the summer of 1349 Geoffroi de Charny, the paragon of French chivalry and the royal commander of the Flemish front, decided to try to regain Calais for his king by means of treason.

Charny's lifestory was a chivalric rags-to-riches tale. He was born around 1305, the younger son of a minor noble family from Burgundy. Peacetime offered him little chances of advancement, but the outbreak of the Hundred Years War in 1337 opened a window of opportunities, and he belonged to the first generation of professional soldiers whom the tide of war raised to the heights of fame and fortune. In the first five years of the war he made for himself a name as a fighter, so that at the battle of Morlaix (1342) he was selected to lead the charge of the French vanguard. The charge and the battle ended in defeat, and Charny had to spend several months as a prisoner in England, yet his reputation seems only to have gained from his conduct. He was eventually ransomed, and rejoined the fray.

When Edward and Philip signed the Truce of Malestroit (1343–5), the disappointed Charny soon joined a crusade to Asia Minor. He returned from the east in time for the great campaigns of 1345–7. During one of the most calamitous episodes of French history, nearly the entire French military leadership disgraced itself at Bergerac, Auberoche, Aiguillon, La Roche-Derrien, and above all at Crécy. Against this bleak background, Charny's heroic defence of Béthune against the Flemings (1346) was a ray of light, and established him as one of the foremost French warriors of his day. His reputation was acknowledged by King Philip VI, who during the subsequent attempt to relieve Calais made Charny the bearer of the *Oriflamme*,[3] the sacred royal standard, which was traditionally entrusted to the best knight of the land. When Philip challenged Edward to come out from the siege lines and face him in the open, he chose Charny to be one of the two emissaries sent to convey this royal challenge.

Charny's reputation was widely acknowledged even outside France. The chronicler Froissart, at a time he was serving the queen of England, described Charny as 'the most worthy and the most valiant' of knights.[4] The English chronicler Geoffrey le Baker, whose chronicle is often a ribald anti-French diatribe, described him as 'a knight more skilled in military matters than any other Frenchman, so that his fame was widespread and who also, through long practice of arms and by a lively, wise character, was until his death … chief counsellor of young French knights.'[5] Charny himself left to posterity three works on chivalry, meant to instruct young knights how they ought to behave and fight.

During the political crisis that followed the fall of Calais, he was appointed to the king's council,[6] and served in various diplomatic capacities. In July 1348 he returned to the field, and was named commander of the forces facing Calais and the rebellious County of Flanders. From the moment of his appointment, he set his heart on recapturing Calais. Though he had hitherto won great honour and riches for himself, he had not really tasted victory. His sole major success was the defence of Béthune against a riff-raff of Flemish weavers. At Morlaix he was decisively defeated, the crusade to Asia accomplished absolutely nothing, and Calais fell. The fall of Calais in particular must have been a humiliating experience, for Charny and the other French knights had to watch impotently as Edward slowly starved a French city to death, while camping on French territory under the eyes of a French relief force that did not dare attack him. If he could recapture Calais, Charny would not only wipe out that shame, but would certainly establish himself as the greatest French commander of the day. Such a feat could easily secure for him even the office of Constable.

Charny first tried to conquer Calais by regular operations. While the plague struck northern France and the world seemed to be coming to an end, Charny utilized the expiry of the truce in July 1348 in order to attack. As the dead piled up in the streets of the cities and macabre processions of flagellants went scourging themselves through the country roads, Charny cut the causeways leading to Calais, harassed the city's communication with Flanders, and built a small counter-fort to watch and pester the garrison. By the time the truce was resumed in November his attacks had achieved very little except proving death's inability to curb human ambitions.

Realizing that he and his royal master simply lacked the military resources needed to storm or starve Calais, and inspired perhaps by events in Brittany and Aquitaine, Charny now decided to try more underhand methods. The resumption of the truce in November 1348 gave him the cover he needed to mount clandestine operations. For during the truce, people travelled freely between Calais and French-held Picardy, and French spies easily mingled with the other travellers.

These spies informed Charny that a knight called Aimeric of Pavia may well be Calais's weakest human link. As his name indicates, Aimeric was a Lombard rather than an Englishman. According to the *Chronique de Quatre Premiers Valois*, Aimeric first served the king of France. However, in April 1348 he was hired by Edward to command the oared galley that formed the nucleus of the small Calais flotilla. Oared galleys were particularly suitable for navigating the shallow waters around Calais. Long after sailing ships gained mastery of the Atlantic and even the Mediterranean, the kings of France kept a force of oared galleys in Calais, Boulogne, Dunkirk, and the nearby ports, and one of the worst punishments that the courts of Louis XIV could inflict on criminals and heretics was condemnation to these galleys. Oared galleys, however, were mainly a Mediterranean specialty, and not much used in fourteenth-century England. It is probably for this reason that Edward entrusted this important command to a Lombard mercenary.

It appears that Edward was impressed with Aimeric's abilities and loyalty, for he soon entrusted to him not only the command of Calais's naval forces, but also the command of one of the citadel's towers, which contained a gate that led into Calais harbour. Most sources claim that Aimeric was actually the commander of the entire Calais garrison, or at least of the citadel. It may be that upon the death of the previous citadel commander from the plague, Aimeric was indeed given temporary command of the citadel. The city itself, however, was governed by John Beauchamp, the brother of the Earl of Warwick. No matter how favourably was Edward impressed with Aimeric, he would never have entrusted him with such an important post.

Charny's impression of Aimeric was somewhat different than Edward's. Reasoning that he was a foreign mercenary who served only for money and whose loyalty was not buttressed either by long-term ties of vassalage or by the burgeoning ties of nationalism, Charny assumed that he could be bought with a large enough sum of money. The fact that Aimeric was a Lombard only strengthened Charny's impression, for in fourteenth-century western Europe Lombards were known for their avarice, and were far more famous as bankers and merchants than as warriors. Froissart derisively writes that Charny thought Aimeric would be inclined to betray Calais because he was a Lombard, and 'Lombards are of their nature covetous'.[7]

Charny soon made contact with Aimeric, perhaps through a Lombard agent of his own called Ambroise. Aimeric was enticed with tempting offers, which he at first resisted. Charny eventually offered the sum of 20,000 gold écus. This was minuscule compared to the price of Calais. Aside from the enormous cost of the city's conquest, between 1347 and 1361 Edward III spent an average of

70,000 *écus* a year on the defence of Calais.[8] Indeed, when a brigand named Bacon captured the far less important castle of Comborn, he first ransomed its lord for 20,000 *écus*, and later sold the castle itself to King Philip VI for another 30,000 *écus*.[9]

Nevertheless, 20,000 *écus* was a respectable sum, enough to make Aimeric a very rich man, and he agreed to betray Calais. According to Jean le Bel, Aimeric met Charny in secret, and swore great oaths that on a night of Charny's choosing he would open his tower's gate, lower the drawbridge over the moat, and admit the French into the citadel. Froissart reports the deal in sarcastic terms, saying that Aimeric agreed *marchander* Calais to Charny,[10] deliberately using a verb of the marketplace rather than of the battlefield. The anonymous Bourgeois of Valenciennes uses the same verb, adding that the decisive meeting took place at Lille in July 1348. This date is extremely unlikely, though the Bourgeois may well have meant July 1349. Charny informed King Philip VI of this mercantile success, and began preparing his forces.

The truce between Edward and Philip was meant to expire on May 1350, but it was never really observed in Brittany and Aquitaine, and in September 1349 the French king himself either annulled it or simply ignored it, sending large armies to invade areas held by his rival in south-western France. In November Edward reacted, sending his most able general, the earl of Lancaster, on a counter-invasion. Hence Charny had no reason to worry about breaking the truce. As for the propriety of subverting an enemy garrison and taking an enemy stronghold by treason, Charny apparently did not think it was unchivalrous. Interestingly, his own chivalric guidebook clearly states that there is nothing wrong with mercenary service or with 'deeds undertaken for rewards',[11] but it is mute on the subject of buying off enemy soldiers, neither recommending nor prohibiting it.

Aimeric's promise did not solve all of Charny's difficulties. First, it was not easy for enemy troops to reach Calais without being detected. The city was surrounded by marshes intersected by numerous streams, and could be approached only by a limited number of roads, which crossed the marshy land over bridges and causeways. These roads were watched over by several outlying strongholds, as well as by scouts and spies.

Secondly, from Charny's viewpoint, Aimeric's tower was located in the worst possible section of Calais's defences. The citadel of Calais was tucked away on the city's north-western edge, surrounded by the harbour on one side and the city on the other side. This allowed Aimeric easy access to his ships, but it meant that his tower was almost inaccessible to a storming party coming from the land side. In order to reach Aimeric's tower without passing through the city, the party would have to come from the Nieulay bridge, sneak past the city's south-western corner, and than traverse a narrow strip of sand wedged between the city's western wall and the harbour. The breadth of that strip varied with the tide, and at high tide it was virtually impassable (see map 3).

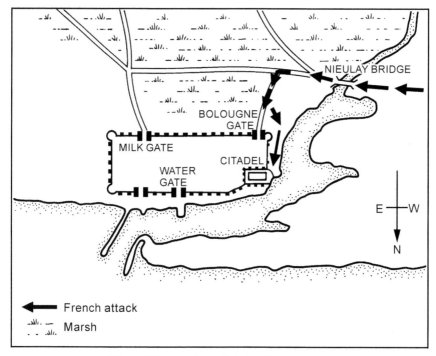

Map 3 The attack on Calais, 1 January 1350

Thirdly, even if a small raiding party managed to storm Aimeric's tower, such an exploit could not lead to the fall of the city. Unlike Antioch in 1098, Calais in 1349 was not besieged by an overwhelming force, and hence it was not enough to puncture a hole in the defences and then allow the weight of numbers to accomplish the rest. If Charny came to Calais with only a small raiding party, even if he managed to take Aimeric's tower he would then be counterattacked by a garrison numbering about 1,200 professional soldiers, which could rely on several hundreds more auxiliaries and militiamen. Thus in order to capture Calais, the storming party had to be quickly followed by a far larger force of perhaps several thousand soldiers. But Calais's peculiar position meant that these reinforcements could not enter the city through the same gate. A few dozen men could perhaps sneak along the beach and seize the tower, but several thousand men could hardly hope to imitate them. If the bulk of the forces tried to follow in the footsteps of the advance party and enter through the harbour gate, the garrison would probably discover them and counterattack before they could force their way in. The French would then find themselves trapped on a narrow beach between the walls on one side and the oncoming tide on the other.

Despite these difficulties, the opportunity was too good to be missed. Charny informed Eustache de Ribbemont, Oudart de Renti, and several other senior French commanders of his plans, and asked for their help. Together they secretly assembled a force of about 1,500 mounted men and 4,000 infantrymen from the garrisons and the feudal levies of Artois and Picardy. The target of this army was kept hidden from most of the soldiers.

Charny sought to utilize several factors in order to overcome the above difficulties. First, whereas combat operations were resumed on the Brittany and Aquitaine fronts in September 1349, no such operations were conducted on the Calais front. This could hopefully lull the Calais garrison into thinking that they were in no immediate danger. The Black Death was also helpful, for, given its catastrophic impact on the surrounding areas, it was easy to conclude that the French had no stomach for warlike activities.

Secondly, the time for the attack was set for dawn of 1 January 1350. The choice of hour was obvious, for it enabled the French to move into position under cover of night. The choice of date was also deliberate. Throughout history holidays have been a favoured time for launching surprise attacks, and Charny could well assume that during the festive season of Christmas and New Year's Eve the garrison would have other things on its mind than keeping watch for French attacks.

Thirdly, Calais had been in English hands for only about two years, and the French had no lack of guides who knew the lie of the land far better than its present occupiers, and who could lead the French forces up to the walls with the greatest discretion.

While the Artois peasants were celebrating the second Christmas season since the coming of the plague, some thanking God for sparing the human race after all, others feasting on the mass of foodstuffs left without owners, Charny gathered his army at Saint-Omer and stealthily made his way westwards. Entering enemy-held territory under cover of a freezing night, they approached Calais from the south-western side and arrived at the bridge of Nieulay sometime after midnight, without encountering any resistance or alerting any of the outlying English strongholds. The bulk of the army was left near the bridge, while Charny, his leading commanders, and an advance party made their way towards the citadel. Ahead of them they sent two squires to investigate.

The squires reached the harbour without alerting the garrison and were met by Aimeric in person. He promised them that all was going well, and that once he received his money, the French could enter the gate. They went back to inform Charny, apparently taking Aimeric's son with them as a hostage, though according to some sources, Aimeric's son had already been sent as a hostage to Charny some time beforehand. Gilles le Muisit's claim that Aimeric actually presented the French with a set of keys, telling them they were the keys of Calais, is probably a fanciful exaggeration.[12]

So far all had gone well, but now came the trickier part. How could the storming party seize Aimeric's tower, and then be reinforced by the main army, without alerting the garrison too soon and without being trapped on the exposed beach? Charny's plan, devised no doubt with the help of Aimeric and of members of the former French garrison of Calais, can be reconstructed with some difficulty from the surviving sources. The main force was never meant to enter Calais through Aimeric's tower. While it gathered and waited in front of the Boulogne Gate, a small storming party of 100 men-at-arms and twelve knights would take possession of Aimeric's tower, and then make its way through the sleeping city towards the Boulogne Gate, seize it by surprise, and let the main force inside. By then the garrison would probably be alerted, but both surprise and numerical superiority would hopefully give the French the necessary edge (see map 3).

Charny gave the crucial job of commanding the storming party to Oudart de Renti, 'a very valiant knight and marvellously subtle'.[13] Renti had recently been a traitor himself. He was banished from France in the mid-1340s for some crimes, and joined the cause of Edward III. He was given command of the Flemish forces that helped Edward capture Calais in 1347. During his tenure as commander of this Flemish army, he had led several unsuccessful attempts to surprise the French-held towns of Béthune and Lille. Only in June 1347 was he pardoned by Philip VI, whence he deserted Edward III and the Flemings, and rejoined the service of the French king. Charny may have picked Renti in order to enable him to redeem his honour. Or perhaps Charny chose him because Renti obviously had an intimate knowledge of Calais's environments, of treacherous plots, and of treasonous minds.[14]

Renti and his men went forward, carrying with them one or two sacks containing Aimeric's 20,000 écus. Synchronizing their advance with the ebbing of the tide, they threaded their way between the overhanging walls and the seashore, their footsteps hushed by the soft sand and the murmur of the waves. As promised, the drawbridge over the citadel's moat was lowered, the gate was open, and Aimeric was anxiously waiting for them at the entrance. Dawn was just beginning to break.

Meanwhile Charny and his companions waited nervously in front of the Boulogne Gate, passing the time and hiding their anxiety by cracking jokes about Lombards. 'How long that Lombard takes!' said Charny (at least according to Froissart), 'He will make us die of cold here.' 'In the name of God, sir,' answered Pepin de Biere, 'Lombards are sly men; he must be going over your florins, to see if none of them is counterfeit, and also to check if the entire sum is there.'[15] Then at last the Boulogne Gate was opened, and out charged hundreds of English soldiers led by King Edward III in person, shouting 'A! Edward, Saint George! A! Edward, Saint George!'[16]

✦ ✦ ✦

KING Edward first heard of the plot to capture Calais a week earlier, while preparing to celebrate Christmas at his rural mansion of Havering. Though Aimeric and Charny thought that their agreement was a complete secret, someone who became privy to it – perhaps one of Aimeric's aides – decided to share it with the English king. When Edward learned of it, he decided to allow the plotters to go ahead with their plans, and use them for his own benefit.

According to Le Bel and Froissart, Edward sent word to Aimeric that his presence was urgently needed in England. Aimeric made the short journey over the Channel, reassuring himself that Edward could not possibly have heard of the plot. However, his worst fears soon came true. According to Froissart, Edward accused Aimeric that, having been entrusted with that thing in the world that Edward loved most after his wife and children – namely Calais – Aimeric now intended to sell it to the French. For this he deserved to die.[17]

While women accused of high treason were burnt, since 1241 the English punishment for males convicted of high treason was to be hanged, drawn, and quartered. This meant first drawing the traitor to the place of execution in full view of the populace; then hanging him, but without breaking his neck, and cutting him down while he was still alive and conscious; then cutting off his sexual organs and burning them in front of his eyes; then disembowelling him and burning the internal organs as well; and finally decapitating the corpse and dividing the headless body into four quarters. These quarters, and the head, were usually exhibited in various public places in order to display the king's justice and power.

If Edward's accusation raised this terrifying spectre before Aimeric's eyes, his next words were like a soothing balm. He was willing to forgive Aimeric's crime, if Aimeric would consent to serve as a double agent. Indeed, if he played his part well and drew Charny into a trap, Edward would even allow Aimeric to keep the 20,000 écus. What Aimeric had to do was in fact very simple. First, he had to keep his mouth shut and not inform anyone of his deals either with Charny or with Edward. Secondly, he had to scrupulously keep his promises to Charny, namely to open the gate, lower the drawbridge, and admit the French into Calais. Edward would take care of the rest. Aimeric agreed, thanking his generous king and his incredible luck. Not only was he allowed to keep his life, he could even keep the money. To be on the safe side, Edward kept Aimeric's brother with him as a hostage.

Le Bel and Froissart may well have embellished actual events for the sake of drama, and it may well be that Edward never summoned Aimeric to England, and made his arrangements with him through some trusted envoys. Alternatively, according to one version of Froissart's chronicle Aimeric never really intended to betray Calais. The minute he concluded his agreement with Charny, he crossed over to England of his own volition and informed Edward of everything. This version, however, is far less convincing. For one thing, Aimeric must have concluded his deal with Charny at least several weeks before New Year's Eve, because it would have taken Charny a considerable time to raise and prepare a force of more than 5,000 soldiers. Edward, however, was informed of it only at Christmas. If Aimeric wanted to betray Charny all along, he would not have waited until the last moment before alerting Edward. Secondly, after the events at Calais Edward removed Aimeric from his command, and seems to have lost his trust in him. If Aimeric was acting from the beginning as an English double agent, Edward should have had no cause to distrust him. On the contrary, by betraying the French in such a spectacular manner Aimeric had made many powerful enemies on the French side, and bound his fortune to Edward.

By whatever means Edward discovered the plot, he had only a few days to prepare a warm reception for Charny. Such a short time hardly sufficed to raise new forces. Edward therefore had to scrape together a small expeditionary force from whatever troops he already had at hand. In the five days he had, he managed to assemble at Dover about 300 men-at-arms and 600 archers. Both Edward and his heir, the future Black Prince, joined this force, but formal command of it was given to Walter Mauny, who was not only one of the architects of Calais's conquest in 1346/7, but was also the city's first English captain. Froissart says that, having played the general at Crécy and Calais, the gallant Edward this time wished to fight as a common knight. If Froissart did not invent this detail and if Mauny was really placed at least in official command of this force, it may well have been done for the sake of secrecy. A force led by the king of England in person was bound to draw far more attention than one led by Walter Mauny.

Some soldiers crossed from Dover to Calais in the preceding nights, but it appears that the bulk of the force together with Edward himself crossed over on the night of 30 December, twenty-four hours before Charny's anticipated arrival. This was again done for the sake of secrecy, for it minimized the chances that these reinforcements could be discovered by French spies and reported to Charny. To limit the chances of detection still further, once in Calais the newly arrived men hid themselves in cellars and secret chambers.

When Renti entered Aimeric's tower, Aimeric led them into a well-prepared English ambush. This is the moment illustrated in a fifteenth-century version of Froissart's chronicle (see illus. 8). The illustration shows – with obvious artistic license – the main French army waiting in the background, while Renti and his men advance to Aimeric's tower. Aimeric receives them on the drawbridge, and relieves them of the sack of coins. According to the accompanying text, Renti told Aimeric that he might count the coins to see if they were all there, but Aimeric responded amiably that there would be time for that later. At present, there was not a moment to lose, for day was dawning. He took the heavy sack and cast it into a nearby room, and then led Renti and his men straight into the English ambush. Caught off guard in the narrow gate-room by a superior English force, Renti's party was quickly overwhelmed. Trumpets gave a pre-arranged signal, and the main English force sortied out from the Boulogne Gate. Simultaneously, a smaller force under the Black Prince exited

Calais from the Water Gate, and went round the city to attack Charny's army from the flank.

As cries of 'Treason! Treason!' filled the air,[18] perhaps half the French army broke and fled in panic. The other half stood firm under the command of Charny, who, according to Froissart, exclaimed to his fellow commanders that they were betrayed by that false Lombard, but that they should nevertheless try to defend themselves as best they could. For a time it seemed as if Edward would get a harder battle than he bargained for. Charny's wisdom in keeping the bulk of his forces in the open, instead of leading them along the beach to Aimeric's tower, now became apparent. Also, in his desire to utilize Aimeric's plot in his favour, Edward perhaps underestimated the army gathered by Charny, which outnumbered the combined forces of the Calais garrison and Edward's small expeditionary force. According to the Chandos Herald, the battle under the walls of Calais was one of Edward's hardest fights.

In the end, however, the English prevailed. The French force was a hastily assembled second-rate army, which expected an easy conquest and was obviously demoralized by the shock of betrayal. Edward's household troops, in contrast, were of far better quality and were reassured by seeing their adversaries trapped unaware. Moreover, the English were constantly reinforced from Calais by men who were previously kept out of the scheme but who now armed themselves and joined the fray, whereas the French soon found themselves attacked from the flank by the Black Prince.

In the growing light of day the French saw that the situation was hopeless. They tried to retreat to the Nieulay bridge, but the marshy terrain hampered them. As the heavily armed knights and men-at-arms fought along the narrow causeways, the lightly armed English longbowmen moved into the marsh and, protected by the mud from French counterattacks, rained arrows on the exposed French flanks. The French broke, but even flight was not easy, for they were still trapped between Calais, the sea, and the marshes. Charny, Renti, Eustace de Ribbemont, and about thirty other important knights were captured, and several hundred more men were killed, including Pepin de Biere.

In the best chivalric tradition, that evening Edward threw a feast to celebrate his victory, and invited his noble prisoners to join in. He went from the one to the other, talking about the events of the day and praising those who distinguished themselves most. When he came before Charny, Edward said to him:

> My lord Geoffroi, My lord Geoffroi! I rightly owe you very little love since you wanted to take from me by night what I have won and what has cost me much money. So I am very pleased to have put you to the rest. You wanted to get it more cheaply than I, for 20,000 écus. But God aided me so that you failed in your intent. He will yet aid me, if it pleases Him, in my greater endeavour.[19]

Then, to show that he had no enmity toward the French, Edward spoke to Eustace de Ribbemont, whom he had fought hand-to-hand during the battle. He praised Ribbemont and exalted his courage and prowess, took off a pearl necklace he was wearing, and placed it around Ribbemont's neck. He then allowed Ribbemont to depart to Paris and report the events to his king, on condition that he later return to English custody, until his ransom was paid. One version of Froissart's chronicle even adds that Edward gave Ribbemont 20,000 écus to defer his travelling expenses, though this is clearly a literary invention meant to contrast Ribbemont's honourable conduct with Aimeric's treachery.

Even the less dubious parts of this story, like so many other stories that emanated from the artful pen of Froissart, have been questioned by modern historians. However, there is nothing implausible about them. Like most of his contemporaries, Edward knew that theatre was the better half of politics, and he was an unsurpassed master in the performative arts of kingship. It is telling that at the height of the Black Death epidemic he had the time and energy to found a new knightly order, namely the Order of the Garter, which is still the most famous and cherished knightly order of the world. And though Edward mercilessly devastated France, bringing death and misery to millions of French commoners, he was careful to show off his magnanimity toward more respectable rivals and prisoners, such as Ribbemont or the rich burghers of Calais.

A few days after their victory, Edward and his men boarded ship and returned to England with their prisoners. Charny stayed behind in Calais to recover from his wounds, and was later transferred to London, were he stayed a prisoner until the summer of 1351, working on his *Livre de chevalerie* – another chivalric guidebook. In section 30 of the book, Charny warns his readers against men

> who some consider to be wise, but they put all their intelligence and concentrated effort into such cunning schemes that their great subtlety sometimes turns them aside from reaching a true, loyal, and sensible conclusion, so that these subtle people are out of step in all undertakings. Like those who leave the good main road to follow minor paths and then get lost, in the same way, through their great subtlety they fail to act according to natural good sense, and therefore they will not profit fully from their natural intelligence through setting their mind to such great subtlety.[20]

Is this tortuous passage referring to Charny or Aimeric?

Aimeric himself received two horses as a present from Edward. He also kept the 20,000 écus. No source records what happened to his son.

✦ ✦ ✦

ON one of the last days of July 1352 the people of Saint-Omer thronged to the town's main square. Geoffroi de Charny, who a year earlier returned from his captivity and reassumed his former position as military captain in Artois, was about to treat them to one of the most awe-inspiring and most popular of medieval public spectacles: a public execution.

A few days earlier, Oudart de Renti had returned from a reconnaissance with welcome news. In order to strengthen their hold on Calais, the English had surrounded the city with a screen of castles and towers. Renti had discovered that the tower at Fretun, which guarded the road along which he and Charny travelled on that unlucky night in December 1349, could be captured by escalade. Renti had also discovered something far more interesting. The governor of Fretun was none other than Aimeric de Pavia.

Charny was a devout Christian. Not only did he go on crusade, but during his life he generously endowed several monasteries, avidly collected relics (he was the first recorded owner of the famous Shroud of Turin), and paid tribute to the spiritual vocation in his chivalric treatises. Nevertheless, forgiveness was not one of his most conspicuous qualities. He quickly gathered a striking force, and arrived before Fretun at dawn of 25 July 1352. This time there was no underhand deal. The French stormed the tower by main force, and captured its luckless governor.

Aimeric was carried back in triumph to Saint-Omer. The fate from which he sought to escape by making his deal with Edward had finally caught up with him. Though it was customary to treat noble prisoners well and ransom them, and though Charny himself had enjoyed such privileged treatment after his defeat at Calais, he was intent on dealing with Aimeric as a traitor rather than as a prisoner of war. Froissart says that Aimeric was taken to Saint-Omer's main market, as would befit a merchant. The author of the *Chronique Normande* recounted how, while the population of the town watched with awestruck fascination, the executioner tore away with red-hot iron pincers Aimeric's two nipples, and then proceeded to similarly tear away his tongue, his heels, and other members of his body. He then chopped off Aimeric's two thighs, two arms, and his head. The dismembered parts were hung on the town's gates, and the head was displayed in the marketplace.[21] Froissart, whose chivalric sensitivity was offended by the Lombard, adds that Aimeric's beautiful English mistress, who was also caught in the raid, subsequently became the lover of a French squire.

Four years later Charny followed his victim to the grave. He was killed while carrying the *Oriflamme* at the battle of Poitiers (1356), an even more catastrophic French defeat than Crécy. He thus died as he lived, a chivalric paragon who gained great honours and riches thanks to a string of almost uninterrupted defeats.

✦ ✦ ✦

AFTER the failure of Charny's raid, Calais remained in English hands for another two centuries. It became the main English beach-head on the Continent, from which countless invasions of France and the Low Countries were launched. It was also the main centre of English espionage on the Continent, a base from which numerous spies operated.[22] In addition, it gradually acquired great economic importance, and much of the English trade with the Continent passed through its harbour. The French repeatedly tried to recapture it, and it was besieged several times, but all these attempts failed due to the city's advantageous position amid the marshes; to the strength of the fortifications; and to the English resolve to hold it at all costs.

Even when, in the 1440s and 1450s, the English lost all their possessions in Gascony and Normandy, Calais remained firmly in their hands. Its possession embittered Anglo-French relations, fuelled repeated English conquest attempts on the Continent, and influenced English relations with the Low Countries as well. It played a major role even in England's internal wars of the late fifteenth century and early sixteenth century, not least because the Calais garrison was the closest thing England had to a standing professional army.

Calais was eventually recaptured by the French only in 1558. It is interesting to note that the duke of Guise's successful attack on the city seems to have been devised with the knowledge of Charny's failed attempt two centuries before. Guise arrived at Calais on the anniversary of Charny's failure – 1 January 1558. He decided to attack at exactly the same place where Charny tried and failed – the citadel. Guise's artillery was posted on the dunes across the harbour, and after a short bombardment breached the citadel's outer walls. The French then waited for low tide, and at night waded their way through the shallow waters at the head of the harbour.[23] They charged the breach exactly where two centuries earlier Renti's party walked into the English trap, and carried the city by storm.[24]

NOTES

1 Sumption, *Hundred Years War*, 1:578.

2 Le Bel, *Chronique*, 2:174. Compare Machiavelli, *Art of War*, 7.118, ed. Lynch, p. 154; Aubigny, *Traité*, p. 17.

3 *Istore et Croniques de Flandres*, 2:64.

4 Froissart, *Œuvres*, ed. Lettenhove, 5:412. See also 5:232.

5 Baker, *Chronicon*, p. 103.

6 *Journaux du trésor de Philippe VI*, pp. 799, 838–9.

7 Froissart, *Œuvres*, ed. Lettenhove, 5:230.

8 Sumption, *Hundred Years War*, 2:23.

9 Le Bel, *Chronique*, 2:175.

10 Froissart, *Œuvres*, ed. Lettenhove, 5:230.

11 *Charny, Book of Chivalry*, sections 10–11, ed. Kaeuper, pp. 92–4.

12 Muisit, *Chronique et Annales*, p. 262.

13 *Istore et Croniques de Flandres*, 2:52.

14 *Istore et Croniques de Flandres*, 2:52–4; Sumption, *Hundred Years War*, 1:565–7.

15 Froissart, *Œuvres*, ed. Lettenhove, 5:237–8. The florin was a popular coin; in the medieval monetary jungle, sums named using one type of coin were usually paid with a frightening mixture of other coins.

16 Murimuth, *Continuatio Chronicarum*, p. 410.

17 Froissart, *Œuvres*, ed. Lettenhove, 5:231.

18 Muisit, *Chronique et Annales*, p. 262.

19 Froissart, *Œuvres*, ed. Lettenhove, 5:247; Le Bel, *Chronique*, 2:181. Translation taken from *Charny, Book of Chivalry*, ed. Kaeuper, p. 12.

20 *Charny, Book of Chivalry*, section 30, ed. Kaeuper, pp. 149–51.

21 *Chronique Normande*, p. 104; Baker, *Chronicon*, pp. 107–8; *Chronographia Regum Francorum*, p. 254.

22 Alban, 'Spies', p. 84.

23 It is impossible to tell why Charny himself did not try to wade through the water at low tide. Calais harbour suffered from a serious problem of sand clogging, and perhaps it was shallower in 1558 than in 1350. In all probability, if Charny had tried to do so in 1350, the results for the French would probably have been catastrophic.

24 The present chapter is based mainly on the following sources: Avesbury, *De gestis mirabilibus*, pp. 406–10; Le Bel, *Chronique*, 2:173–82; Baker, *Chronicon*, pp. 103–7; *Chronique Normande*, pp. 91–2, 104; *Chronographia Regum Francorum*, 2:247–54; Muisit, *Chronique et Annales*, pp. 259–63; Froissart, *Œuvres*, ed. Lettenhove, 5:148–9, 220–51, 271–4; *Charny, Book of Chivalry*, ed. Kaeuper, pp. 3–18, 84–199; *Récits d'un bourgeois*, pp. 264–6; *Istore et Croniques de Flandres*, 2:52–71; Sumption, *Hundred Years War*; 1:535–86, 2:60–2, 93; Rogers, *War Cruel and Sharp*, pp. 273–85; Contamine, 'Geoffroy de Charny'; DeVries, 'Hunger, Flemish Participation';

It is based to a lesser extent on: Rymer, *Foedera*, vol. 3, part 1, pp. 1–51; *Journaux du trésor de Philippe VI*, pp. 799, 838–9; Lescot, *Chronique*, pp. 85, 91; *Chronique des quatre premiers Valois*, pp. 29–30; *Prince noir*, lines 410–55, ed. Michel, pp. 27–9; *Chronicon Angliae*, pp. 27–8; Walsingham, *Historia Anglicana*, 1:273–4; *Lettres de rois*, 2:78–101; Neillands, *Hundred Years War*, pp. 113–17; Cazelles, *Sociétié politique*; Keen, *Chivalry*, p. 12; Boulton, *Knights of the Crown*, p. 186; Doig, 'New Source for Siege of Calais'; Grummitt, 'Financial Administration'; Harriss, 'Struggle for Calais'; Munro, 'Economic Aspect'; Oman, *Art of War in the Sixteenth Century*, pp. 267–73; Prestwich, *Three Edwards*, pp. 172–3; Potter, 'Guise and the Fall of Calais'; Power, 'English Wool Trade'.

6

Princes in the Cross-Hairs:
The Rise and Fall of Valois Burgundy, 1407–83

MANY medieval and early modern empires were founded on the sterility of princely houses. Kingdoms and principalities that resisted conquest for centuries were gobbled up whole if their ruling dynasty died out. Whenever a prince failed to provide a legitimate heir, greedy relatives and neighbours could soon be seen circling him like a pack of vultures, and conquest or civil war were bound to follow. When a prince sired only daughters, he was just as quickly surrounded by suitors, anxious to put their hands on the dowry. It was in such a way that Scotland and England, and Aragon and Castile – hitherto bitter enemies – found themselves united into Britain and Spain. It was in such a way that the Habsburgs constructed the greatest empire of the early modern age.

During the late Middle Ages no dynasty preyed on its infertile neighbours with more ruthlessness and success than the Valois of Burgundy. Since their stepping stones to empire were the heads and wombs of princes and princesses, the focus of their military efforts too was on these heads and wombs as much as on armies and fortresses.

The house of Valois was a cadet house of the Capetians, the ruling dynasty of France since 987. (See genealogical table overleaf.) It came to power in 1328 when the last Capetian king of France, Charles IV, died without leaving any male heir. The Capetian inheritance – which constituted the most powerful kingdom in Christendom – was then disputed between Charles IV's cousin, Count Philip of Valois, and his nephew, King Edward III of England. Philip won, due to a combination of many causes, but the legal excuse given was that Edward had inherited his claim to the French Crown through his mother, and in the Kingdom of France, a female could allegedly neither inherit land nor pass rights of inheritance to her sons.

Philip's son, King Jean II of France, fathered a number of sons, and while the crown went to the eldest, each of the others was compensated with a dukedom. One of these younger sons, Philip 'le Hardi', received the duchy of Burgundy. Soon after, he married the richest heiress of his time, Margaret de Mâle. She inherited from her father the County of Artois, the Franche-Comté and above all the rich County of Flanders – the most urbanized and industrialized area of medieval northern Europe. Thanks to his wife's rich dowry, Philip was transformed from just another duke amongst many into one of the foremost princes of Christendom and the most powerful force in French politics. (See map 4.)

The Houses of Capet, Plantagenet and Valois

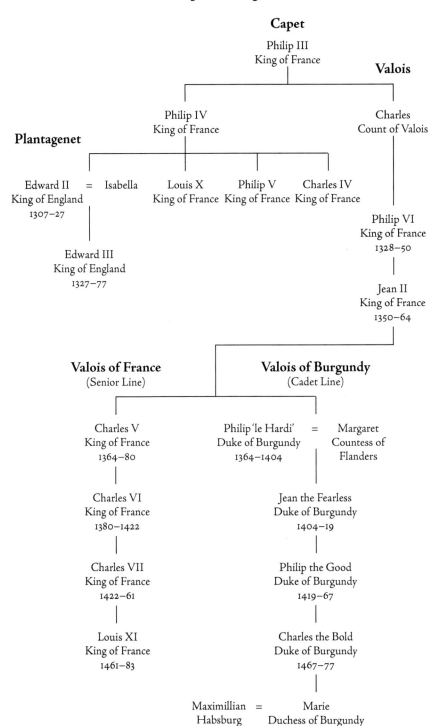

When in 1392 the young king of France went mad, Philip 'le Hardi' sought to take over the royal government itself, and was kept in check only by a rival contender for power – Duke Louis of Orléans. For several years France tottered on the brink of armed conflict, a prey to the rival factions. When Philip 'le Hardi' died, he was succeeded as duke of Burgundy and head of the Burgundian faction by his son, Jean the Fearless. The fearless new duke quickly had his rival Orléans assassinated (1407), which pushed France into a murderous civil war.

For a time, Duke Jean gained control of Paris and of the government, but

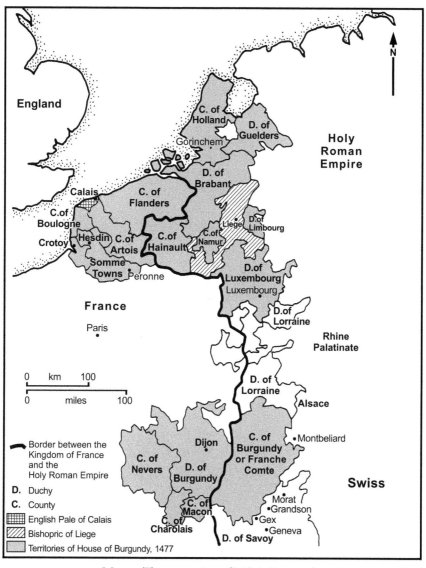

Map 4 The expansion of Valois Burgundy

the main beneficiary of the conflict was King Henry V of England. He had his own family claims to the French crown, and utilized the Burgundy–Orléanist war to invade the kingdom. He annihilated the largely Orléanist army that opposed him at Agincourt (1415), and then set about slowly conquering the forts and cities of Normandy. The English invasion hardly interrupted the French civil war, now waged between the duke of Burgundy on one side, and the young French crown prince, the Dauphine Charles, on the other. Only when Henry conquered Rouen, the capital of Normandy (1419), did the rival parties agree to come to terms. Duke Jean and the Dauphine Charles met for a peace conference on the bridge of Montereau, in order to arrange a permanent peace between themselves – and a common war against England. However, the peace conference turned ugly. Either in the heat of the moment or due to a premeditated plot, one of the Dauphine's followers split Duke Jean's head with a battle-axe.

Jean was succeeded by his son, Duke Philip the Good. Philip at first made a firm alliance with the English invaders to avenge his father. It was later quipped that the English entered France through the hole in Duke Jean's head. With Burgundian help, the English gained momentary control of Paris and large parts of northern France, and for a time seemed poised to unite France and England under Plantagenet rule. However, the premature death of Henry V, the meteoric career of Jeanne d'Arc, and Burgundian defection in 1435 decided otherwise.

In fact, already long before 1435 Philip the Good turned his attention away from the Anglo-French conflict. He offered only limited assistance to the English, and after switching sides, offered even more limited assistance to the French. Instead of becoming embroiled in French politics like his father, Philip preferred to follow the less risky path of his grandfather. While the French monarchy was busy fighting for its survival, Philip sought to create a Burgundian empire in the Low Countries by picking the inheritances of dying dynasties.

His first prey was the County of Namur. Its count, Jean III, had no children, and Philip convinced him in 1420 to name him as his heir in exchange for a huge sum of money. Jean died in 1429, and Philip duly became the new count of Namur. Next came the Duchy of Brabant. In 1427 Brabant belonged to a youthful cousin of Philip the Good, called Philip of Saint-Pol. He too agreed to name Philip as his provisional heir, provided he did not have children of his own. Shortly thereafter, Philip of Saint-Pol asked for the hand of a princess of the House of Anjou, enemies of the House of Burgundy. However, he died before marrying his intended bride, on 4 August 1430, and Brabant passed into Burgundian hands. Malicious tongues whispered that the duke of Burgundy had Philip of Saint-Pol murdered.

The acquisition of Namur and Brabant paled in comparison to Philip's next conquest. Throughout the 1420s the flourishing territories of Holland, Zeeland, and Hainault were disputed between another of Philip the Good's cousins – the young Duchess Jacqueline – and his uncle, John of Bavaria. John spent most of his life in church service, and had no children. On 6 April 1424 Philip convinced John to name him as his heir, agreeing in return to help him in his war against Jacqueline. Exactly nine months later John died; murdered, said many, by his impatient nephew – or perhaps by Jacqueline. One of the suspected agents even confessed under torture that a poisoned prayer-book was used to eliminate the ex-bishop.[1]

Philip the Good now proclaimed himself John of Bavaria's heir, and stepped up the war with Jacqueline. The unlucky duchess, who tried to establish her headquarters at the city of Mons, was betrayed by the citizens. They delivered her to Philip the Good on 13 June 1425 in order to save their city from siege and assault. Philip placed her under house arrest in Ghent, and set himself up as her guardian.[2] It was not the last time that the dukes of Burgundy would lock a princess in a tower in order to get possession of her lands.

Yet victory slipped from between the duke's fingers. In early September, when she learned that Philip was about to move her to the more secure castle of Lille, Jacqueline resolved to escape. She disguised herself in men's clothing, and while her guards were eating, she escaped from the house together with two companions. She slipped out of the city unnoticed and rode to Antwerp still disguised as a man. There she felt safe enough to declare her true identity, and made her way to Holland, which still supported her cause. The war of inheritance, which seemed to be over, flared up again with even greater intensity.[3] It took three more years of intense military efforts to defeat Jacqueline's adherents. In 1428 she was forced to surrender. By then the young duchess had had two disastrous marriages, but no children. In the treaty of peace she agreed to recognize her cousin, Philip the Good, as her provisional heir and guardian. It was also stipulated that she could not marry again except with Philip's approval. If she broke this term, she would forfeit her lands, which would immediately revert to Philip, who had very little intention of endangering his inheritance by allowing Jacqueline to marry. When in 1433 he discovered that she had secretly married Frank van Borselen, he kidnapped and imprisoned the unlucky husband, and forced her to renounce all her rights.

According to Monstrelet, the aggrieved Jacqueline and her mother, Margaret of Hainault, tried to avenge themselves on Philip by having him assassinated. One of Margaret's household knights, Gille de Postelles, conspired with several other Hainault noblemen to surprise the duke of Burgundy while he was hunting in the woods. However, the plot was discovered, and Postelles and his accomplices were captured and executed.[4]

Shortly afterwards Philip made his peace with King Charles VII of France at Arras (1435). In exchange for abandoning the English alliance, Charles gave Philip in mortgage the Somme towns – a strategically and economically important belt of towns on France's northern border. Philip, however, was reluctant to wage war on his former friends for the sake of his father's murderer, and with the exception of a few noisy demonstrations, continued to focus his efforts on the Low Countries.

There another childless relative had meanwhile entered Philip's sights. This was Elizabeth of Görlitz, duchess of Luxembourg, who had first married Philip's uncle Anthony, and after his death married John of Bavaria, but without bearing any living children. Philip pestered his ageing aunt for two decades until she finally agreed to name him as her heir, in exchange for a yearly stipend of 7,000 florins (1441).

There were, as usual in such cases, other claimants to the inheritance. Duke William of Saxony, who enjoyed the support of many Luxembourgers, occupied the duchy and garrisoned its main strongpoints. After two years of desultory skirmishes, a Burgundian army invaded Luxembourg in 1443 to dislodge the Saxon. The countryside was easily overrun, but the two chief strongholds of Thionville and Luxembourg seemed to be beyond the invaders' reach. Two experienced Burgundian *eschelleurs* named Robert de Bersat and Johannes de Montagu, accompanied by a German interpreter, were sent to infiltrate the two cities and see whether they could spot any weakness in the defences. They first infiltrated Thionville, but found nothing of use. They then infiltrated Luxembourg, climbing over the walls by means of a silk ladder, and disguised in German robes. This time Montagu discovered a hidden postern that was used by the townspeople in peacetime and was now barred. After carefully reconnoitring the postern gate and its surroundings, Montagu concluded that it could be captured with relative ease by a sudden onslaught.

On one of the darkest nights of the year, 21/2 November 1443, the walls of Luxembourg were approached by a Burgundian force of about 200 men, guided by Montagu the *eschelleur* and a number of local guides. Half a league away from the city they dismounted from their horses and proceeded the rest of the way on foot. They reached their destination without being detected at about 2 o'clock in the morning. A scaling party of between sixty and eighty men threw their ladders against the walls and climbed up. Montagu led the way, followed by a few other notable warriors and six archers of Duke Philip's personal bodyguard, who carried with them a huge pair of iron pincers. Once the advance party mounted the wall they dispatched the few guards they encountered, and ran towards the postern gate, capturing it without difficulty and breaking it open using the pincers.

The rest of the Burgundian force now entered the city. They raised the war cry, shouting 'Our Lady, the town is taken! Burgundy! Burgundy!' The defenders woke up in alarm, and showed almost no resistance. Some fled from the city; the rest locked themselves up in the citadel. The capital of Luxembourg fell with hardly a blow being struck or a Burgundian soldier being injured. The citadel surrendered after a few weeks. The Saxon duke, disheartened by the defeat, sued for peace and agreed to evacuate Thionville too and sell Philip all his claims to the duchy for a handsome sum.[5] Another claimant to the duchy subsequently appeared in 1457, in the shape of King Ladislas of Bohemia. However, just as the seventeen-year-old Ladislas began pressing his claims in earnest, he suddenly died. This time we can safely discount the rumours that he too was poisoned by Burgundian agents, though enemies closer to home may have had a hand in his death.

Luxembourg was Philip's last major acquisition. Thanks to the barrenness of his relatives and neighbours, and thanks to the English invasion of France, which occupied the attention and resources of the king of France, the House of Burgundy now controlled not only the Duchy of Burgundy, but also a patchwork of territories covering the greater part of modern Belgium, Holland, and Luxembourg, together with sizeable chunks of northern France and western Germany. Since the English were by 1453 expelled from all their Continental possessions save Calais, Philip could expect a showdown with a resurgent and vengeful king of France. Yet he was ready for that eventuality as well. With the Hundred Years War over, the duke of Burgundy was not the only French nobleman fearful of a resurgent French monarchy. In the 1450s and 1460s a coalition of territorial French princes gathered around the Valois duke of Burgundy, all anxious to curb the power of the French king.

The stage was thereby set for a collision between the two branches of the House of Valois. The senior branch, now headed by a new king, Louis XI, aimed to reunite France and transform it into a centralized kingdom. The cadet Burgundian branch aimed both to keep France a motley collection of autonomous principalities, and simultaneously to fuse its own disparate dominions into a centralized polity.

However, Burgundy had for some time been facing an enemy far worse than the king of France. The same type of genealogic calamity that had been so far the fountain of its power was now threatening the House of Burgundy itself with extinction. Philip the Good had several sisters, but no brothers. His father sought to safeguard the family inheritance by marrying Philip off at the relatively tender age of thirteen (1409). However, the chosen wife, Michelle of France, failed to provide Philip with any children before she died in 1422. She was poisoned, some believed, by one of her ladies-in-waiting.[6] Philip quickly remarried, taking as his wife one of his many aunts, Countess Bonne of Nevers. She died in 1425, leaving to Philip the County of Nevers, but no heirs.

In 1430 Philip married again, this time Princess Isabel of Portugal, who bore him a son in 1431, and another in 1432, but both died in infancy. By this time Philip had already sired an entire troop of bastards – as many as twenty-six are recorded.[7] Yet none of these could succeed to the family fortune. Another legitimate son was born in 1433, and was christened Charles. After him, Isabel bore no more children.

Charles, who at birth was made count of Charolais, survived the dangerous years of infancy. His birth had momentarily brightened the family prospects, but they remained precarious. If he died, or failed to produce legitimate offspring of his own, the family inheritance was likely to break up between a host of distant relatives, foremost among whom were the Valois kings of France. To ensure the succession, Philip married off Charles when he was a child of five. However, the chosen bride died in 1446, and the question of succession remained as open as ever. Charles was again married, to his cousin Isabel of Bourbon, who lived until 1465, but bore Charles only one child, Marie. This daughter, born in 1457, was Charles's sole heir and the richest prize in the European marriage market. With her the story of Valois Burgundy came full circle. It began with a rich heiress, and now it seemed destined to end with one.

From 1457 the question of the Burgundian inheritance came to dominate European dynastic politics. Could Marie – a woman – inherit the vast Burgundian patrimony? This was far from certain, at least regarding the Burgundian dominions within the Kingdom of France. And even if Marie could inherit her father's empire, who would marry her and add that empire to his own patrimony?

Since Marie's rights of inheritance were doubtful, Charles ought to have married her off as soon as possible, in order to establish her husband and children in place, and secure their position before his own death.[8] But he failed to do so. During his reign he arranged for Marie numerous marriage alliances, and broke them all one after the other. His behaviour resulted partly from a psychological reluctance to give up control of his daughter and set up a foreign man as his heir. But partly, she was just too valuable for him as a diplomatic pawn. He repeatedly gained allies by promising them her hand, and almost as often broke up hostile combinations by promising her to one of his would-be enemies. These short-term advantages, however, greatly exacerbated Charles's long-term position. For as long as Marie remained without husband and children, the future of the Burgundian inheritance continued to be in doubt.

Hence from the moment of his birth till his dying day, Charles knew that the fate of his house and of the burgeoning Burgundian state depended solely on his own life. The numerous conquests his father had made were poignant reminders of the fate installed for Burgundy in case Charles died without a legitimate male heir. The numerous true and false stories of poisoning and assassination that circulated around the Burgundian court were equally poignant reminders of the precariousness of his life. In particular, the fate of his grandfather at Montereau was never far from people's minds in the ducal court. During Charles's childhood, more anxiety was added by the rising reputation of George de la Trémoille as a master of dirty warfare. La Trémoille was the power behind King Charles VII for much of the 1420s and 1430s. In 1427 he arranged the murder of Charles VII's previous two favourites, the Lords of Giac and of Beaulieu, and was later credited with the kidnapping, assassination, and attempted assassinations of other rivals and enemies. In 1432 he plotted to kidnap the Burgundian chancellor, Nicolas Rolin, from deep within Burgundian territory. Rolin had two lucky escapes in 1432 and 1433, following which he was allowed to keep about him a personal bodyguard of twenty-four archers. Duke Philip the Good himself raised his own personal bodyguard from twelve archers to twenty-four. In 1438 he increased their number again to fifty.[9]

As Charles grew up, the close ties he established with Italy and his suit of Italian courtiers could only have exacerbated his home-grown fears. For Italy had a reputation as a land of assassins and poisoners, and every year news of fresh assassinations or assassination plots streamed north from the glittering and turbulent courts of the peninsula. The news from the British Isles were hardly more assuring. The uncouth islanders lacked the Italians' finesse in the use of poison and dagger, but throughout the fifteenth century the royal and noble clans of both England and Scotland devastated one another with barbarous ferocity. At least three kings and two crown princes, as well as numerous dukes and earls, were imprisoned and murdered during those violent decades.

Charles's mother, Isabel of Portugal, added to the fearful atmosphere. She was, according to her husband's testimony, 'the most apprehensive lady he had ever known'.[10] Not surprisingly, her son too was a rather paranoid prince.

Charles became fearful of assassination plots already before he became duke. In the late 1450s and early 1460s his position in the ducal court was uneasy. His father was gradually sinking into senile atrophy, and several factions fought for control of the old man and of the Burgundian government. Charles was a defiant son and an incompetent courtier, and his relations with his father gradually deteriorated. The old duke deprived his heir of any share in the Burgundian government, and instead relied more and more on the powerful noble clan of the Croys, who for a time became virtual rulers of Burgundy.

A deep hostility naturally developed between Charles and the Croys, whom Charles feared might become *de facto* regents of Burgundy. He also suspected them of plotting with King Louis XI of France his own elimination. The Croys had been receiving French bribes on a regular basis since 1435, and if they were not downright traitors, they were certainly of mixed loyalty. As long as Duke Philip lived, their chief loyalty was still to him, particularly since through their control of the old duke they amassed more and more lands and riches in Burgundy. Yet it was obvious to them that sooner or later Philip would die, and if Charles then succeeded as duke, the day of reckoning could be extremely harsh.

In July 1462 Charles accused Jehan Coustain, one of the Croys' protégés at the ducal court, of attempting to poison him. He had Coustain apprehended in Brussels, then brought him to the castle of Rupelmonde and quickly executed him before either the Croys or Duke Philip could intervene. Contemporary chroniclers made much of the juicy story Charles spread about, but it is impossible to say how much truth it contained. Perhaps the Croys really intended to get rid of him, then govern Burgundy in the name of Philip the Good and his infant granddaughter, whom they could marry off as they pleased. Perhaps Coustain and the Croys were innocent, and Charles concocted the whole story to incriminate them and regain favour with his father. Perhaps the Croys were indeed innocent, yet the fearful and disgruntled Charles actually believed that they were plotting his elimination. At the very least, the Coustain affair heightened the tension in the Burgundian court, and raised the question of assassination in unequivocal terms.[11] A year later, Charles accused another rival at court, the count of Étampes, of making wax images of him in order to cast spells on him.

The Coustain affair failed to improve Charles's standing with his father. Philip did not believe his son's story and continued to put his trust in the Croys. In fact, the Croy family now reached the apogee of its power, and succeeded in securing a major coup for King Louis. When King Charles VII gave Philip the Good the Somme towns in order to buy his alliance (1435), it was stipulated in the treaty that the kings of France could redeem these towns for a large sum of money. Charles VII never managed to do so. One of Louis's first aims upon succeeding his father was to regain this vital area. In 1463 the Croys convinced Philip to agree to sell the towns back to the king of France, despite Count Charles's vehement protests. The deal led to another major crisis between father and son, and manifested the power of the Croy family. Charles was reportedly haunted now by fears that the Croys would apprehend and imprison him.[12] He distanced himself from the court, and attempted to build up an independent power base in Holland, in case his father might completely disinherit him.

Shortly after gaining the Somme towns, Louis came up with another suggestion. Anxious to exploit to the full the hold he had over Philip through the Croys, Louis offered to buy from Philip the towns of Lille, Douai, and Orchies. These towns also possessed great economic and strategic importance, yet unlike the Somme towns, they were an old Burgundian territory, part and parcel of Margaret de Mâle's dowry. Louis argued that these particular towns were given a long time previously by the kings of France to the counts of Flanders and their *male* heirs, but they could not be inherited by or through a woman. The Croys pressured Philip to sell the towns and avoid war, and Philip met Louis several times at Hesdin to discuss the offer, as well as several other outstanding issues. Charles fiercely objected to this new venture, rightly depicting the Croys' stance as treasonous. However, his opinions carried little weight. While Philip and the Croys were at Hesdin negotiating with King Louis, Charles was left to sulk in his castle of Gorinchem, in Holland, which stood about 40 kilometres east of Rotterdam, on the river Merwede.

At this moment, an even more serious scandal than the Coustain affair exploded. Louis XI had in his service a shady character, the Bastard of Rubempré, who was reputed to be 'a courageous and enterprising man',[13] but was also known as 'a man of ill-repute, a murderer and a bad lad',[14] and as 'a man of an evil name, of light counsel, and of bad doings'.[15] The Bastard was also a nephew of the Croys. In September 1464 he was given secret instruction by Louis to undertake a delicate mission deep within Burgundian territory. He gathered a band of forty to eighty cut-throats, hired a light corsair vessel at the port of Crotoy, and sailed northwards. 'None of the crew,' says the chronicle of Wavrin, 'knew whither the bastard intended to carry them, nor what orders he was charged with, except that they were told they must follow him wherever he should choose to lead them, and do anything he commanded them.'[16]

Rubempré's ship arrived at Armuyden on the coast of Zeeland sometime in the middle of September. Rubempré left his ship at anchor there, took with him a few of his most trusted companions, and together they made their way on foot inland, towards the town of Gorinchem. Once they reached the town, they took up lodging in the best hotel, pretending to be merchants on business. They stayed there for three weeks, according to the chronicle of the Hague, and began making inquiries about Charles's habits and household arrangements: When did he use to go out to sea? In which kind of ship did he usually sail? When did he go hunting? Did he go about with a large or a small company? Did he go in the morning or in the evening? Rubempré then made a reconnaissance of the castle and its environs, climbing the walls and examining with particular interest the route back to the sea-coast.

Though the courts of princes always attracted many hangers-on eager for information about their activities, Rubempré's inquiries aroused suspicions. According to the chronicle of the Hague, it was the hostess of their hotel who became suspicious of her guests and reported them to the authorities. According to Chastellain, Rubempré had served Charles in the past, and was now recognized by some of Charles's household members. His activities were reported to the count, and when Rubempré heard of it, he became frightened and took shelter in a church, from where he was taken and thrown into prison. According to another version, it was not Rubempré but rather one of his companions who was recognized in an alehouse and asked about his business. The man said that he was part of an armed force under the command of the Bastard of Rubempré, sent to Holland by the king of France. What their mission was, however, he did not know. The report alarmed Charles, who immediately sent men to apprehend Rubempré, and another force to capture the ship.

In prison Rubempré at first claimed that he was a merchant on his way to Scotland. He then changed his story and said he was actually going to visit the Lady de Montfort, daughter of the lord of Croy. Yet soon enough he broke and confessed everything. What he confessed, though, remained a closely guarded secret. This did not prevent rumours from spreading, probably with active encouragement from Count Charles. Rubempré, it was reported in alehouses, churches, and palaces throughout the Low Countries and France, was sent to Holland by King Louis in order to kidnap Charles and bring him to France. Some added knowingly that if Rubempré failed to kidnap the count, he was instructed to kill him instead.

Thomas Basin, a source extremely hostile to Louis XI, writes that Rubempré confessed in front of numerous trustworthy persons, and without being subjected to any torture, that he meant to kidnap Charles on one of his excursions, take him to the ship, and bring him to Louis either alive or dead. Once Charles was imprisoned or killed, some of the reports continued, Louis intended to sweep down on Duke Philip at Hesdin and secure his person too. He would then marry off Marie of Burgundy to whomever he liked, and carve up the Burgundian inheritance as he pleased.

The chronicle of the Hague gives the most detailed explanation how Rubempré supposedly planned to kidnap Count Charles. The Bastard's ship was of a unique design, and its master mariner promised Rubempré that he could take him to Holland and back safely even if all the fleets of England and Holland tried to block his way. Charles was extremely fond of the sea and of sailing. His intimate friend Olivier de la Marche confirms that 'more than anything, he had a natural love of the sea and ships'.[17] Rubempré therefore believed that if he spread word in Gorinchem of his wonderful ship, Charles would become curious and come to inspect it in person. Once the count boarded ship, Rubempré's men could overpower his guards and carry him away. Alternatively, Charles could be ambushed on one of his frequent excursions to the coast and the sea, and taken on board forcefully. The chronicle further says that when Rubempré was captured, a letter was found on him sealed with the private seal of Louis XI, in which the king promised Rubempré great rewards if he brought him Count Charles. The last detail, however, casts doubts on the veracity of this report. Rubempré would have been crazy to carry on his person such incriminating evidence.[18]

As soon as Rubempré was taken and questioned, Charles sent to Hesdin the commander of his bodyguard, Olivier de la Marche, to beat the wave of rumours and inform Duke Philip of the affair in carefully chosen words. La Marche arrived at Hesdin on 7 October, while Philip was taking his midday meal. He apparently told the duke that Count Charles had barely been saved from a kidnapping attempt, and that Philip too might be in danger. According to a letter sent to Duke Francesco Sforza of Milan, La Marche also brought with him a written copy of Rubempré's interrogation, in which the Bastard confessed that he was ordered by the king of France to take with him about eighty people and kidnap Count Charles.

Philip became alarmed. Though he had discounted his son's allegations during the Coustain affair, there were enough reasons to suspect King Louis. Not least of these was the fate of Philip, the younger son of the duke of Savoy. King Louis had always shown great interests in the affairs of Savoy, the Alpine duchy bordering France and Burgundy to the south-east, which controlled the vital mountain passes connecting Italy and north-western Europe. He had even taken one of the duke of Savoy's daughters as his wife, whereas his sister Yolanda was married to the Savoyard crown prince, Amadeus. Philip of Savoy was leader of the anti-French faction in Savoy, and strongly objected to French intervention in Savoyard politics. A few months before the Rubempré affair, Louis had invited Philip to visit his court and settle their differences, providing him with all the necessary promises and safe-conduct letters. Yet once the Savoyard prince arrived, Louis broke his word and imprisoned him in the dreary fortress of Loches. Such dishonourable conduct aroused outcries throughout the courts of Europe, but Louis did not yield.

The duke of Savoy was Philip the Good's cousin, and Philip of Savoy was actually named in honour of the Burgundian duke. In August 1464 the sorrowful duke of Savoy paid Hesdin a visit, and for twenty-five days implored the duke of Burgundy to intervene with King Louis and set his son free. The issue was raised during Philip's meetings with Louis, but nothing came out of it. In early September, the disappointed duke of Savoy left Hesdin. Philip of Savoy continued to languish in Loches for two more years, where he composed a mournful chanson about the treason of the king of France. Could the news from Holland mean that King Louis was trying to betray the house of Burgundy in a similar fashion?[19]

Chastellain says that people at Philip's court also began to talk of the bridge of Montereau and other past French treacheries. Suspicions were fuelled by the circumstance that, shortly before La Marche's arrival, Duke Philip had received a message from Louis, saying that he was on his way to Hesdin, and intended to visit Philip the following day. Louis was reportedly accompanied by a strong guard, whereas Philip had only a small force at Hesdin. After a short deliberation, Philip decided to take no chances. He hardly waited to finish his meal, and hastily departed Hesdin with only six or eight horsemen, letting as few people as possible know of his departure. He first made his way to Saint-Pol, about 20 kilometres away, which he reached by nightfall. Early next morning he continued on his way, reaching Lille, deep within Burgundian territory and far from the menacing king of France, by 10 October.

Louis was disappointed to hear of Philip's sudden departure. Not knowing what prompted the move, he made his way back to Abbeville, and from there to Rouen. So far, he had heard nothing from or about Rubempré. But within days news began to stream in. Everywhere it was said that King Louis had sent the Bastard of Rubempré to Holland in order to kidnap or assassinate the count of Charolais. Louis was flabbergasted. This was a political and diplomatic disaster of the first order. He responded quickly, sending messengers far and wide to spread his own version of events. Yes, he had sent Rubempré with fifty men to Holland. And yes, they were ordered to kidnap an important personality there. But their target was not Count Charles of Charolais; rather it was Jehan de Renneville, the vice-chancellor of the Duchy of Brittany.

Brittany, like Burgundy, was a French duchy in theory and an independent principality in practice. The dukes of Brittany had never really accepted the authority of the king of France, and for much of the preceding century had allied themselves with his enemies. In the 1420s it was a triple alliance of Brittany, Burgundy, and England that came close to eliminating the king of France.

After Louis XI acceded to the throne the fearful duke of Brittany tried to revive that alliance. He had therefore sent his vice-chancellor on an embassy to England to conclude a treaty. From there he was instructed to proceed to Holland, meet the Burgundian heir apparent, and induce him to join the alliance. Louis XI, who was closely informed of events in Brittany by a network of spies, heard of Renneville's mission, and had sent Rubempré to Holland to kidnap Renneville before he could meet Count Charles. By such means Louis hoped to foil or delay the formation of the alliance, and also to be intimately informed of its proposed details.

Louis protested that since the duke of Brittany was technically his vassal, such kidnapping was really just a legal arrest of one of his own subjects. He also vehemently emphasized that he never had the slightest intention of kidnapping Charles or harming him in any other way. It was solely due to his own excessive fearfulness that Charles suspected Rubempré and had him apprehended. To strengthen his point, Louis added that it would have been quite impossible to kidnap Charles using only fifty men, and that if he really wanted to do so, he would not have entrusted the job to the riff-raff pirates of Picardy.

Was Louis telling the truth or trying to extricate himself by means of an ingenious lie? As usual in such cases, the truth cannot be known for sure after half a millennium. All details of the Rubempré affair were quickly buried beneath a mountain of propaganda, for the case developed into a major political and diplomatic crisis with far-reaching consequences. Count Charles recognized that this was his best chance to regain his father's favour and undermine the influence of Louis and the Croys in the Burgundian court. Louis on his side was frantic to defend his good name, save the Croys, and prevent an open rupture with Burgundy.

Assuming that the best defence was a vigorous attack, Louis quickly went from confessions to accusations. Laying aside the fact that even by his own admission he had sent a gang of pirates into a friendly country in order to kidnap a senior diplomatic emissary, he began acting as if he was the wronged party. Within days of hearing the news from Holland, he sent an express and aggrieved message to Duke Philip. He was surprised and dismayed, he said, that Duke Philip departed so suddenly from Hesdin without waiting to meet him. He had furthermore heard that some preachers in Bruges were spreading rumours that he had intended to kidnap or murder Count Charles. He was extremely angry about this libel, and expected the duke of Burgundy to quash these rumours immediately and punish those guilty of spreading them.

Shortly afterwards, another demand was forwarded to the duke of Burgundy. King Louis wrote that he had now heard that the real culprit was not some anonymous Bruges preachers, but rather Olivier de la Marche. It was he who brought about the capture of Rubempré;[20] it was he who subsequently brought Duke Philip the first news of Rubempré's arrest; and it was he who wrongfully told the duke that the Bastard intended to kidnap Charles.

Moreover, Louis asserted, while riding from Holland to Hesdin, La Marche did not keep his mouth shut, but spread the same false rumours far and wide. The king demanded that Philip turn over to him both the Bruges preachers and La Marche. Finally, Louis wrote to Philip that he would like to have Rubempré himself back.

By making such demands, Louis put Charles in a tight corner, and forced a power struggle within the Burgundian court. If the Burgundians handed over La Marche, it would have meant that Charles invented the whole thing, and was either a liar or a fool. Even worse, it would have shown that the count of Charolais was incapable of defending even his staunchest and closest servants. His honour and his position in Burgundy and abroad would have suffered a fatal blow.

To decide the issue, Charles, the Croÿs, and the ambassadors of the king of France came before Duke Philip at Lille, on 4/5 November 1464. The ambassadors restated the French version of events, and demanded that Rubempré, the Bruges preachers, and La Marche be handed to them. Charles then fell on his knees, and remonstrated with his ageing father. According to an unpublished chronicle, Charles argued that Louis's version of events made little sense. If Rubempré intended to intercept the Breton vice-chancellor on his way from England, why did he leave his ship anchoring on the Zeeland coast, and make his way to Gorinchem, which is perhaps 60 kilometres inland? Moreover, if he was a royal French agent employed on the lawful mission of arresting a traitor, why was it that when he reached Gorinchem, he did not present himself before the count of Charolais, as normal etiquette demanded?

The latter argument was obviously disingenuous, but the former certainly made sense. Charles carried the day. Philip was either convinced that Charles's story was true, or at last realized where his true interests lay. Regardless of whether Charles was telling the truth or not, Philip owed his loyalty and support to his son and heir rather than to the Croÿs and Louis. Philip answered all of Louis's demands in the negative. He had no intention of handing back Rubempré: that pirate had been arrested in Holland, where Philip was sovereign and recognized no lord save God, and he would be judged there according to his merits and crimes.[21] As for the Bruges preachers, Philip excused himself that he was a secular prince and refrained from intervening with the clergy. Moreover, he explained to Louis, 'many preachers are not very wise, and they quickly say things without advice and without authority.'[22] Finally, regarding La Marche, to the best of Philip's knowledge, he had done and said nothing wrong.

The French ambassadors left in dismay. Making their way back to King Louis, they passed through Tournai, Douai, Arras, Amiens, and several other important French towns. In each place they convened the town's estates, formally repudiating the ugly rumours spread about Louis and swearing on the honour of the king that he did not attempt to kidnap Charles. If anyone repeated these rumours again, they were to be arrested and sent to the king, to face his wrath and justice.[23]

The Rubempré affair thus ended as a decisive victory for Charles. Either he or the Breton ambassador were saved from Louis's clutches. The king's honour suffered a severe blow both within and outside his domains. Most importantly, from November 1464 onwards Charles and Philip were reconciled; the Croys lost their grip on the Burgundian court; and Charles became the real power there instead. Within months the Croys were fugitives in France, while Charles launched a war against Louis XI in alliance with the duke of Brittany and several other leading French princes, which came within a hair's breadth of toppling Louis and fragmenting the kingdom of France.

✦ ✦ ✦

THE war which Charles and his fellow princes launched against King Louis XI in 1465, commonly known as the War of the Public Weal, involved various special operations. For example, on the night of 3/4 October 1465 a Burgundian raiding party captured by escalade the town of Péronne together with its lord, the voodoo-practising count of Étampes. The only interesting incident in terms of assassination attempts, however, took place shortly after the battle of Montlhéry.

When the Burgundian army joined its allies at Étampes after this battle, the soldiers of both armies enjoyed themselves in the streets while Count Charles of Charolais and Prince Charles of France – the rebellious brother of King Louis XI – conferred in one of the town's houses. As the two commanders were 'at a window, talking to each other very intimately', a poor Breton soldier called John Boutefeu was amusing himself at the expense of his comrades. He stood in a house overlooking the street, and threw firecrackers at the soldiers who passed below. One such firecracker accidentally fell against the window frame where the princes were conferring, and both were startled, thinking it was an assassination attempt. They immediately gave orders to arm their bodyguards and other household troops. Within minutes, two to three hundred men-at-arms and archers surrounded the house and mounted a search to find the would-be assassin. The trickster eventually confessed and was forgiven, and all ended well.[24]

This incident shows how edgy the princes were. Curiously though, it also shows how flimsy their security measures were. Nobody prevented the Breton soldier from approaching the princely residence with a load of explosives, and a guard was mounted at the entrance only after the firecracker exploded. Perhaps in the mayhem that followed the battle of Montlhéry, normal procedures were momentarily suspended. Then again, perhaps the security measures taken by Olivier de la Marche – the commander of Charles's bodyguard – were simply inadequate. No wonder that La Marche does not mention the incident in his memoirs.

The War of the Public Weal ended as a qualified Burgundian victory. The power of Louis XI was curbed, and he was even forced to return the Somme towns to Burgundy. For the next couple of years Louis was put on the defensive, whereas Charles grew strong. He became duke of Burgundy upon the death of his father in 1467. He was also the leader of a formidable, albeit fragile, alliance of French princes whose goal was to keep Louis XI in check. In 1468 Charles married for a third time. Whereas his first two wives were French princesses, he now wed Margaret of York, sister of King Edward IV of England. She bore him no children, but greatly strengthened Burgundy's relations with England.

Louis XI, already fearful of Charles's rising power, was now alarmed by the spectre of an Anglo-Burgundian alliance. When hostilities between Louis and the French princes were renewed in 1468 Louis decided that he had better meet the new duke of Burgundy in person and settle their differences. Given the precedent of Montereau and Charles's past fears of assassination and kidnapping, Louis took a bold step. He told Charles he was willing to come to visit him in the Burgundian town of Péronne, accompanied by only a few of his men. Charles agreed. And thus the fox entered the wolf's den, of his own free will, trusting solely in his cleverness. Louis brought with him into Péronne only fifty men, whereas Charles firmly controlled the town and had an army of several thousand men camped nearby. It was 9 October 1468, exactly four years since Rubempré had been caught.

What followed has been described and analysed numerous times. Charles, always suspicious of Louis, had hardly received the king of France into the castle of Péronne when he heard news that the city of Liège had attacked his rear. Liège, one of the most powerful and turbulent cities of the Low Countries, had been a pain in Burgundy's side for decades, and in 1465 it rebelled against its prince-bishop, Louis of Bourbon, who was an ally and relative of the Burgundian duke. The duke of Burgundy came to the bishop's aid, and had to mount three successive expeditions against the rebels until he finally defeated them in battle, destroyed their city's fortifications, and forced the rebel leaders to flee into exile.

In September 1468, when King Louis saw that another confrontation with Burgundy was imminent, he encouraged the Liégeois to rebel again. With his encouragement, the exiles returned to Liège on 9 September, massacred their opponents and prepared for war. Duke Charles took the news lightly. He continued to concentrate most of his forces against France, and dispatched towards Liège only a small army, several thousand men strong, assuming that it would not be too difficult to crush the new rebellion.

While King Louis was asking Charles to meet him for a peace conference, he continued to send agents to Liège, promising his aid to the rebels and inciting them to attack their prince-bishop and his Burgundian allies. When Charles agreed to meet Louis at Péronne, Louis did not know what fruits his agents' efforts bore. To wait until he had sent new agents to Liège to countermand his previous moves and urge peace on the Liégeois would have taken far too long. He hoped the Liégeois had not had time to undertake any major operations, and confidently rode to Péronne.

Unfortunately for Louis, the Liégeois had taken his bait, and had moved with unusual celerity and boldness. On the night of 9/10 October a small raiding party left Liège under command of Jehan de Wilde and Gossuin de Streel and headed towards Tongres, the headquarters of the prince-bishop and his Burgundian army. The Burgundians were taken completely by surprise. They believed that Liège was defenceless and that its sole hope lay in receiving French assistance. On the evening of the 9th they heard of Louis's arrival at Péronne, and concluded that no French help would be forthcoming and that Liège was consequently doomed. When the raiders arrived at Tongres a few hours later, in the middle of the night, the surprised Burgundians offered no resistance. The entire army collapsed and fled in panic. The Liégeois did not bother to pursue the fugitives, but they did capture Bishop Louis and carried him back in triumph to Liège. During the march back the burghers killed several of the bishop's servants and councillors. Reportedly, they amused themselves by cutting the hated Archdeacon of Liège Cathedral, Robert de Morialme, into small pieces, and throwing them at one another's heads.

The townsmen now hoped to reach a separate peace agreement with their captive bishop, thereby making any further Burgundian intervention redundant. According to several medieval and modern authorities, the prince-bishop himself by this time may have been quite happy to strike an independent deal with Liège, realizing that a peace agreement dictated by the duke of Burgundy would reduce him to a powerless puppet.

News of this disaster reached Charles at Péronne on the evening of 11 October. The first reports stated that the Burgundian army was destroyed, that the bishop of Liège was murdered, and that royal French agents were seen amongst the attacking forces. Though Charles knew of Louis's dealing with the Liégeois before, he had previously discounted them as insignificant. Now defeat stung his pride and rekindled his deepest suspicions. In 1419 Louis's father had ostensibly come to Montereau to talk peace with Charles's grandfather, but in fact had him assassinated. In 1464 Louis himself was talking peace with Duke Philip at Hesdin while sending Rubempré to Holland to kidnap or kill Charles. Now in 1468 Louis had come to talk peace with Charles at Péronne, while inciting the Liégeois to kidnap or kill their bishop. Charles worked himself up into an overpowering rage. He was going once and for all to pay the French monarch for his treacheries. In addition, Charles perhaps could not resist the temptation to inflict upon his chief enemy the fears that haunted him for years.

The gates of Péronne were shut tight, and armed guards were placed around Louis's quarters. He was not formally imprisoned, but he was constantly watched. Not a person dared speak with the king except by loud voice, to assuage any suspicions that he was planning a secret breakout. Some chroniclers state that

Charles contemplated killing Louis there and then, and crowning Louis's weak brother in his stead. For several days the king lived in fear of this possibility. He was made apprehensive by the presence of several of his mortal enemies around Charles, most notably Philip of Savoy, who had only recently been set free from Loches. Louis was hardly comforted when Charles reminded him that a king of France had previously been held prisoner in the castle of Péronne. This was King Charles the Simple, whom a count of Vermandois seized in 923 and held there for six years, until he expired.

Duke Charles eventually decided to spare the king, but to impose upon him the harshest possible peace conditions. These were formulated in the peace treaty of Péronne, which gave Charles anything and everything he thought of demanding from Louis. The treaty virtually secured the establishment of an independent Burgundian state, and well-nigh insured the permanent fragmentation of the Kingdom of France. The helpless Louis duly signed, but Charles realized his signature would be worth very little once he were be allowed to depart.[25]

In order to keep Louis in his possession for a little longer and in order to humiliate him further, Charles came up with a new demand. When news of events in Liège first reached Péronne, Louis said that in order to prove his innocence, he was willing to march along with Charles and together subdue the recalcitrant city. Now that peace was made between them, would Louis make good his promise, and join Charles for the expedition against Liège? Louis tried to wriggle out, but eventually he had little choice but to agree. Thus Charles set out for Liège carrying the king of France in his baggage. To keep up appearances, both the Burgundian duke and the French king pretended that Louis was accompanying Charles from his own free volition. Charles even allowed Louis to bring along a small French contingent, including the royal guard of 100 mercenary Scottish archers and another 300 men-at-arms. They were, however, badly treated. Ludwig von Diesbach, a Swiss page of Louis XI who accompanied him to Péronne and Liège, and who later composed an autobiography, writes that he and his companions suffered greatly from hunger and cold, and feared for their lives due to the hatred of the Burgundians around them.

When the Liégeois heard of the events at Péronne, they naturally lost heart. Unable to face Burgundy by themselves, they quickly released the prisoners they had taken at Tongres, including their prince-bishop, and pleaded for peace. But Charles would have none of that. It was the fourth campaign he was leading against Liège in three years, and he was now determined to raze the city to the ground once and for all. The desperate Liégeois mounted a few bold sorties against the advancing Burgundian steamroller, but it availed them little. On 27 October Charles, Louis, and the main Burgundian force arrived before the ruined walls of Liège. The bulk of the forces encamped to the west of the city, in front of the Sainte-Walburge Gate. Another large force was posted to the north of the city. Charles did not bother to block the eastern or southern approaches. Given the state of its fortifications and forces, he assumed that the city would easily fall to a direct assault.

Charles set up his quarters about half a kilometre from the Sainte-Walburge Gate, in one of the still standing suburban houses. Louis was lodged in a nearby house. Two days and nights of desultory skirmishes followed, during which several Liégeois sorties were repulsed, while the majority of the population fled the doomed city, and the besiegers prepared for the final assault. The assault was first set for 29 October, but it rained heavily, and Charles decided to postpone it until the following morning. As Philippe de Commynes writes, by now the Liégeois 'had not one professional soldier in their garrison ... They had neither gate, nor wall, nor fortification, nor one piece of cannon, which was good for anything.'[26] The few remaining Liégeois contingents suffered heavily in the abortive sorties. Everyone in the Burgundian camp therefore expected it to be a walk-over. The soldiers went to sleep happy, dreaming of the following day's easy conquest and of the orgy of rapine, loot, and destruction that awaited them. Since the duke planned to annihilate Liège anyhow, there would be even fewer curbs on their behaviour than usual.

The Liégeois indeed seemed to be helpless prey. However, Gossuin de Streel, commander of the raid on Tongres, came up with a desperate plan. They had brought destruction on their heads by raiding Tongres at night and capturing their bishop by surprise. Why not repeat the same performance, only this time direct it at the duke of Burgundy himself? If a few resolute souls could make their way into the Burgundian camp and kill or capture the duke, Liège might still be saved. In fact, if they managed to kill the duke, the entire Burgundian state was likely to disintegrate. Streel convinced the remaining Liégeois leadership that this was their only chance to save the city, and they decided to give it a try. They would kill Duke Charles or perish in the attempt.

Charles was surrounded by thousands of Burgundian soldiers. Strong pickets were placed in front of the ruined walls, to give advance notice of any sortie. Charles also had a permanent bodyguard of forty crack archers, under the command of Olivier de la Marche, who never budged from his person during either wartime or peacetime.[27] Apparently, shifts of twelve archers took turns guarding the duke's person around the clock, and they were now lodged in the same house as Charles, occupying the upper floor. Another complication was posed by the presence of King Louis. The king of France posted his 100 Scottish archers around his house, and the rest of his men-at-arms camped nearby. Charles feared that Louis might try to escape, or worse, might try to attack him under cover of night with this elite force. Charles therefore chose 300 of his best and most reliable men-at-arms, and posted them in a big barn that stood between the two princely dwellings. This group of men was meant primarily to safeguard Charles against a sudden onslaught by the royal French bodyguard, but it could also fall upon any force coming from Liège.

No Liégeois sortie could hope to defeat these forces in open combat. However,

Streel hoped that a small and resolute force could infiltrate the Burgundian camp under cover of darkness, and reach the duke before the alarm was raised. He knew exactly where Charles and Louis slept. The houses in which they were quartered were marked with all the pomp and circumstance of princely residences, and stood but a few hundred metres from the ruined ramparts. The lie of the ground was perfectly familiar to the Liégeois. Most importantly, the previous owners of the two houses which now sheltered the duke and the king were in Liège, and they gave Streel all the information he needed about these dwellings and their immediate surroundings. One vital piece of information was that Charles's lodging was placed near a deep and rocky ravine, called the Fond-Pirette. The ravine secured Charles against any conventional attack from his flank, but it was also an ideal conduit for secret infiltration. The two vengeful landlords further agreed to serve as guides and personally lead the strike force against their unwanted new tenants.

According to Commynes, Streel received information on 29 October that the final assault on the city was planned for 8 o'clock on the following morning, and that therefore during the coming night the duke ordered all his army and even his guards to disarm and refresh themselves. This greatly enhanced his hopes of success. Streel also hoped that the weather might work in their favour. The 29th was a stormy day, and the bad weather was likely to help conceal secret moves.

Between 200 and 600 men were detailed to undertake the strike, commanded by Vincent de Bures and Streel himself. They were not special forces in any sense, but probably contained the best of the remaining Liégeois troops. Particularly conspicuous among them was a large contingent of men from the mountainous district of Franchimont. The rest of the Liégeois forces were also put on alert. Once they heard the war cries rising from the Burgundian camp, they were to sortie out of the city and create as much havoc as possible, to confuse the Burgundians and prevent them from sending reinforcements to the one place where they could still lose the war.

Only one big question mark remained: what about King Louis? It is impossible to say what Streel and the Liégeois intended to do with him. Their chief aim was without doubt Duke Charles. Perhaps they wanted to liberate the king of France, if they could. Perhaps, as many sources indicate, they wished to kill him, in retaliation for his betrayal. Perhaps they hoped that in the dead of night, when the alarm sounded, the king would order his guards to join the attackers and help them liquidate Duke Charles.

About ten o'clock on the night of 29/30 October, Streel and his men set out from the Sainte-Marguerite Gate, which was not guarded or watched by the Burgundians. Walking in a circuitous route, they made their way cautiously towards the Fond-Pirette ravine, and were swallowed inside without being observed by any Burgundian outpost. They then slowly threaded their way amongst the rocks until they emerged from the other side of the ravine.

The Burgundian camp was silent. The duke and the king were in their lodgings, fast asleep. The information Streel received was correct, and even the guards in the nearby barn had taken off their armour a mere two hours previously, and were now resting. For the last three days and nights they had been engaged in constant skirmishing, and Charles wanted them to be fresh for the next day's assault. The twelve archers on duty as Charles's personal bodyguard were busy playing dice in the room above Charles's bed. Only the Burgundian sentinels were alert. The lord of Gapannes, their commander that night, had spread a cordon of scouts and sentinels between the camp and the ruined walls, ready to sound the alarm. But neither he nor any of his men had detected the Liégeois' flank march. Apparently, no sentinels were placed along the Fond-Pirette ravine.

The Liégeois began dribbling into the camp. The camp contained thousands of soldiers and camp-followers belonging to different units, countries, and languages, and it was in place for only the last three days. The Liégeois could therefore hope that in this Babel they would not be recognized as enemies until it was too late. Several sources affirm that to blend in more easily, the raiders sewed on their tunics the cross of St Andrew, the Burgundian badge, and when questioned, claimed to be Burgundian soldiers. They nearly reached the duke's quarters when something went wrong. According to Commynes, who slept that night in Charles's own room, the fault lay squarely with the Liégeois. Charles would surely have been killed, writes Commynes, except that some of the raiders prematurely attacked the nearby tent of the duke of Alençon and the fortified barn, either due to their impatience or because they mistook them for Charles's quarters.

Jean de Haynin and Onofrio de Santa Croce say that the raiders made no such mistake, and were halted a short distance from the duke's bed only by the alertness of some women camp-followers. Haynin writes that the raiders' vanguard had reached the kitchen of Charles's house without being detected. Yet just as they were about to enter the house itself, they were stopped and questioned by a washer-woman called Labesse (or perhaps nicknamed, 'the Abbess'), who was apparently accompanied by some other female camp-followers. The raiders claimed to be Burgundian soldiers, but either Labesse or some other woman became suspicious of their accent, and said aloud that these were men from Liège. Fearing that their presence would be betrayed, the Liégeois drew their weapons and fell upon the unfortunate camp-followers.

The women were quickly killed, but one of them, who according to Onofrio fell or jumped into a pit, managed to cry out. Haynin writes that one of the raiders was already entering the duke's lodging, but when the alarm was raised the raiders panicked and fled. Most other sources confirm that just the contrary happened. Realizing that it was now or never, some of the raiders spread out to create as much havoc as possible, setting fire to tents and baggage, while two special strike forces pressed straight for the bedrooms of the duke and king, guided home by the vengeful landlords. The main assault was launched on Charles's lodging, to the cries of 'Vive le Roi!' The Liégeois still claimed to be the staunch allies of the king of France, and they may also have hoped to sow confusion amongst their enemies, and lead the Burgundians to believe that they were being attacked by the royal guards.

Charles awoke into a nightmare. The raiders were storming the entrances of his house, and had apparently killed one of his valets as well as two squires inside the house. The archers in the room above forgot about their game of dice, reached for their weapons, and ran down the stairs to save the duke. A fierce struggle ensued, the archers trying to buy a few precious seconds at the price of their own lives. The men-at-arms in the barn meanwhile snatched whatever weapons were at hand and rushed to the duke's rescue. Inside Charles's bedroom, Commynes and Charles's two other pages were frantically trying to arm the duke, but had time only to put on his cuirass and breastplate and clap a steel cap upon his head. Commynes describes in his memoirs the din and confusion of those moments. All around the house and in the street outside there was terrible noise and uproar, the cries of 'Long live Burgundy!' mingling with the battle cry of both the royal guard and the Liégeois raiders: 'Vive le Roi!' Nobody knew for sure what was happening. Was it a Liégeois attack, or perhaps some more foul play by the treacherous Louis?

The king himself also woke up in trepidation. According to his page, Ludwig von Diesbach, the king's lodging was set on fire, and the raiders almost managed to kill Louis. Commynes affirms that the raiders actually penetrated the house before they were repulsed by the Scottish guards. The Scots then placed themselves as a human shield all around Louis, and rained a hail of arrows on the confused *melee* outside, shooting down indiscriminately both Liégeois and Burgundians.

With each passing second, the raid's chances of success diminished, as the raiders were beaten back from the two houses and more and more Burgundian soldiers armed themselves and joined the fray. Torches were brought to light the scene and clarify the situation, and soon the Liégeois were in full retreat. More light could have been thrown on these eventful moments by Olivier de la Marche. However, La Marche does not even mention the raid in his memoirs. According to a letter of Anthoine de Loisey, the Liégeois killed altogether about 200 men, including many camp followers and pages. They themselves appear to have suffered lighter losses. Haynin says that only fourteen of them were killed. Commynes writes that the landlord of the duke's house, who guided and led the attack, was the first one to be struck down, though he survived a few hours more, and Commynes had personally heard him speak. The rest, headed by Streel, made it safely back to Liège.[28]

The following morning Liège was stormed. Little resistance was offered to the assailants. The city was thoroughly pillaged and burned to the ground. Charles personally supervised the destruction, and then sent a punitive expedition to wreak havoc in the region of Franchimont, from where most of his would-be killers hailed. He held on to Louis for a few more days, but ran out of excuses for delay, and had to either allow the king to depart, or to publicly confess Louis was now his prisoner. He opted for the former course. After exacting from Louis a few more worthless promises to abide by the treaty of Péronne, Charles reluctantly set him free.[29]

✦ ✦ ✦

THE treaty of Péronne became a dead letter within less than two years. By 1470 king and duke were again eyeing each other suspiciously, readying themselves for the next round. The propaganda war between them continued unabated. Charles continued to harp on his old themes of assassination and kidnapping, accusing Louis of fighting a dirty war. On 13 December 1470 Charles published an open manifesto in which he alleged that Louis stood behind a recent plot to assassinate or kidnap him. According to the most extravagant version of the events, Jehan d'Arson, a Burgundian nobleman who secretly joined the service of King Louis, contacted one of Duke Philip the Good's many bastards, Baudouin of Burgundy, and made him a tempting offer. If Baudouin managed to rid the king of Duke Charles, by one means or another, Louis promised to give him the greatest rewards imaginable. Arson explained that Duke Charles had no children, save a single daughter, and if he died, his lands would be estranged and would be divided between many hands. Louis would then be able to reward Baudouin with any share of this inheritance that Baudouin might desire.

Baudouin agreed, and collected a group of disaffected noblemen to help him carry out the project. They intended to surprise Charles either at the park of Hesdin, where he often went hunting with only a small company, or during his visit to the port of Crotoy on the Picard coast (from where Rubempré had once set sail). They hoped to overcome his guards, and either kill him or carry him off to France. The plot was uncovered, though Baudouin and most of his accomplices managed to flee Burgundy in November 1470. Whether this story is true is not easy to judge. The only fact we can be certain of is that Baudouin and several other noblemen had indeed defected from Burgundy to France in November 1470, and received rather meagre rewards from Louis.[30]

In May 1472 Louis's younger brother died, dashing any hopes that Charles of Burgundy and the leading French noblemen had of using him to check Louis's power. Charles and his confederates immediately spread allegations that he had been poisoned on Louis's orders, and even kidnapped a few of the dead man's close servants who confessed their guilt, under torture. Modern scholars habitually discount these allegations as propaganda. Fifteenth-century public opinion took them more seriously, and Charles of Burgundy and his confederates seized upon them as a pretext for launching a combined military attack on Louis.[31] At about the same time, Charles himself instituted elaborate precautions in his kitchens and dining halls against the threat of poisoning.[32]

Louis, for his part, responded with counter-accusations whose truthfulness is equally impossible to tell. In 1473 a poisoner named Jehan Hardy was caught in Louis's kitchen. French propaganda accused him of being a Burgundian agent attempting to poison the king of France. In 1476 another poisoner was caught in the royal kitchens. This time the alleged target was the French crown prince.[33]

The heavy atmosphere of suspicion is best attested by the elaborate precautions taken during several summit conferences that were held in the wake of Péronne. When Louis met his brother, Charles of France, at Niort (1469), a bridge of boats was made to span over the river Sèvres, and in its middle was built a stout wooden grille. The two royal brothers met with this barricade separating them, so that they could talk and shake hands, but could not kill or kidnap one another. In 1475 a similar bridge was constructed over the river Somme at Picquigny for the peace conference between Louis and King Edward IV of England. In the middle, writes Commynes, a strong wooden trellis was placed, 'such as lions' cages are made with, the hole between every bar being no wider than to thrust in a man's arm'.[34] The two kings spoke and hugged each other through the trellis. To further diminish the danger of assassination, some of the attendants of both kings came to the meeting dressed exactly like their masters.

In 1477 King Alfonso V of Portugal, who was a relative and ally of Duke Charles, visited France and tried to negotiate a peace treaty between the duke of Burgundy on the one hand and the king of France and his allies on the other. At some point, while he was residing in Paris, the Portuguese monarch grew suspicious that Louis was about to seize and deliver him to his bitter enemy, the king of Castile. Alfonso therefore disguised himself, and taking only two servants with him, tried to flee France. One of Louis's lieutenants captured Alfonso, who aroused his suspicions. Louis, according to Commynes, was greatly ashamed of the entire episode. He had no intention of doing any harm to the Portuguese king, and to prove his innocence, conducted him safely back to Portugal.[35]

Despite these apparently widespread fears of Louis's underhand methods, it was the abductor of Péronne who seemed to have acquired during those years a taste for kidnapping foreign princes. The first to learn this lesson were Dukes Adolf and Arnold of Guelders. During the 1450s and 1460s Adolf had been engaged in a bitter feud with his father, Arnold. Adolf, frustrated by his father's extraordinary longevity, asserted that Arnold had ruled long enough, and it was time he stepped aside and allowed his son to have his turn. Arnold refused, and a state of virtual civil war ensued. For mediation the rivals turned to the duke of Burgundy, their powerful neighbour and long-time ally. For a time it seemed that Burgundian intervention forced a peaceful settlement on

Guelders. However, on 10 January 1465 Adolf mounted a surprise attack on Duke Arnold's castle of Grave, allegedly with Burgundian assistance. Arnold was captured, and spent the next five years locked up in the castle of Buren. Adolf became duke in his stead, but Arnold's supporters refused to acknowledge his authority, and open war resulted.

In 1470 Adolf and his rivals travelled to the court of Duke Charles, then at the height of his power, to plead their cases and secure his support. In January 1471, either with or without Adolf's consent, Charles sent Henric van Horne with a small Burgundian force into Guelders. Horne extricated Arnold from his prison, and brought him too before Duke Charles. Charles then kept both father and son at Hesdin, while the negotiations crept slowly on and the civil war in Guelders continued unabated.

Adolf grew apprehensive, fearing that Charles was intending to hold both him and his father as virtual prisoners, while taking over Guelders himself. On the night of 10 February 1471 Adolf secretly escaped from Hesdin. Charles combed the Low Countries for the fugitive duke. Adolf disguised himself as a travelling Frenchman, and accompanied by a single servant, tried to get back to Guelders. He nearly reached his destination, but while boarding a ferry near Namur he was recognized by a priest and apprehended. He spent the next six years under heavy guard in several Burgundian castles, despite repeated requests from foreign powers to release him. His father meanwhile disavowed him and adopted Charles of Burgundy as his heir, on 7 December 1472. This time, the old duke of Guelders did not keep his heir waiting for long. He died three months later. Charles quickly collected his armies and invaded Guelders to enforce his rights. By July the conquest was complete, and Guelders became part of the Burgundian patrimony.[36]

A year later, it was the turn of Count Henry of Württemberg. This seventeen-year-old youth inherited the strategically vital town of Montbéliard in the Upper Rhine region, which then absorbed most of Duke Charles's expansionist ambitions. He had also inherited several fiefs within Burgundy. Though his rights there were infringed upon, he seemed to have been on good terms with Duke Charles.

In April 1474 Henry was travelling near Thionville with a small escort; he may have been intending to meet Duke Charles to settle the question of his Burgundian lands, or have been on a pilgrimage, or was on his way to meet the German emperor. When Charles heard of it, he dispatched a small force that intercepted and captured Count Henry. In prison the count promised to surrender Montbéliard to Charles in exchange for his freedom. Olivier de la Marche was given charge of the delicate mission. Taking the count along with him, La Marche appeared before the walls of Montbéliard and threatened the garrison that if they did not surrender the place, he would behead their lord and master. The garrison shut their ears to La Marche's threats as well as to Count Henry's desperate pleas. Since this psychological attack failed, and since a conventional attack on the heavily fortified town was out of the question, La Marche had to return to Charles empty-handed. The angry duke threw Count Henry back into prison, holding him first at Maastricht and then at Boulogne. The young count was devastated by this turn of fortune's wheel, and went insane. Charles kept him in prison nevertheless; he was finally released only after the duke's death, a broken man.[37]

Duke Charles himself was also beginning to show signs of insanity. He had now reached the pinnacle of his power, but success went to his head, and he started overreaching himself. During the next four years, while King Louis watched and held his armies at bay, Charles got bogged down in messier and messier adventures. He attempted almost simultaneously to conquer Alsace, Lorraine, and Cologne, as well as to establish a protectorate over Savoy. These attacks, coupled with adroit French diplomacy, forged a powerful anti-Burgundian coalition of German powers, led by the cities of the Rhine basin and Switzerland. The stubborn Charles repeatedly hurled himself against this coalition, losing campaign after campaign. The flower of the Burgundian army was squandered during the barren siege of Neuss (1474/5). Another army was routed on 2 March 1476 by the rising power of the Swiss at the battle of Grandson. By June Charles had reassembled a third army, which was massacred by the Swiss at Morat on 22 June 1476.

This string of disasters broke Burgundian military power, and Charles lost his most recent conquests one by one. King Louis seemed poised to attack his rear, and the many allies that flocked to join Charles during the rosy day of his success now turned their backs on him. While trying to collect a new army, Charles made desperate attempts to retain the alliance of at least one crucial alley, the Duchy of Savoy. Savoy not only guarded his south-eastern flank and threatened the southern flank of his Swiss enemies, but it also controlled the routes to Burgundy from Italy, from where Charles now obtained most of his mercenary soldiers.

After the death of Duke Amadeus IX in 1472, his son Philibert was proclaimed duke of Savoy. Philibert, however, was merely seven years old, so his mother Yolanda ruled as regent. Though Yolanda was sister of the king of France, she was a firm ally of Burgundy throughout the 1470s, partly because Charles tempted her with promises of marrying his daughter Marie to Philibert. Indeed, the conflict between Burgundy and the Swiss was largely a result of Burgundian attempts to protect Savoy against Swiss imperialist encroachments, and the campaigns of Grandson and Morat were both fought on Savoyard territory in order to repel Swiss invasions. It is interesting to note that by 1475 Yolanda had around her person a guard of eighty Burgundian mercenaries, though it was not absolutely clear whether they were protecting her or supervising her.[38]

After Grandson, Burgundian control over Savoy was only strengthened, as Yolanda became completely dependent on Burgundian help to ward off the

Swiss. On 22 March 1476 Yolanda and her five children came to meet Charles at Lausanne to reassure him of their continued loyalty. They also sent 4,000 men to join Charles's resuscitated army. They remained under Burgundian supervision henceforth, while Charles placed Burgundian garrisons in several Savoyard strongholds. It is not easy to understand how any princess could have willingly entrusted herself and her children to the Burgundian serial kidnapper at this date.

Exactly three months after Yolanda and Charles met at Lausanne, Charles's army was annihilated at Morat. At that time Yolanda was staying at Gex, a small town in the Duchy of Savoy, on its border with the Burgundian Franche-Comté, about 100 kilometres south-west of Morat and 15 kilometres north-west of Geneva, which since 1444 also formed part of the Savoyard dominions. The first news of the defeat arrived at Gex sometime on 23 June, closely followed by a tide of fugitives. Charles himself first fled to Morges, on Lake Geneva, and from there to Gex, apparently more anxious to safeguard his hold on Savoy than his crumbling position in Lorraine. He arrived at Gex on the evening of the 23rd, a gloomy man. He went directly to the castle where Yolanda and her children were staying. Charles kissed Yolanda and her children, and secluded himself with the Savoyard regent for a private talk. Yolanda then surrendered her apartment for the duke's use while she moved to Philibert's chamber. The Burgundian duke, visibly suffering from the effects of his defeat, shut himself up in his room, refusing to see anyone till morning.

When Yolanda heard the news from Morat and saw the fugitives and the broken duke, she finally realized that she had bet on the wrong horse. She immediately opened communications with the king of France, sending messengers to her brother and trying to reach some accommodation with him and the Swiss. Meanwhile Charles began suspecting her of treasonous intents. Not only did he accuse her of trying to defect in his hour of need, but in his desperate search for a scapegoat, he began to say that she had been a traitor all along, and had conspired with her brother from the beginning of the war to bring about Charles's downfall.

Yolanda did her best to assuage his fears, but smarting from the experiences of the dukes of Guelders and Count Henry of Würtemberg, and realizing she could not negotiate with the French and Swiss as long as she remained under Burgundian surveillance, she decided to put as many miles as possible between herself and the unstable duke of Burgundy. Pretending to remain Charles's staunch alley, she told him that for the interests of them both, she must retire towards Turin, the Savoyard capital, to strengthen Savoy's defences against the triumphant Swiss and the growing menaces of the duke of Milan and the king of France. Charles tried to persuade her to stay in Gex, where it would be easier for him to protect her, but she refused. Eventually, he consented, and on 26 June Yolanda gathered her children and attendants, and prepared to travel to her city of Geneva, guarded by a troop of loyal Savoyards.

As Yolanda left Gex, Charles came to accompany her part of the way. A short distance outside the town, as evening was descending, he dismounted from his horse and came before the duchess. He again tried to persuade her to remain. For an hour and a half she apologized and negotiated, until finally the duke relented. By now the sun had set on one of the longest days of the year. They exchanged kisses and pleasantries, and Charles returned to Gex. Yolanda and her retinue, extremely happy to finally see the duke's back, continued on their way toward Geneva, in complete darkness.

Yet Charles was hardly willing to allow the duchess to slip out of his hands. The prolonged farewell ceremony was merely a ploy to allow time for a more sinister undertaking. In order to safeguard his control of Savoy, and in order to punish Yolanda for her supposed betrayal, Charles resolved to seize the duchess and her children, and govern Savoy as their 'protector'. Why he did not simply arrest the Savoyards at Gex is impossible to say. Instead, while the duchess was making her preparations, Charles sent a swift message to the faithful La Marche, who by a stroke of good fortune was already in Geneva with a select company of troops. A few days before the battle of Morat Charles sent La Marche towards Turin with a force of about 600–1,200 men to safeguard Savoy against the mounting threat of a French or Milanese invasion. La Marche was passing through Geneva when news reached him on the evening of 22 June that the Burgundian army had been annihilated at Morat. He stopped in his tracks, waiting for more precise information. On the morning of the 23rd more news arrived, confirming the defeat but reporting that Duke Charles himself escaped safely.

La Marche was still at Geneva on 26 June, when an express rider arrived with a secret message from Charles to inform him that Yolanda and her children were making their way towards Geneva. He was ordered to intercept and capture them at all costs. If he failed or refused the job, he would have to answer for it with his own head. La Marche was by then one of the world's leading experts in the business of princely abductions. Yet in his memoirs he writes that this particular order was 'against my heart'. He nevertheless obeyed it, he explains, to save his life.

At first sight, it seemed an easy job. La Marche was already placed athwart the duchess's route of escape. Moreover, aside from his own men, there were several other Burgundian contingents in Geneva, mostly Italian mercenaries. Several factors, however, complicated the task. First, Geneva was well inside Savoyard territory, and if it came to an open fight, the Geneva militia and the local population were bound to support their rulers rather than the foreign Burgundians, especially since the Burgundians had already managed to incur the hatred of the populace. Secondly, there were in Geneva some loyal Savoyard troops as well, and they too would surely come to Yolanda's help.

Thirdly and most importantly, La Marche's task was not merely to defeat Yolanda's armed escort, but rather to capture the duchess and her children, particularly Philibert and his two brothers. If Yolanda, the eleven-year-old duke, or even one of Philibert's brothers escaped, Duke Charles's entire plan could fall apart, for any such escapee could serve as a figurehead for an anti-Burgundian government in Savoy. This meant that La Marche could hardly concentrate the Burgundian forces in Geneva and attack Yolanda openly. Such a move would give the duchess advance warning of his intentions, and a few minutes would be enough time for the ducal family members to disperse and be hidden or spirited away by loyal subjects. If that happened, only a meticulous search of the countryside amidst a hostile population could hope to unearth the missing princes, and La Marche did not have either the time or the forces necessary for that.

La Marche therefore decided to mount a covert operation, and bag the entire ducal family in one bold strike. He would leave Geneva with only an elite company of about 600 horsemen, without utilizing or even alerting the other Burgundian contingents in the city, for fear of a leak. He would then surprise Yolanda and her children somewhere along the way, and make his escape towards Burgundy before news of the coup reached Geneva. Charles's delaying actions at Gex were apparently meant to insure that Yolanda's cavalcade approached Geneva in the dead of night.

When darkness settled on Geneva, La Marche gathered his men and left the city. It was well known in the city that Yolanda was on her way there, but apparently nobody suspected La Marche's intentions. Perhaps he announced that he was proceeding on his course towards the mountain passes and Turin, in accordance with his initial orders. But he did not march south-eastwards toward Turin. Rather, he rode a short distance north-westwards, towards Gex. He then carefully placed his men in ambush, on the very outskirts of the city, close enough to the gates to be certain of intercepting Yolanda's caravan, but far enough to prevent any noise from reaching Geneva or any assistance from reaching the duchess in time.

Either at 2 a.m. or two hours after darkness, the Savoyard caravan fell into the trap. The Burgundians quickly surrounded it, to prevent anyone from escaping, and then closed in. The escort fought a desperate action to save the ducal family, but was overcome. La Marche came before Yolanda's carriage, and courteously said to her: 'My most illustrious lady, it is needful that you should come into Burgundy because thus it pleases our lord duke.' To intimidate her, he added that he had 4,000 men with him. 'I will never go there,' the duchess replied acerbically, but La Marche seized her and forcefully placed her behind him on his own horse. Her three sons and two daughters were also secured by other members of La Marche's force. The raiders then put spurs to their horses, and rode as quickly as possible in the darkness of night over the mountains towards Saint-Claude, in order to outrun any pursuit that might be mounted from Geneva.

To La Marche's horror, somewhere along the way he discovered that two of the birds had flown. Both Jacques-Louis, the youngest sibling, and Duke Philibert himself, had disappeared. It later transpired that two of La Marche's own men, who were mercenaries of Savoyard origins, felt they owed their loyalty to their own ducal family rather than to their paymaster, and utilized the darkness and the confusion to rescue the two princes. Philibert was first concealed under the mantle of Ludovic Taglianti or Goffredo di Rivarolo, and then hidden in a cornfield while the Burgundian force rode by. In their eagerness to outrun any pursuit, neither La Marche nor any of his subordinates noticed the disappearance of the two princes, thinking that someone else had them in his possession. When the truth was found, it was far too late to ride back to Geneva. Besides, by then looking for the missing duke would have been like searching for a needle in a haystack. With a heavy heart they therefore rode on, passing through Mijous, about 7 kilometres north-west of Gex, and eventually reaching the Burgundian town of Saint-Claude.

Savoyard loyalists meanwhile left Geneva in a hurry, after fugitives brought news of the attack to the city. While some tried ineffectively to catch up with the raiders, others, carrying torches and weapons, combed the countryside, and were overjoyed to find Duke Philibert hidden in the corn. The population of Geneva was incensed by news of the kidnapping, rioted against the Burgundians, and massacred many of those Burgundian soldiers who, oblivious of La Marche's move, had remained behind in the now hostile city.

It is noteworthy that in his memoirs La Marche does not condemn the men who betrayed him and rescued the two princes. Though they had proven false to him, he says, they had in fact done nothing but their duty. He confesses that he himself performed this odious task only because his head was at stake. When Duke Charles heard of the mishap, he took it badly, and La Marche was for a time in danger of losing his head after all. The duke, however, could hardly afford to kill the loyal commander of his bodyguard, and eventually forgave him. Yolanda, her son Charles, and her two daughters Marie and Louise were taken first to the castle of Rochefort, near Dole, and then to Rouvres, near Dijon.

The possession of Yolanda hardly availed Duke Charles. Public opinion in Savoy was outraged by his act, and swung decisively in favour of France. Already on 29 June a Milanese diplomat reported from Geneva that the Savoyards were sending ambassadors to negotiate with the Swiss, and now looked upon the duke of Burgundy as their mortal enemy. Burgundian representatives in Savoy were arrested, and Burgundian garrisons were attacked and expelled. Simultaneously, Louis XI sent armed forces into Savoy to forestall any further Burgundian intervention. With French protection, and pressure, Duke Philibert was installed at Chambéry, on the Savoyard–French border and a safe distance from Burgundy. The Savoyard estates chose pro-French regents for him, and for the next few years Savoy became a French protectorate. Charles's blow thereby acted as a boomerang, delivering Savoy into the hands of his bitterest enemy. He thought of retaliating by invading Savoy under the pretext of upholding Yolanda's rights to the regency, but the threat to Burgundy's position in Lorraine deflected his attention northwards. In addition, Yolanda's kidnapping provided Charles's last Italian allies with the excuse they sought to desert him on some honourable pretext.

In Rouvres Yolanda was guarded by a band of English mercenaries, one of the few remaining forces in whom Charles still had confidence. The conditions of her imprisonment were relatively lax. While she and her children could not leave the castle, her servants were quite free to come and go as they pleased. Through them she was in regular communication both with Savoy and with her brother, the king of France, with whom she conducted clandestine negotiations. She promised Louis to become his faithful servant if he would rescue her. He agreed, and gave the chivalrous task to Charles of Amboise, one of his ablest commanders.

Rouvres was in the middle of the Duchy of Burgundy, near the Burgundian capital of Dijon. However, Duke Charles was concentrating all his available forces on the eastern frontier of the duchy, which itself was denuded of troops. Apparently Rouvres's English garrison, despite Duke Charles's trust, also had little stomach for a fight. Amboise was informed of the situation around Rouvres by Yolanda's envoys. He figured that if he relied on speed and surprise rather than on force, he could make it to Rouvres and back without encountering any resistance. Heading a force of between 700 and 1,200 men, he made a dash to Rouvres, reaching the castle on 2 October 1476. He easily overcame the surprised and demoralized garrison, liberated Yolanda and her children, and brought them to Louis's residence of Plessis-les-Tours. There brother and sister were reconciled.[39]

In November 1476, supported by French forces, Yolanda returned to Savoy and was acknowledged as regent for her son. In September, while still in French territory, she instituted a ducal bodyguard to protect herself and her sons, numbering 100 loyal archers. In June 1477, after she had re-established herself in Savoy, the number was reduced to seventy-two.[40]

By then Duke Charles was dead. In January 1477 he was besieging Nancy at the head of a small and dispirited army. When he heard of the approach of a much superior relief army, he refused to retreat. By now, either his view of reality was completely distorted, or he was suffering from an acute death wish. His army disintegrated upon the first contact. He himself was killed by a halberd blow that split his head from top to chin. The fate of his grandfather had finally caught up with him.

His twenty-year-old daughter was still single and childless at the time. King Louis immediately claimed the vast Burgundian lands in France, arguing that these could not be inherited by a woman and backing up this legal argument with military force. Town after town opened its gates to the French forces, and within a short time almost all the Burgundian lands in France passed into Louis's hands. Louis also hoped to marry his son, the future Charles VIII, to Marie, and thereby lay his hands on the rest of the Burgundian patrimony. However, Marie chose to marry Maximilian Habsburg, son and heir of Emperor Frederick III, and a war of succession ensued between the couple and Louis.

Marie and Maximilian managed to retain control of most of the Burgundian territories in the Low Countries. These eventually passed to the couple's son, Philip, along with the rest of the Habsburg lands. Philip Habsburg continued the family tradition by marrying Juana, sole heiress of Ferdinand of Aragon and Isabella of Castile. The offspring of that union was Charles V, the greatest of early modern European emperors, who inherited a united Spain, much of the Low Countries, vast territories in Italy and Germany, and eventually came to rule much of the New World as well. A famous proverb about the Austrian Habsburgs summed up their rise to the pinnacle of world power: 'While others make war, you happy Austria, marry.'

Louis, for his part, annexed to his royal dominions almost all Burgundian lands in France, including the Duchy of Burgundy itself, Picardy, and Artois. However, like the hero of some mythic tale, when Louis swallowed his dead rival's territories, he incorporated his weaknesses and fears along with his powers. From the moment he conquered the Duchy of Burgundy until his death in 1483, Louis became the prisoner of mounting fears for the safety of his person.

The seeds of these fears had already been sown in his early childhood. In the 1430s his father Charles VII shut him up in the fortress of Loches in order to ensure that Louis would not be kidnapped and used as a puppet by one of the rival court factions. (Interestingly, Louis later imprisoned Philip of Savoy in the very same fortress in 1464.) These fears were then fanned by events of the 1460s and 1470s, and were well cultivated even before Péronne. For example, when Duke Jean of Anjou came to visit Louis in 1466 at his castle of Meung-sur-Loire, Louis feared that his guest, who was known as a volatile and violent man, might attempt to kidnap or murder him. Hence before Jean arrived, Louis is said to have inspected the castle room by room, and, discovering a secret passage he did not know about, had it quickly blocked up.

Péronne certainly did nothing to assuage Louis's fears. Yet it was only after 1477 that they broke out in the most aggressive manner and completely took hold of Louis. The ageing monarch became paranoid that his relatives or some disaffected noblemen might seize either himself or his son and set themselves up as regents, under the pretext that he was too feeble or too insane to rule France.

Consequently, he imitated his father and shut his own son Charles in the castle of Amboise. Little Charles was kept isolated and under tight guard. Strangers were forbidden even to approach the castle's environs, and few people received permission from the king to visit him. Louis locked himself inside the manor of Plessis, almost never daring to leave its narrow confines. He allowed as few people as possible to visit Plessis, especially from amongst his relatives and the high nobility. Even when his beloved daughter and her trusted husband visited him, he had their servants closely searched for weapons. Seeing would-be spies, assassins, and kidnappers all around him, he dismissed all his old servants, and constantly changed his new ones. He apparently avoided setting up any predictable schedule for himself, to help foil plots.

To protect himself from armed attacks, Louis surrounded the manor with a ditch and a wall with a lattice of iron bars. He also constructed four watch-towers of thick iron at the manor's corners, where he placed twenty crossbow-men with orders to fire on anyone who approached the place before the gate was opened. The gate was always kept closed at night, and never opened before 8 o'clock in the morning. 400 more archers guarded the gate and patrolled the environs day and night to prevent surprise attacks. They were specifically ordered to supervise the nearby villages and towns, and expel any newcomers who aroused suspicion. Commynes, who was one of the few people in whom Louis still had some trust, writes that Plessis was guarded as closely as if it was a frontier fortress.[41]

As Commynes himself explains, these security measures and fortifications could not hope to withstand a siege or a full-scale attack by a large army. How-ever, Louis had no fear of such an attack. Rather, his great apprehension was that some great lord or a group of noblemen, having intelligence within, might attempt to capture the place by escalade, and then hold Louis captive and pro-claim themselves regents. Plessis's defences were therefore designed specifically to thwart a surprise attack by a small raiding party.[42] Commynes reflects on the vagaries of human fortunes, writing that the victorious king spent his last months imprisoned by his fears, as if he was a captive criminal.

✦ ✦ ✦

THIS chapter has discussed a large number of abduction and assassination operations. A few of them were quite successful, such as the abduction of the dukes of Guelders, which enabled Charles of Burgundy to acquire their duchy with relative ease. Perhaps many more such operations were successful, if we believe that Louis XI, for example, really did poison his brother Charles. After all, the most successful poisonings are the ones which remain concealed.

Yet even if we take into account these shady cases, all of the most spec-tacular abductions and assassination attempts discussed in this chapter still ended in failure. The Bastard of Rubempré was sent to Holland to strengthen the king of France's position, but his mission ended in a palace revolution in Burgundy that toppled the pro-French Croys and brought to power the anti-French Charles. By abducting King Louis in 1468 Charles imposed on him the treaty of Péronne, but this became a worthless piece of paper within months of Louis's release. The abduction of Bishop Louis of Liège at Tongres was a calamitous move which scuttled the peace efforts and ensured the destruction of Liège. The subsequent attempt to assassinate Duke Charles could have saved Liège and ruined Burgundy, but it failed. The abduction of Count Henry of Würtemberg achieved nothing except to further tarnish Duke Charles's honour, whereas the abduction of Yolanda completely backfired: Instead of safeguarding Savoy, it pushed the duchy right into the expectant hands of the king of France.

The direct political damage caused by these failures, particularly those of Rubempré and of the abductions of Bishop Louis and Yolanda, was immense. The long-term damage to the perpetrators' image and diplomatic standing was also great. In addition, these sinister operations, including the successful ones, created an atmosphere of fear and suspicion, which harmed the involved heads-of-state more than anyone else. This, however, was not necessarily bad, and would have surely been approved of by Thomas More's Utopians. While in most wars the princes initiated hostilities while the common people bore the brunt of the misery, 'dirty warfare' had the advantage that its chief victims, in physical and psychological terms alike, were those most responsible for the conflict. As Ludwig von Diesbach wrote about the failure of the Liégeois to kill Duke Charles: 'It was unfortunate for many good knights and servants that his life was saved, because they later lost their own lives on his account.'[43]

NOTES

1 Vaughan, *Philip the Good*, p. 36.

2 Monstrelet, *Chronique*, 4:239.

3 Monstrelet, *Chronique*, 4:248–9; Wavrin, *Recueil des croniques*, 3:193–4; Lefèvre de St Rémy, *Chronique*, 2:116–17.

4 Monstrelet, *Chronique*, 5:67; Chastellain, *Œuvres*, 2:85.

5 Monstrelet, *Chronique*, 6:87–93; La Marche, *Mémoires*, 2:35–40; Chastellain, *Œuvres*, 8:34–8; Emerson, *Olivier de la Marche*, pp. 30–2.

6 Monstrelet, *Chronique*, 4:118–19.

7 Emerson, *Olivier de la Marche*, p. 159.

8 The situation could be compared with that of the eighteenth-century Habsburg emperor, Joseph I, who devoted much of his career to securing the doubtful rights of inheritance of his daughter, Maria Theresa.

9 Vaughan, *Philip the Good*, p. 140.

10 Commynes, *Mémoires*, 1.1, ed. Mandrot, 1:6.

11 On the Coustain affair, see Chastellain, *Œuvres*, 4:235; Du Clercq, *Mémoires*, 3:212–19; Collard, 'Assassinat manqué'.

12 Vaughan, *Philip the Good*, p. 345.

13 La Marche, *Mémoires*, 3:3.

14 Du Clercq, *Mémoires*, 4:77.

15 Chastellain, *Œuvres*, 5:84.

16 Wavrin, *Recueil des croniques*, 5:443.

17 La Marche, *Mémoires*, 2:217.

18 The account of the chronicle of the Hague is quoted in Chastellain, *Œuvres*, 5:85–6.

19 On Philip of Savoy, see in particular Chastellain, *Œuvres*, 5:8–10, 38–42.

20 La Marche, *Mémoires*, 3:4.

21 Rubempré was indeed kept in prison for four years. Charles released him in 1468, whence he rejoined the service of Louis XI.

22 Du Clercq, *Mémoires*, 4:78.

23 On the Rubempré affair, see Du Clercq, *Mémoires*, 4:65–82; La Marche, *Mémoires*, 3:3–5; *Briefwechsel Karls des Kühnen*, 1:104–5; Haynin, *Mémoires*, 1:7; Chastellain, *Œuvres*, 5:81–151; Commynes, *Mémoires*, 1.1, ed. Mandrot, 1:4–8; Basin, *Histoire*, 2:87–93; Roye, *Journal*, 1:35; But, *Chronique*, pp. 447, 455; Wavrin, *Recueil des croniques*, 5:441–54; Plancher, *Histoire*, 4:318–20; Emerson, *Olivier de la Marche*, pp. 59–63.

24 Commynes, *Mémoires*, 1.5, ed. Mandrot, 1:47–8.

25 On Péronne, see La Marche, *Mémoires*, 3:81–5; Commynes, *Mémoires*, 2.7–9, ed. Mandrot, 1:135–50; Basin, *Histoire*, 2:187–200; Haynin, *Mémoires*, 2:67–70; Bricard, *Serviteur et compère*, 106–9; Roye, *Journal*, 1:212–15; *Briefwechsel Karls des Kühnen*, 1:327–33; Oudenbosch, *Chronique*, pp. 208–14; Pauwels, *Historia*, pp. 210–16; Maupoint, *Journal parisien*, pp. 107–10; *Lettres de Louis XI*, 3:285–99; Commynes, *Mémoires*, ed. Dupont, 3:226–37; *Lettres-missives … de Thouars*, pp. 47–50; *Analecta Leodiensia*, pp. 371–8; Diesbach, *Autobiographischen Aufzeichnungen*, pp. 42–4; But, *Chronique*, p. 491; Chastellain, *Œuvres*, 5:431–2; Buser, *Beziehungen*, pp. 437–40; Vaughan, *Charles the Bold*, pp. 53–9; Paravicini, *Guy de Brimeu*, pp. 177–89; Plancher, *Histoire*, 4:371.

26 Commynes, *Mémoires*, 2.12, ed. Mandrot, 1:158.

27 Vaughan, *Charles the Bold*, p. 195.

28 In 1327, when the Scottish and English armies faced one another on the bank of the Wear river, James Douglas led 200 Scottish men-at-arms in a daring night raid on the English camp. The Scots reached King Edward III's tent and came close to killing or abducting the king, though in the end they only managed to cut two or three of the tent's ropes (Le Bel, *Chronique*, 1:70).

29 On Liège, see Commynes, *Mémoires*, 2.11–13, ed. Mandrot, 1:154–67; Commynes, *Mémoires*, ed. Dupont, 3:238–52; Pauwels, *Historia*, pp. 220–1; Los, *Chronicon*, pp. 59–60; Henrici de Merica, *Compendiosa Historia*, p. 177; *Analecta Leodiensia*, pp. 254–6, 380–1; Oudenbosch, *Chronique*, pp. 215–16; La Marche, *Mémoires*, 3:84–6; Haynin, *Mémoires*, 2:76–7; *Briefwechsel Karls des Kühnen*, 1:335–6; Basin, *Histoire*, 2:200–3; *Speierische Chronik*, pp. 497–9; Roye, *Journal*, 1:215–17; Maupoint, *Journal parisien*, pp. 110–11; But, *Chronique*, pp. 491–2; Wavrin, *Recueil des croniques*, 5:569–71; *Lettres de Louis XI*, 3:299–302; Diesbach, *Autobiographischen Aufzeichnungen*, pp. 44–8; *Chronique de Lorraine*, p. 87; Onofrio de Santa Croce, *Mémoire*; Vaughan, *Charles the Bold*, pp. 31–2; Kurth, *Cité de Liège*, 3:318–27, 360–3, 385–8; Fairon, 'Six cents Franchimontois'; Plancher, *Histoire*, 4:371–2.

30 On this affair, see Chastellain, Œuvres, 5:470–83; Basin, Histoire, 2:234–44; Haynin, Mémoires, 2:94–5; Oudenbosch, Chronique, pp. 231–2; Vaughan, Charles the Bold, pp. 238–9.

31 Commynes, Mémoires, 2.8–9, ed. Mandrot, 1:228–38; Basin, Histoire, 2:285–8, 295–6; Roye, Journal, 1:262–3, 268–70; Vaughan, Charles the Bold, pp. 76–7; Kendall, Louis XI, pp. 246–8.

32 La Marche, Mémoires, 4:27.

33 Collard, 'Assassinat manqué', p. 11; Kendall, Louis XI, p. 261.

34 Commynes, Mémoires, 4.9, ed. Mandrot, 1:313.

35 Commynes, Mémoires, 5.7, ed. Mandrot, 1:381–3.

36 On Guelders, see Commynes, Mémoires, 4.1, ed. Mandrot, 1:259–62; Basin, Histoire, 2:314–20; Vaughan, Charles the Bold, pp. 112–22.

37 La Marche, Mémoires, 3:207–8.

38 Vaughan, Charles the Bold, p. 305.

39 On the abduction and rescue of Yolanda, see La Marche, Mémoires, 3:234–6; Chroniques de Yolande, pp. 22–5, 140–75, 302–4; Commynes, Mémoires, 5.4, ed. Mandrot, 1:364–9; Haynin, Mémoires, 2:220–1; Dépêches des ambassadeurs milanais sur les campagnes de Charles-le-Hardi, 2:302–43, 365–8; Lettres de Louis XI, 6:66–71, 92–4, 99–100; Roye, Journal, 2:17–22; Briefwechsel Karls des Kühnen, 2:384–431; Buser, Beziehungen, pp. 459–71; Schilling, Berner Chronik, 2:75–6; Etterlin, Kronicat, pp. 254–60; Basin, Histoire, 2:391; Bonivard, Chroniques de Genève, pp. 104–5, 203–6; Favier, Louis XI, pp. 710–12; Gabotto, Stato sabaudo, 2:180–213; Perret, Histoire, 2:75–81; Guichonnet, Histoire de Genève, 117–18; Emerson, Olivier de la Marche, pp. 70–2.

40 Chroniques de Yolande, p. 174.

41 Compare Aubigny, Traité, pp. 20–1, where the arrangements for opening the gates of frontier fortresses are discussed.

42 Commynes, Mémoires, 6.6–7, 10–11, ed. Mandrot, 2:41–2, 48–52, 56, 69–70, 75–80.

43 Diesbach, Autobiographischen Aufzeichnungen, p. 46. The present chapter is based mainly on the following sources: Chastellain, Œuvres; Du Clercq, Mémoires; La Marche, Memoires; Haynin, Mémoires; Monstrelet, Chronique; Basin, Histoire; Roye, Journal; Lettres de Louis XI; Commynes, Mémoires, ed. Mandrot; Molinet, Chroniques; Dépêches des ambassadeurs milanais en France; Dépêches des ambassadeurs milanais sur les campagnes de Charles-le-Hardi; d'Escouchy, Chronique; Lefèvre de St Rémy, Chronique; Briefwechsel Karls des Kühnen; Maupoint, Journal parisien; Buser, Beziehungen; Bonenfant, Actes; Chronique de Lorraine; Diesbach, Autobiographischen Aufzeichnungen; Etterlin, Kronica; Speierische Chronik; Wavrin, Recueil des croniques; Linden, Itinéraires de Philippe; Linden, Itinéraires de Charles; Schilling, Berner Chronik; Vaughan, John the Fearless; Vaughan, Philip the Good; Vaughan, Charles the Bold; Vaughan, Valois Burgundy; Emerson, Olivier de la Marche; Bittmann, Ludwig XI; Le Cam, Charles le Téméraire; Kendall, Louis XI; Cauchies, Louis XI et Charles le Hardi; Paravicini, Karl der Kühne; Paravicini, Guy de Brimeu;

Plancher, *Histoire*, vol. 4; Bricard, *Serviteur et compère*; Dufournet, *Destruction des mythes*; Harari, *Renaissance Military Memoirs*; Collard, 'Assassinat manqué'; Gabotto, *Stato sabaudo*, vol. 2; Dufayard, *Histoire de Savoie*; Favier, *Louis XI*; Bonenfant and Stengers, 'Rôle de Charles le Téméraire'; Bonenfant, *Philippe le Bon*; Mandrot, 'Jean de Bourgogne'; Guichonnet, *Histoire de Genève*. For individual episodes, see the previous notes.

7

The Mill of Auriol: Auriol 1536

IN the early sixteenth century two dynastic states struggled for mastery over western Europe. At first it was the Valois kings of France, who seemed poised to become the arbiters of Europe, after expelling their English rivals from the Continent, vanquishing their over-mighty Burgundian vassals, and forging a centralized state out of their feudal jigsaw puzzle. Their attempts to conquer Italy were only barely held in check by the Italian powers, the Holy Roman (i.e. German) emperor, and the newly unified Kingdom of Spain.

In 1516, however, the crown of united Spain was inherited by Charles Habsburg, who was also head of the House of Austria, ruler of the Low Countries, and from 1519 Holy Roman emperor. The same year that Charles became emperor, the Spanish adventurer Hernando Cortés landed in Mexico, and soon a stream of treasure from the New World began to enrich Habsburg coffers in Europe.

By the mid-1520s France was thrown on the defensive, encircled by Habsburg territories from the north, south-east, and south-west. The first war between King François I of France and Charles V ended with the battle of Pavia (1525), in which the French army was annihilated and François himself taken prisoner. The captive king signed the humiliating treaty of Madrid in 1526, but repudiated it immediately after being set free. In the second war the French suffered a succession of defeats, and managed to hold their own thanks only to the help of the schismatic Protestant princes of Germany and of the infidel Ottoman Turks, both of whom were alarmed by the rising power of the Habsburgs. In 1529 Charles V, anxious about the Ottoman threat, granted France a tolerable peace at Cambrai.

François licked his wounds and prepared for the next round by reorganizing his armies. Charles utilized the peace to concentrate his efforts against the Ottomans. In 1536 François felt it was time to take the offensive again, partly in order to avenge past defeats, but more importantly in order to help his hard-pressed Ottoman allies. A French incursion into Italy overran Savoy, threatened Milan and forced Charles to abandon his plans for further campaigns against the Ottomans in the Mediterranean. Meanwhile, the French were also actively assisting Muslim pirates in the Mediterranean. Turkish fleets were regularly welcomed into the ports of Provence, where they were resupplied and from where they pounced on Christian shipping.

Charles V decided that this time, he would not settle merely for the expulsion of the French from Italy. The French king had already violated two peace treaties within the span of a decade; was assisting infidel pirates to attack

Christians; and had stabbed the emperor in the back when the latter was leading a crusade. It was time to crush François once and for all.

Charles could invade France from three main directions: from Spain over
the Pyrenees, from the Low Countries, and from Italy over the Alps. He chose
the last course. His forces first swept the French invaders from northern Italy.
On 24 July 1536 Charles crossed the river Var into Provence at the head of
the largest army he ever assembled against a Christian enemy. He had about
60,000 men with him,[1] under his best generals: the duke of Alba, the marquis
del Vasto, Fernando de Gonzaga, and above all Antonio de Leyva. Leyva was
reckoned to be one of the greatest captains of his day, and was the chief architect of the invasion. Charles's fleet, commanded by the redoubtable Genoese
admiral Andrea Doria, sailed along the Provençal coast. A smaller Habsburg
army simultaneously invaded France from the Low Countries, whereas threatening noises were made on the Pyrenees front as well, in order to prevent the
French from concentrating their forces in Provence. Charles was so certain of
his success that he ordered his official historian, Paulus Jovius, to make a large
provision of paper in order to record the forthcoming victories.[2] Martin du
Bellay writes that the emperor had obtained a detailed military map of Provence from a traitorous mercenary general who switched sides. Military maps
were still a novelty in the early sixteenth century. The emperor was so pleased
with his acquisition, and he studied the map so thoroughly, 'applying to it all his
desires and affections', that he imagined he had possessed the province itself by
possessing the map.[3]

Facing the emperor the French had at first only about 30,000 men, largely
mercenary forces of varying quality. By August their numbers nearly doubled,
but the French army was of markedly inferior quality compared to the Habsburg
forces. Many of the troops were raw recruits, some of the mercenary forces were
unreliable, and there were even several outbreaks of violence between different
sections of the army. The French commander, Anne de Montmorency, decided
he could not risk battle under such conditions. Indeed, even if he had more
reliable troops at his disposal it would have been an extraordinarily dangerous
gamble to fight a pitched battle, for defeat would have left France completely
defenceless.

Instead, Montmorency adopted a Fabian strategy. He heavily fortified and
guarded the only bridges over the lower Rhône river, at Arles and Tarascon.
He entrenched his main field army in a strong position near Avignon, blocking the route along the Rhône's eastern bank. King François himself camped
upriver at Valence, from where he supervised the campaign and sent supplies
and reinforcements downriver. Provence's main port of Marseilles was similarly
well fortified, and a strong garrison of about 6,000 men was placed there, commanded by the lord of Barbezieux. The rest of the Provençal towns, including
the capital of Aix, were abandoned without a fight, after their supply maga-
zines were destroyed. The Provençal countryside was similarly devastated by

the retreating French, despite the sometimes violent resistance of the Provençal peasants. Stores that could not be removed were burned and spoiled; farm animals were slaughtered; the wheat was torched in the fields; wells were blocked or polluted; and mills were destroyed. Only vines and fruit trees were deliberately spared, for excessive eating of fruit was likely to induce dysentery amongst the invaders.

Montmorency thus invited Charles's troops to advance into a barren cul-de-sac. They would find nothing to eat in Provence itself. They would be unable to supply themselves through the port of Marseilles. Behind them the towering Alps would prevent supplies from reaching them overland from Italy. Their way north was barred by the same Alps, and the way south by the Mediterranean. They could advance only eastwards, but there all the crossings of the Rhône were heavily fortified, and the way along the Rhône's eastern bank was blocked by Montmorency's camp at Avignon. (See map 5.)

The city of Avignon itself threatened to provide the Imperialist forces with a way out of the trap. Avignon was a papal city, and the pope was Charles's alley. The French had no time to besiege the city, whereas storming it could prove costly. Besides, France was a Catholic country, and if possible, François preferred not to have to storm a papal city. If his Protestant German mercenaries,

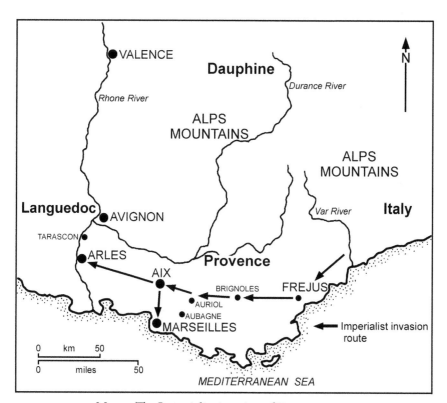

Map 5 The Imperialist invasion of Provence, 1536

who made up the best part of his infantry, pillaged the place, it could turn into a public relations disaster. Instead, Avignon was captured by a ruse.

François de Vieilleville, escorted by only six men, came before the city's walls and demanded in the name of the king of France to speak with the governor, the papal vice-legate. The vice-legate appeared on top of the wall, but Vieilleville asked him to come down to speak more intimately, for he had important business to discuss. Vieilleville had only a handful of men, but the vice-legate could bring with him as big an escort as he wished. The vice-legate consented, opened the city's gate, and came out accompanied by twenty soldiers and a few of his main subordinates.

Vieilleville told him that King François had no wish to occupy Avignon, but wanted to ensure that no Imperialists would be allowed inside either, so the vice-legate should hand over some hostages to vouch for his conduct. The vice-legate replied that he was under strict orders from the pope not to allow troops of either side into the city, but that the French would have to take his word for it, as he was not going to give them any hostages. Vieilleville pretended to become angry, and started shouting and threatening the vice-legate. While all attention was drawn to him, four of his men stationed themselves near the gate to prevent the guards from shutting it. Vieilleville jumped on the vice-legate, forced him to the ground, and threatened him with his sword. The two men left with Vieilleville immediately discharged their arquebuses at point blank range, killing two of the papal guards. Putting hands to their swords, the three then charged the rest of the guards, who, stunned by this undiplomatic behaviour, fled before them into the city. In the ensuing confusion Vieilleville's other four soldiers managed to prevent them from closing the gate. At that moment 1,000–1,200 French soldiers who were hidden in the cornfields a short distance from the gate charged forward and streamed through the opening. The city surrendered without further resistance.[4]

With the fall of Avignon, the trap Montmorency had set for the Imperialists was completely corked. It was impossible to tell, however, whether this trap was strong enough to hold in the prey. After crossing the Var, Charles occupied Fréjus without a fight, and then Brignoles. His forces overran almost the whole of lower Provence, but found the countryside devastated and the food supply short. Provençal peasants, who had previously resisted the French scorching parties, now resisted with still more vehemence the Imperialist foragers, and even attacked Imperialist regular formations.

Such guerrilla attacks were a nuisance, but they could hardly hope to stop the Imperialist steamroller. A band of fifty peasants who had realized as much, made an attempt to kill Emperor Charles himself sometime around 10 August, hoping that the giant war engine might fall apart if its main linchpin was removed. The emperor was crossing a narrow mountain path approaching the village of Muy. The band armed itself with arquebuses and hid in a tower in the village – later known in local parlance as the 'tour de Charles-Quint'. The peasants intended to wait in hiding until they saw the emperor approach, and then simultaneously discharge all their firearms at him, in the hope that one of them might score a hit. (Sixteenth-century arquebuses were notoriously inaccurate.) Their main problem was that none of them knew what Charles looked like. To their misfortune, they mistook one of Charles's generals, who was richly dressed and accompanied by a huge entourage, for the emperor himself. When the general approached, they shot him as planned, and he was apparently killed. The entire Imperialist column was brought to a stand-still, and cannon had to be brought forward to dislodge the band. Only after cannonballs began crashing into the tower did the peasants surrender. Charles ordered them all to be hanged.[5]

While Charles thus had a narrow escape, the French crown prince, the Dauphine François, suddenly died at Tournon on 10 August. Hysterical accusations were made that he was poisoned by Imperialist agents. A servant of the dead prince, an Italian called Sebastiano de Montecuculli, admitted under torture that he had poisoned the prince at the command of Leyva and Gonzaga. French propaganda took up the theme and accused Charles of murder. Meanwhile in France itself fingers were pointed at another Italian, Catherine de Medici, wife of François's brother Henry, who thanks to François's death was soon to become queen of France. This was not the last time such accusations were levelled at that sixteenth-century Livia, and they certainly did not contribute to the atmosphere at the French camp.[6]

While King François mourned his son and the French camp filled with rumours and accusations, Emperor Charles continued his march and entered Aix, the Provençal capital, on 13 August. He established a camp on the nearby plain of Aillane and sent advance parties towards Avignon, Arles, Tarascon, and Marseilles to take the measure of the French defences. He had to capture at least one of these keys in order to break out of Provence or safeguard his conquest. Yet he had to do it fast, and the time at his disposal was being measured by a gigantic grain clock. His supply difficulties were mounting quickly, and if he failed to break out of the trap by the time his supply ran out, his army would either starve to death or be forced to beat a hasty and shameful retreat. Montmorency's scorched-earth strategy and the guerrilla campaign conducted by the Provençal peasants dashed Charles's hopes of living off the land, and the planned provisioning by Doria's fleet failed to materialize. The fleet was first delayed by contrary winds, and even after the winds changed, the absence of a good harbour greatly reduced the volume of supply that reached Charles from his ships.

Montmorency and King François were nevertheless worried. Charles's army may have began to fill the pinch of hunger, but it was still greatly superior to theirs, and even starving armies could win battles and conquer towns, as happened for instance at Agincourt (1415). If Charles stormed the defences of Arles, for example, and crossed the Rhône into Languedoc, or if he marched on Montmorency's camp and defeated the French army in battle, few would remember his momentary supply difficulties. Similarly, if Charles conquered Marseilles and established there a secure maritime supply base, he could remain in Provence indefinitely, annexing the province to his domains. The French leaders therefore resolved to do anything in their power to tighten the screw on the emperor and cut short the time at his disposal.

French spies active in occupied Provence informed François that the Achilles' heel of the already shaky Imperialist supply system was the handful of mills which provided the Imperialists with their flour and bread. Mills were as important as corn for medieval and early modern military supply systems. Without mills, soldiers had great difficulties in consuming the available corn. They could hardly be expected to grind the grains themselves, and though various gruels could be made from unground corn, their preparation was time-consuming. Moreover, eating too much unground corn caused digestive problems and often resulted in sickness and even death.[7] Defenders relying on scorched-earth strategies therefore always took care to destroy mills. Invading armies occasionally sought to counter the problem by taking along mortars and hand-mills, yet these were obviously far less efficient than the large stationary mills powered by water, wind, and animal-traction.[8]

As the French retreated from Provence, Montmorency had all the local mills put out of action. Du Bellay writes that 'the mills were destroyed, the millstones were broken to pieces, the mills' ironworks were carried away, and all those who could be found in the country who knew how to build mills were sent to our camp under the pretext that they would be employed there, but in fact out of fear that they might help the enemy repair the destroyed mills.'[9] Yet French spies now reported that a few mills remained standing – one at the town of Auriol, and a couple more near the city of Arles.

François and Montmorency decided that their best way to put pressure on the Imperialists was to destroy those remaining mills. The Arles mills were attacked first. Arles was held in force by the French, the front line in the area had not yet stabilized, and the mills were not heavily defended. A well-executed raid by the lord of La Garde managed to seize and burn the mills without encountering much resistance.

The mill of Auriol was a completely different story. Auriol was a small fortified town on the river Huveaune, about 25 kilometres north-east of Marseilles and roughly the same distance south-east of Aix. It was now deep within Imperialist occupied territory. How its mill escaped the French scorched-earth strategy is not completely clear. Perhaps it was because the mill belonged to the Abbey of Saint-Victor, and the abbey's superior, the Cardinal Trivulzio, was the papal legate negotiating for peace between François and Charles.[10] If so, the king came to sourly regret this particular case of favouritism. For after the destruction of the mills of Arles, the Auriol mill became a cornerstone of the Imperialist supply system. French spies informed François that flour from that single mill fed the emperor himself, the entire Imperial household, and the 6,000 veteran Spanish infantrymen of the Naples and Sicily *tercios* who constituted Charles's elite force and who were always kept about the emperor's person.

When the king learned of this, he sent Barbezieux – his lieutenant in Marseilles – repeated orders to put the mill of Auriol out of action, even if he had to sacrifice an entire troop of men. Barbezieux and his chief lieutenant, Montpezat, who had no particular special force for the execution of such exploits, turned to Christophe Guasco, one of their most capable subordinates, and asked him to take some regular units and go to Auriol to burn the mill. Guasco, an experienced Italian mercenary, flatly refused. He told his superiors that they were asking him to undertake a suicidal mission. It was 25 kilometres as the crow flies from Marseilles to Auriol. The countryside was infested with Imperialist scouts and forces. The main Imperialist camp outside Aix was only 20 kilometres away from Auriol. The town of Auriol was guarded by an entire company, which in the Spanish army of 1536 meant about 250 men. The mill itself was guarded by another sixty men under an experienced captain, who were ordered never to budge from it, day or night. To ensure that they remained at their post even if the town itself was attacked, the mill's garrison was constituted as an independent command, and its captain was made responsible only to the emperor, not to the commander of Auriol. The emperor knew as well as François how important this mill now was.

In order to achieve surprise, Guasco explained, his men would have to march at least 25 kilometres and immediately fight a hard action. Even if they overcame the Auriol garrison, the exhausted raiders would have no chance of marching the 25 kilometres back to Marseilles without being intercepted by Imperialist forces coming from the Aix camp. Indeed, marching more than 50 kilometres without a break, with a hard battle into the bargain, was more than most troops in history were capable of.

François was informed of Guasco's refusal, and it was explained to the king that he was demanding the impossible. François was not impressed. He had already heard several reports accusing Barbezieux of being an incompetent and sluggish general, and was in no mood for receiving negative answers from him. He sent back an even more clear-cut order, demanding that Barbezieux and Montpezat find someone who would be willing to undertake the mission. François assured them that they need not be worried about losing even a thousand men, for the benefits of burning the mill were well worth the loss.

Barbezieux and Montpezat now offered this hot potato to the lord of Fonteraille. The latter, flattered by the offer, at first agreed, but then his friends remonstrated with him that he would certainly be ruined in this attempt, and Fonteraille changed his mind. François still continued to press the Marseilles commanders to destroy the mill, growing increasingly discontented with their inaction. As in a classic fairytale, word spread around the French camp in Marseilles that after the failure of these first two champions, anyone who was willing to undertake the hazardous task would be rewarded with royal munificence.

Enter Blaise de Monluc, an obscure infantry officer in his mid-thirties. Monluc was born sometime around 1501, offspring to a noble Gascon family of eleven children and very little money. The meagre family lands could hardly feed such a host of children, let alone finance their unbounded social aspirations in an age when every minor nobleman, and particularly a Gascon, looked upon himself as equal to kings. Just south of the Pyrenees, in Spain, men of noble birth were known to go begging at night, whereas by day they went about puffed up, saying that 'they are as good gentlemen as the king himself, minus a few coins'.[11] Like so many impoverished Gascon cadets before and since, Monluc knew that the only honourable way to fulfil his aspirations and climb the slippery social scale was through the army. Hence at the age of twenty, his spirit inflamed by tales of bravery and riches from Italy, he left his home and enlisted as a simple light cavalryman. Men were still expected to pay for their own equipment, and he soon discovered that he could not defray the costs of a cavalryman's post. He therefore transferred himself to the less demanding infantry, securing through family connections the position of a junior officer.

His burning ambition was to make for himself a worthy name in arms and gain both fame and fortune. In his memoirs, Monluc boasts that in order to further his military ambitions he completely weaned himself from play, wine, avarice, and romantic follies, to which youths are normally prone, and which have been the ruin of many officers. 'I can proudly say,' he wrote, 'that never any affection or [amorous] folly diverted me from undertaking and executing what was given me in command.'[12] Yet, Monluc stressed, it was not enough to be a virtuous man and to fight bravely. These brave deeds must make a favourable impression on one's superiors. On one's first campaigns, he instructs, limb and life must be risked in bold adventures to catch the attention and win the favour of some great man.[13] For only a helping hand from above could help a subordinate climb up the slippery scale.

Monluc spoke from bitter experience. He had served with distinction in numerous campaigns in Italy and along France's Spanish and German borders from 1521 to 1528, sustaining several injuries and almost losing his hand. He particularly distinguished himself as a gifted commander of small forces on bold strikes, first in a skirmish at Saint-Jean-de-Luz (1523), later at another skirmish on the river Maddalena (1528). Yet the only important commanders who took notice of him died soon after, and consequently, when the disgruntled Monluc left the service in 1528, he was still a junior officer. The only booty he brought with him from Italy was 30 ells of taffeta – the cloth with which his injured arm was bandaged and cushioned. For six years he lived the life of an impoverished Gascon landlord, serving as a simple man-at-arms in the local host of the king of Navarre, raising a family, dreaming of war, and chafing at the bit.

When François I began to raise new troops in 1534, in expectation of renewed hostilities, the thirty-something Monluc joyfully re-enlisted, leaving his wife to take care of the land and the troop of toddlers he had meanwhile fathered. He joined the Languedoc Legion, a novel unit of native French foot soldiers. The four legions François raised consisted of six bands of 1,000 men each. The captain of one of the 1,000-man strong Languedoc bands, Antoine de Rochechouart, appointed Monluc to be one of his two lieutenants. This time Monluc was determined to fulfil his youthful dreams. He took part in the invasion of Savoy and in the subsequent retreat, but did not perform any memorable deed. In August 1536 he was serving in the garrison of Marseilles along with the rest of Rochechouart's band.

When Monluc heard how anxious the king was to destroy the mill of Auriol, and how displeased he was with his subordinates' inaction, his hopes rose. Perhaps he could accomplish this great deed, and thereby win the undying gratitude not just of his embarrassed superiors, but of the king himself? The problem was, of course, that the job was not easy. Guasco's excuses were valid and very daunting. Nevertheless, as he mulled things over in his mind, Monluc resolved to undertake the mission and execute it or die in the attempt.

The Marseilles garrison had no barracks or camp. Rather, the soldiers were quartered on the civilian population. By a stroke of fortune, the landlord on whom Monluc was quartered was a native of Auriol. Monluc therefore unburdened his soul to this unnamed civilian, and asked for his advice. The landlord explained that Auriol was a small town, enclosed by high walls and commanded by a well-fortified castle. The mill itself was outside the walls, near the river Huveaune. A long street connected the town to the mill, along which a suburb of many houses sprang up. A high tower was built at the town's gate and completely dominated the way to the mill. Anyone who ventured into it could easily be shot from the tower. Thirty to forty paces from the mill, to the side further from the town, stood the parish church. (See map 6.)

As for the way to Auriol, explained the landlord, from Marseilles Monluc would first have to go to Aubagne. From there, he could take either of two roads. The main road went through the Huveaune valley, and could be traversed by foot and horse alike. However, the road passed at least one major watercourse, and the bridges were at present broken. Moreover, anyone going along the main road would find it difficult to conceal his movements from enemy troops. Monluc could also leave the main road at Aubagne, and make his way to Auriol over the Roussargue range, which stood to the east of the Huveaune valley. This range could be crossed only on foot. The going there was much slower, but enemy cavalrymen could not enter and patrol the area.

Monluc thought things over. Like Guasco, he concluded that the biggest problem he faced was the way back. He was quite confident in his ability to

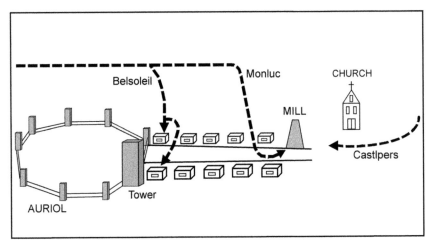

Map 6   The raid on Auriol, 19/20 August 1536

storm and destroy the mill, but how could he hope to cover at least 25 kilometres back to Marseilles with exhausted soldiers, while avoiding the inevita-
ble pursuit? In particular, even if he could outrun any pursuit mounted from
Auriol itself, how could he avoid being intercepted by Imperialist forces coming
from Aix?

He decided that his best chance would be to take an elite party of about
120 men on foot and make his way to Auriol and back through the mountains.
The small size of his force would make it more difficult for enemy outposts to
observe it on the outward journey, and for enemy patrols to track it down on
its return. It was one thing to locate a host of 1,000 soldiers, quite another to
locate a band of 120. The biggest danger during the pursuit was from light cavalry. Going through the mountains greatly lessened that particular danger, but
it had one obvious disadvantage, namely the difficulty of the terrain. However,
Monluc assumed that a small elite force of fit and highly motivated men could
overcome these difficulties better than a large regular formation.

The downside of taking only 120 men was, of course, that instead of storming Auriol with superior forces, he would actually be attacking a well-fortified
enemy who outnumbered him by more than two to one. Still, Monluc was quite
certain that since he had only to destroy the mill rather than conquer the town,
if he could manage to surprise the Imperialists, he could perform this task even
against a superior enemy. Weighing things over carefully, he calculated that it
was better to reduce the assaulting force to a bare minimum in order to maximize its chances of getting back to Marseilles in one piece. In addition, if the
enterprise miscarried, the loss of a large force might endanger the defence of
Marseilles itself, whereas the loss of 120 men would hardly change the overall
situation.

He announced his decision to his landlord, who was acting now as both his intelligence officer and his operations officer. Together they computed how many hours of darkness the short August nights provided and how many hours the march to Auriol would require. They concluded that if Monluc set out from Marseilles at twilight, marched briskly, and did not lose his way *en route*, he should be able to reach Auriol two hours before dawn. The way back, though, would have to be covered in daylight.

The landlord now undertook an even more delicate and important task, namely to find Monluc three guides who could find their way to Auriol at night through the mountains. Tellingly, Monluc preferred to rely on local civilians rather than on army scouts. The well-connected landlord quickly found three qualified men. When they heard what was wanted of them, they lost heart. The landlord strengthened their resolve with words, whereas Monluc distributed to them a handful of glittering *écus*. To prevent any word of his intentions from leaking out he then shut them up in his lodging and went to see Montpezat. It was now midday on 19 August.[14] To prevent any leakage of his intentions, Monluc hoped to be on his way to Auriol that very evening.

Monluc told Montpezat that he was willing to undertake the raid on Auriol. He would, however, take with him only a small force of 120 men, which he would personally choose from Rochechouart's Languedoc band. Montpezat was an old friend of Monluc's. They had served together in Italy in the 1520s, and Montpezat knew that Monluc was a capable and experienced officer. He was glad that someone had finally taken up the gauntlet and was willing to try to destroy the mill. But he thought Monluc was crazy. He told him that if he really wanted to raid Auriol, he had better take along at least 500 men. Monluc would not hear of it, and said he would rather have only 120. Montpezat was hardly convinced. Monluc writes in his memoirs that he so tormented Montpezat, that the latter eventually agreed to lay Monluc's plan before Barbezieux, and hear what the commander-in-chief thought.

Barbezieux was even more doubtful of Monluc's chances than Montpezat. He demanded that Monluc explain to him in detail exactly how he meant to destroy the mill with such a small force, when both Guasco and Fonteraille declined to undertake the same mission even with a thousand men at their command. Monluc refused, saying that he would not disclose to anyone how he planned to do it. Montpezat then intervened on behalf of his friend. 'Let him go,' he told Barbezieux, 'for if he be lost with so few people, it will not endanger the city, and at least we will satisfy the king.'

The lord of Villebon, who was also present at the meeting and with whom the volatile Monluc had previously quarrelled, now mocked Monluc's suggestion, telling Barbezieux in jest that he should indeed allow Monluc to go, for 'he will capture the emperor and we shall all be ashamed when we see him bring the emperor into the city tomorrow morning.'[15] Monluc, who was by his own admission an irascible Gascon firebrand and could never keep his big mouth shut, turned on Villebon and told him he was like a dog in a manger that would neither eat himself nor allow others to eat. A few more words were said, half in anger and half in jest. Finally Rochechouart, Monluc's direct superior, convinced Barbezieux to give him a free hand. Monluc was then authorized to choose his 120 men, and leave within a few hours for Auriol.

Monluc acted speedily. He immediately went and chose 120 of the best soldiers in the Languedoc band, taking care to select only noblemen. They were such a good company, he writes, as to make them better than 500 ordinary soldiers. He comments that in every formation he ever commanded, he always got acquainted with his soldiers and studied them well, so that he would know what each was capable of, and for what usages to employ which men.[16] This habit, he says, stood him in good stead on this occasion.

Within an hour all of Marseilles knew of Monluc's intentions. To ensure that no brave souls followed him and encumbered his force, and that word of his plans could not be sent to the Imperialists, Monluc had Barbezieux shut tight the city's gates.[17]

At sunset Monluc and his chosen band marched to the city's gate. The exit was virtually blocked by a crowd of soldiers, all clamouring to join the raiders. Gaspard de Saulx-Tavannes, later a marshal but at that time a junior officer like Monluc, pressed Monluc particularly hard to allow him and a score of other noblemen under his command to volunteer. Monluc was finally convinced to leave behind twenty of his chosen men, and take Tavannes and his companions instead. These altercations and arguments cost precious time, and it was already night when they finally set out on their long march.

Monluc divided his force into two parts. He kept sixty men and two of the guides under his direct command. He entrusted the other sixty men and the one remaining guide to Captain Belsoleil, telling him to march behind at a fair distance from Monluc's own party. Just as they began their march, twenty riders suddenly arrived from Marseilles. These were twenty Gascon cavalrymen commanded by the lord of Castelpers. Castelpers explained to Monluc that he must be allowed to come along with him, for the honour of all Gascons was at stake, and if Monluc failed, the Gascon soldiers in Marseilles would never hear the end of it from the French. After some discussion, which consumed another half an hour, Monluc accepted the reinforcement. He gave one of his troop's two guides to Castelpers, and told him to make his way to Auriol on horse, along the main road. If he arrived at Auriol before they did, he was to hide himself behind the parish church and do nothing until their arrival.

They made good time to Aubagne, marching about 17 kilometres through the Provençal plain. It was 12 kilometres more, as the crow flies, to Auriol. At Aubagne Castelpers with the horse continued on the main road, whereas Monluc and Belsoleil took to the mountains. They walked up and down the steep slopes of the Roussargue, conducted by their guides through narrow goats' tracks. After an arduous march they emerged from the mountains, and made a halt a few hundred metres south-west of Auriol. Most of the night had already passed and dawn was approaching. There was as yet no sign of Castelpers, but Monluc knew there was no time to lose.

Monluc left his troop under Tavannes's command and went to convene with Belsoleil. He ordered Belsoleil and his guide to take their sixty men and march behind Monluc's force. While Monluc pressed forward to attack the mill, Belsoleil should swerve aside, and make his way through the unwalled suburb directly towards the town's gate. Belsoleil should seize the two houses adjacent to the gate and fortify himself inside. He should then devote himself solely to blocking the gate and preventing the garrison from sallying out or sending reinforcements to the mill. To make sure that there would be no mistakes, Monluc explained his plans to Belsoleil's sixty soldiers as well. They were to devote all their attention to blocking the gate, and nobody under any circumstances was to go to help the attack on the mill itself.

Monluc's entire plan rested on the assumption that he could defeat the sixty defenders of the mill with only sixty men of his own. He was more apprehensive about the enemy company garrisoning the walled town. If they sallied out in force, he would have no chance of beating them back, let alone capturing and destroying the mill. However, he believed that as long as it was dark, the garrison would not be able to tell how small the raiding force was, and as long as it was oblivious of their numbers, it would be reluctant to risk an all-out sally for fear of falling into a trap or being attacked by another enemy force from behind.[18] At most, the garrison would make only hesitant attempts to reinforce the mill and try to take the measure of the attacking force. If Belsoleil showed spirited resistance to any such half-hearted attempts, Monluc would have enough time to take and destroy the mill before the light of day took the blindfold from the garrison's eyes. (See map 6.)

Returning to his own men, Monluc led them to the attack. They first had to skirt around the walled town. Imperialist sentinels on the wall heard their movements and called out, 'Who goes there?' The French made no reply, but hurried their steps. Passing by the gate, Belsoleil swerved to the side, whereas Monluc led his force onwards toward the mill. The mill's garrison was asleep, but three or four armed sentinels stood guard outside its entrance. One of them saw or heard the raiders approaching, and cried the first part of the Imperialist password, 'Qui vive?' Monluc answered 'Espaigne', guessing that this was the right retort. He was wrong. The pass was actually 'Impery'. The sentinel fired on them, but missed.

Monluc and Tavannes now charged the mill at the head of the raiders. The sentinels ran inside, and tried to close the two heavy folding doors behind them. They managed to shut one completely, and placed a great chest behind it to hold it tight. They shut the other door too and secured it with an iron bar, but enough space was left between the two doors to allow a man to squeeze in. The sentinels then positioned themselves at the entrance, ready to fire at any who ventured to enter. The shot and the following cries meanwhile woke up the rest of the mill's sixty guards, and they could be expected to come into action within a minute or two.

Monluc's mind worked fast. The sentinel who had fired at them was probably busy reloading his arquebus, which would take him at least a minute under the most favourable conditions. At present, there were therefore just two or three other loaded arquebuses to deal with. Tavannes sprang forward, intending to gallantly poke his head into the trap. Monluc grabbed him by the arm and pulled him back. He then grabbed a soldier who stood behind him, and pushed him inside by force. Apparently, honour had its limits. It is interesting to note that twenty years later, when Monluc commanded the storming of Thionville (1558), he repeated the same trick. When his soldiers declined to storm a dangerous position, he grabbed one of them and offered him 20 écus if he jumped in first. The soldier refused, saying that 20 écus will be useless for a dead man. Monluc then turned to his subordinate officers. Together they seized the soldier and threw him into the enemy position by force, head first. 'We made him brave against his will,' quipped Monluc.[19] Mercifully for that soldier, the position at Thionville turned out to be empty.

At Auriol the Imperialist sentinels were armed and ready. The moment the soldier was pushed inside, two arquebus shots rang out. 'Now enter,' said Monluc to Tavannes, 'if you want.'[20] Tavannes entered, followed by Monluc and a few other men. A hand-to-hand combat developed in the darkness, lit by a single lamp. The raiders quickly overcame the sentinels. The half-asleep and half-armed Imperialists on the ground floor offered little resistance, and fled to the upper floor. A fierce struggle then took place on the staircase. Monluc realized that he could not take the stairs by force. He sent an order to those of his men who remained outside the mill to climb unto its roof, make holes in it, and then fire down on the Imperialists in the second floor. The men quickly followed his orders. As soon as the shots began to rain down on the Imperialists, they lost heart. Breaking open a window at the back of the mill, most of them jumped out into the river that skirted the building. Monluc then stormed the upper floor, killed all who still offered resistance, and took prisoner their wounded captain as well as seven other wounded men.

While Monluc took the mill, Belsoleil seized the two houses near the gate and foiled three lukewarm attempts by the garrison to sally out. Arquebus shots flew thick about the street leading from the gate towards the mill, but no Imperialist soldiers managed to exit the town and help their compatriots. As Monluc foresaw, they assumed they were being attacked by a superior French force, and were reluctant to leave the security of the walls. After capturing the mill, Monluc sent most of his men to reinforce Belsoleil and bade him to take courage and continue blocking the exit at all costs. With the remaining men, Monluc removed all the spindles and other ironwork from the mill, rolled the millstones into the river, and burned the structure itself to the ground.

He completed the work of destruction just in time. Day was beginning to break. Soon the Auriol garrison would realize the truth of the situation and storm out in force. Just as Monluc was about to give the order of retreat, Castelpers finally arrived. He left his men behind the parish church and came to the burning mill to ask Monluc for instructions. Monluc told Castelpers to stay behind the church, where he was protected from the hail of shot issuing from the town. He commanded Tavannes to collect the men from around the mill and join Castelpers behind the church. Monluc himself then went to draw off Belsoleil. One by one the men left the houses near the gate, and ran for their lives from cover to cover towards the church. Monluc now feared that as he drew the last of Belsoleil's men away, the garrison might sally out and overwhelm them. Luckily, Castelpers on his own initiative, and wishing to see some fighting after coming all the way from Marseilles, showed up with his twenty cavalrymen on the far side of the street. His presence deterred the Imperialists, who feared to follow Monluc through the street lest they be charged down by Castelpers. They therefore remained inside the town, and Monluc and the last of the men made it safely to the church.

In the growing daylight Monluc surveyed his force for the march back to Marseilles. To his delight, he discovered that only seven or eight of the raiders were injured throughout the whole engagement, and only one of them, a man called Vignaux, was seriously wounded. Apparently, the soldier who was thrown first into the mill had a lucky escape, which is not impossible given the notorious inaccuracy of sixteenth-century arquebuses (or alternatively, Monluc may have already written him off). They placed Vignaux on a donkey and the rest began to march back towards Aubagne, on foot. Castelpers's cavalrymen led their horses by the bridle. Their pace was extremely slow, for the soldiers were exhausted and the terrain was difficult. They nevertheless managed to outrun the pursuit mounted by the Auriol garrison, and made it safely to the mountains. They then continued marching without a break, refreshing themselves by munching on some loaves of bread. They still had a long way ahead of them, and feared that their route might be blocked by forces coming from the Imperialist camp at Aix. Monluc knew that though he had done everything he could to maximize their chances of success, they were now dependent on the vagaries of fortune.

They reached Aubagne safely, without being detected by any Imperialist force. The enemy light cavalrymen, the eyes and ears of early modern armies, may have scanned the plain for them, but could not venture into the mountains. Having reached Aubagne, Monluc at first hoped to rest and refresh his men in the town. Yet as they entered the town, they heard the sound of cannonades from the direction of Marseilles. Unbeknownst to them, during the night, while they were marching from Marseilles to Auriol, Emperor Charles marched from Aix to Marseilles with about 8,000–12,000 men, aiming to test the city's defences. He was greeted by a furious cannonade from the city's outlying forts as well as from the French naval squadron.[21]

This was actually a great stroke of fortune for Monluc. When his raiders attacked the mill, the first thing which the defending captain did was to send a messenger to Aix to inform the emperor of the raid. According to Monluc, when the messenger arrived at Aix, he found that Charles had already departed, and had to ride in his trail towards Marseilles in order to deliver his message. Had Charles remained in camp, any forces he sent to intercept Monluc would surely have caught up with the French raiders, just as Guasco feared. As it was, Charles heard of the attack on Auriol only after daybreak, when he was nearing Marseilles. He immediately sent about 400–500 horsemen to intercept the raiders. These rode swiftly from Marseilles towards Aubagne, which they were approaching just as Monluc and his tired men were making their way into it from the other side.

Monluc could not know what the sounds coming from Marseilles meant. He and his men were convinced at first that the entire Imperialist army had marched on the city during the night, and was now preparing to either assault it or lay a regular siege to it. If they hurried, perhaps they could still slip inside. If they waited, they might well be cut off. He decided they could not risk a halt in Aubagne. Furthermore, whereas he previously intended to march from Aubagne to Marseilles along the main road, he now resolved to abandon it for fear of encountering Imperialist columns. Only Vignaux on his donkey and the other wounded, who could no longer cope with the mountains, took the level road. The rest, led by Monluc, again turned to mountain tracks, climbing up and down the slopes of the Carpiagne and Marseilles-Veyre ranges.

Monluc abandoned the level road not a moment too soon. Vignaux and the other wounded hardly walked 500 paces from Aubagne when they fell in with the Imperialist cavalry detachment coming from Marseilles. They were all taken prisoner. Monluc and his men, struggling through the mountains to the south, escaped unnoticed.

However, they could not escape the attention of the August Provençal sun. As the day progressed and the miles lengthened, the temperature too rose, and the sweat streamed. The raiders had no water with them, and could find none in the scorched countryside. Still they went on climbing up and down the slopes, thinking that they will die of thirst any moment. At last they reached the fort of Nostre Dame de la Garde, one of Marseilles's outlying forts. At first, they were fired upon, but eventually they were recognized and allowed to enter. The Imperialists meanwhile broke off their attack, and retired towards Aix. They found Marseilles's defences too formidable for them.

When they saw the Imperialists retreat, Monluc and his men left Nostre Dame de la Garde, and marched to the city's gate. There stood Barbezieux, Montpezat, and the other captains. At first they thought Monluc's men were the vanguard of another Imperialist attack, but they soon recognized them, and received them with great joy. They were extremely glad to hear the good news that Monluc's party brought, and were also keen to interrogate the captive captain of the Auriol mill. Monluc confesses in his memoirs that his safe return to Marseilles was due as much as to luck as to reason. Though he was quite confident from the start in his ability to capture and burn the mill, like the Armenians at Khartpert, he had to trust fate, or God, to get him back safely to Marseilles. Unlike the poor Armenians, Monluc had no reason to regret his faith.

The mill's destruction contributed greatly to the subsequent Imperialist defeat. It aggravated the supply difficulties of the Imperialist forces, which now had to rely ever more heavily on fruit and grapes, and on bread made from corn pounded in mortars. The production of this bread was time-consuming, and its quality was so bad that the French made fun of captured loaves, and Montmorency sent specimens to the ministers in Paris, in order to lift their spirits and convince them that the Imperialists were close to collapse.[22] The unwholesome diet resulted in the outbreak of a dysentery epidemic amongst the Imperialist troops. Thousands died, and thousands more were incapacitated. By 2 September, without fighting a single battle, the Imperialist army had already lost up to 8,000 men. On 7 September Leyva, his great enterprise falling to pieces around him, died too.

It is impossible to say how important the destruction of the Auriol mill was to the deteriorating situation of the Imperialist forces. Monluc understandably presents it as the straw that broke the camel's back. No other source singles out the destruction of the mill as a chief cause for the Imperialist defeat, but many claim that the destruction of all available mills was indeed one of the main difficulties from which the Imperialists suffered.[23] Emperor Charles himself, in several letters he wrote to explain his failure, said that he resolved to retreat from Provence mainly due to the lack of supply, and that one of the principle causes of this lack was the destruction of the mills.[24]

On 11 September Charles acknowledged defeat, and decided to retreat back to Italy while his men were still capable of walking and defending themselves. He accordingly abandoned the Aix camp, and took the way eastwards towards Fréjus and the border. The road that the Imperialists trod with such confidence in early August was now covered with their sick, their dead, and their stragglers. French marauders stalked them, from time to time falling upon the weakest of the herd. Martin Du Bellay, who led a light cavalry unit in pursuit of the Imperialists, writes that from Aix to Fréjus 'all the roads were strewn with dead and sick, with harnesses, lances, pikes, arquebuses and other weapons, and with exhausted horses … There you could see … the dying mingled with the dead corpses, presenting a horrible and piteous spectacle.'[25] Of the 60,000 men who crossed the Var river on 24 July, less than half managed to cross back to Italy. Thousands had deserted, many had switched sides to join the French, and many others were taken prisoner. Thousands more were dead. The French main army did not budge from its fortified camp near Avignon. They had won a tremendous victory without fighting a single engagement.

When the coast was clear François I came down from Valence to tour the ravaged province and to commend the French forces for their efficient defence. On 20 September he visited Marseilles.[26] This was the day Monluc had been dreaming of since his youthful years. In his mind's eyes he already saw himself being presented to the victorious monarch, who had pressed so hard for the destruction of the Auriol mill, and who had been repeatedly informed of the impossibility of that mission. In glowing terms Barbezieux would tell François how Monluc nevertheless succeeded in destroying the mill, and the grateful monarch would surely take note and reward Monluc handsomely.[27]

Monluc was in for a rude awakening. Barbezieux was at the time fighting hard to defend his name and his conduct, which were severely criticized during the campaign. Needing all the credit he could get, he did not disdain to take credit even for other men's achievements. Hence when he sent Montmorency and François word of the mill's destruction, he attributed the honour of it to himself alone, saying that it was he who laid out the ingenious plan through which the mill was destroyed. He did not even mention Monluc's name.

Montmorency too was quick to attribute the success to himself. In a letter he wrote on 2 September, he informed the French commander in the Dauphiné, the lord of Humières, that 'I sent [to Auriol] a good number of cavalrymen and infantrymen, who completely demolished and burned the mill, and also cut to pieces 100 or 120 Spaniards who guarded it. This is a great damage [to the Imperialists], for it is believed that they cannot obtain flour except from there, and now we shall see what they will do.'[28] Not a word was said about the commander of the successful raid.

When the victorious François entered Marseilles, Barbezieux again presented himself to the king as the chief architect of the raid, and reaped all the praise and honours. As luck would have it, Montpezat was at the time stricken with severe illness, and could not speak up for Monluc. The Gascon officer was never presented to François, who apparently did not enquire about the identity of the man who executed 'Barbezieux's plan'. As Tavannes' son, the memoirist Jean de Saulx, wrote, many a time the glory of war went to the superior officers who were often asleep in their beds while their subordinates commanded in the field. Of the resulting victories, he says, the field commanders got all the dangers, whereas the superiors got the glory.[29]

Thus Monluc's name remained unknown to King François, to Anne de Montmorency, and to the majority of French generals. Monluc's relations with the one important general who knew him well, namely Barbezieux, understandably turned sour. When François and Charles signed the truce of Nice (1538), the almost forty-years-old Monluc had reached the rank of only a captain of foot.

To his joy, however, the wars were renewed in 1543, and did not really end until the peace of Cateau Cambrésis in 1559. They were immediately succeeded by the French Wars of Religion. The endless campaigns gave Monluc a few more chances to show his worth, and he eventually fulfilled his youthful dreams beyond his wildest expectations. In 1543 he excelled himself in several engagements, including several special operations such as the destruction of the vital Po bridge at Carignano (1544).[30] Later the same year he finally met King François in person. The king, who grew to appreciate the advantages of caution in war, absolutely forbade his commander in Italy, the duke of Enghien, to engage in battle. Enghien sent Monluc to François to convince him to rescind the order. By dint of a forceful and heroic speech, Monluc carried the day. He rode back to the army, and was joyfully welcomed by Enghien, who exclaimed: 'I knew well that you will not bring us peace!'[31] The following battle of Ceresole (1544) nearly ended in defeat, but thanks in part to Monluc's vigorous conduct, in the end the French carried the day. Monluc was knighted on the battlefield, though it was such a close call, that for three nights afterwards, he writes, he woke up in fright in the middle of the night, dreaming of defeat.[32]

Now he began to swiftly rise through the ranks, winning one engagement after another. He eventually became marshal of France and the Catholic governor of Guienne during the Wars of Religion. In the latter capacity he led a campaign of terror against the Huguenot rebels. The streaks of ruthlessness that appeared at the door of Auriol's mill, and that later showed themselves in his abominable treatment of Italian civilians at Siena (1555), now erupted in full force. The dashing special operations officer became in old age a brutal tyrant, conducting what almost amounted to an ethnic cleansing campaign against the Guienne Huguenots. He died in 1577.[33]

NOTES

1 The army's nominal roll call amounted to almost 64,000 men (Oman, *History of the Art of War in the Sixteenth Century*, p. 61; Tracy, *Emperor Charles V*, pp. 161, 176–7; Valbelle, *Histoire journalière*, 2:314, 316; Du Bellay, *Mémoires*, 3:136–7, 297).

2 Robertson, *History of the Reign*, 2:265.

3 Du Bellay, *Mémoires*, 3:118–19.

4 Vieilleville, *Mémoires*, pp. 15–16. Note that Vieilleville's story of the way he almost single-handedly captured Avignon is not corroborated by any other source. Avignon apparently did fall to a French ploy, but whether it happened as Vieilleville describes it is uncertain.

5 Du Bellay, *Mémoires*, 3:242–3.

6 On this affair, see Decrue, *Anne de Montmorency*, pp. 280–1; Knecht, *Renaissance Warrior*, pp. 337–8; *Correspondance du Cardinal François de Tournon*, p. 132; Du Bellay, *Mémoires*, 3:132–5, 215, 336–8; Valbelle, *Histoire journalière*, 2:320; Sandoval, *Historia de la Vida*, 3:17–18, 24–5.

7 See Perjés, 'Army Provisioning', pp. 7–9; Harari, 'Strategy and Supply', p. 304.

8 Harari, 'Strategy and Supply', p. 304; Du Bellay, *Mémoires*, 3:257; Pizan, *Book of Deeds*, p. 111.

9 Du Bellay, *Mémoires*, 3:192. See also Du Bellay, *Mémoires*, 3:115, 148, 192, 257, 282; Arena, *Meygra Entrepriza*, pp. 28–30.

10 Courteault, *Blaise de Monluc*, p. 119 n. 1.

11 Brantôme, *Œuvres complètes*, ed. Lalanne, 7:56.

12 Monluc, *Commentaires*, pp. 23–9.

13 Monluc, *Commentaires*, p. 31. See also Tavannes, *Mémoires*, pp. 86–7.

14 Monluc does not give the date of the event. It might have been 30 August rather than 19 August. See note 21.

15 Monluc, *Commentaires*, p. 65.

16 See also Monluc, *Commentaires*, pp. 24–5.

17 Compare Aubigny, *Traité*, p. 22.

18 Compare Aubigny, *Traité*, p. 20; 'Excerpts of Polyaenus', sections 54.12–13, ed. Krentz, 2:982.

19 Monluc, *Commentaires*, p. 439.

20 Monluc, *Commentaires*, p. 68.

21 On the Imperialist attack on Marseilles, see Valbelle, *Histoire journalière*, 2:305–6; Du Bellay, *Mémoires*, 3:244–8. Monluc's reference to the Imperialist attack on Marseilles is the only way we can date the Auriol raid with certainty. There was, however, another Imperialist attack on Marseilles on 31 August, and there is some circumstantial evidence supporting the idea that the Auriol raid actually coincided with this second Imperialist attack, and hence took place on the night of 30/31 August. Nevertheless, there are equally strong circumstantial reasons to believe that Monluc is referring in his memoirs to the 19 August Imperialist attack. It is particularly notable that, whereas the first attack was led by Emperor Charles in person, the second was not. Most scholars therefore assign the raid to the night of 19/20 August rather than that of 30/31 August.

22 Monluc, *Commentaires*, p. 902; Decrue, *Anne de Montmorency*, p. 279.

23 See for example Arena, *Meygra Entrepriza*, pp. 28–30; Decrue, *Anne de Montmorency*, pp. 278–9.

24 *Correspondenz des Kaisers Karl V*, 2:249; *Corpus Documental de Carlos V*, 1:522.

25 Du Bellay, *Mémoires*, 3:299.

26 On this visit, see also Valbelle, *Histoire journalière*, 2:314–15.

27 Monluc, *Commentaires*, p. 72.

28 Quoted in Courteault, *Blaise de Monluc*, p. 122.

29 Tavannes, *Mémoires*, p. 19.

30 Monluc, *Commentaires*, pp. 132–8.

31 Monluc, *Commentaires*, p. 149.

32 Monluc, *Commentaires*, p. 165

33 The present chapter is based mainly on the following sources: Monluc, *Commentaires*, pp. 61–74; Du Bellay, *Mémoires*, 3:115–301; Tavannes, *Mémoires*, 81–2; Vieilleville, *Mémoires*, 15–18; Valbelle, *Histoire journalière*, 2:294–317; Courteault, *Blaise de Monluc*, pp. 112–23; Monluc, *Habsburg–Valois Wars*, pp. 1–27; Decrue, *Anne de Montmorency*, pp. 253–89. It is based to a lesser extent on: Arena, *Meygra Entrepriza*; *Du glorieux retour de Lempereur*; La Noue, *Discours*; Rochechouart, *Mémoires*, p. 602; Sandoval, *Historia de la Vida*, 3:7–25; *Correspondenz des Kaisers Karl V*, 2:239–41, 248–52, 259–64; *Corpus Documental de Carlos V*, 1:500–25; *Catalogue des actes de François Ier*, 3:231–41; *Correspondance de Joachim de Matignon*, pp. 35–8; *Correspondance du Cardinal François de Tournon*, pp. 103–7, 131–8; Harari, *Renaissance Military Memoirs*, pp. 21, 95–8, 102–3, 144–9, 191; Knecht, *Renaissance Warrior*, pp. 329–38; Oman, *History of the Art of War in the Sixteenth Century*, pp. 45–8, 56–62, 213; Procacci, 'Provence', pp. 243–52; Robertson, *History of the Reign*, 2:245–75; Tracy, *Emperor Charles V*, pp. 158–63, 176–8; Perjés, 'Army Provisioning'; Harari, 'Strategy and Supply'; Parker, 'Political World'; Chaunu and Escamilla, *Charles Quint*, pp. 268–71; Sournia, *Blaise de Monluc*; Bouche, *Chorographie*, 2:580–90; Le Gras, *Blaise de Monluc*, 44–7.

8

Conclusions

S PECIAL operations are not a novel late modern phenomenon. They were an integral and very important part of the military and political tool-kit already in the Middle Ages and the Renaissance. The main targets of medieval and Renaissance warfare in general, namely strongpoints and leaders, were often more vulnerable to special operations than to regular ones.

The extensive usage of special operations demonstrates that medieval and Renaissance warfare did not always obey the conventions of chivalric fair play. Commanders habitually relied not only on guile and ruse, but also on bribery, treason, assassination, and abduction. Chivalry was nevertheless an important part of medieval and Renaissance wars. It still had a restraining effect on the use of special operations, especially assassination and abduction. Conversely, the potential usefulness of assassination and abduction was so great in the Middle Ages and the Renaissance precisely because political loyalties were still feudal and chivalric in nature.

Several important questions are left open by the present book, to await future research. The methods and importance of assassinations and poisoning in chivalric culture deserve much further study. Such study might confirm or disprove Franklin L. Ford's hypothesis that assassination was of comparatively smaller importance in the military and political culture of high medieval Europe, and that it became far more important only during the sixteenth-century wars of religion.[1] Though the present book indicates that assassination was of great importance throughout the Middle Ages, a much more detailed study is needed before any firm conclusions can be reached.

Similarly, a more detailed study of medieval and Renaissance siege warfare is needed in order to determine the relative importance of regular and special operations. From a cursory survey it appears that special operations were considerably more important in siege warfarse than were, say, mechanical artillery, but a more thorough research is needed to either confirm or disprove this hypothesis. If it is true, it would mean that military historians should pay much more attention not merely to special operations but also to psychological warfare, which was often the key for securing traitors.

One field of study that has been intentionally neglected in the present book is the naval arena. Naval special operations often differed from inland ones in their execution and targets, but they could have equally important strategic and political results. Future studies of medieval and Renaissance naval warfare would therefore benefit from taking these operations into account.

Finally, the present book stops at 1550, in the midst of the gunpowder revolution and somewhere along the earlier stages of the Military Revolution. Though up to 1550 these two revolutions seem to have had little impact on special operations, it is clear that between 1550 and 1914 both inland and naval special operations underwent important changes in their methods, targets, and cultural standing. The story of these changes merits a book of its own.

NOTE

1 See Ford, *Political Murder*.

Works Cited

Abbreviations

RHC   *Recueil des historiens des croisades*, Academie des inscriptions &
               belles-lettres (France), 16 vols. (Paris, 1841–1906)
RHC Ar.   *Historiens Arméniens*
RHC Oc.   *Historiens Occidentaux*
RHC Or.   *Historiens Orientales*

Primary Sources

Abū'l-Fidā, 'Imād al-Dīn Isma'īl ibn 'Alī al-Ayyūbī, *Muntaḫabāt min al-mukhtaṣar fī akhbār al-bashar*, RHC Or. 1 (Paris, 1872), pp. 1–165.

Aeneas Tacticus, 'On the Defence of Fortified Positions', in *Aeneas Tacticus, Asclepiodotus, Onasander*, ed. the Illinois Greek Club (London, 1962 [1923]).

al-Ansarī, Umar ibn Ibrahim al-Awsi, *A Muslim Manual of War, being Tafrij al-Kurub fi tadbir al-Hurub*, ed. and trans. George T. Scanlon (Cairo, 1961).

Albert of Aachen, *Historia Hierosolymitana*, RHC Oc. 4 (Paris, 1879), pp. 265–713.

Amatus of Montecassino, *The History of the Normans*, trans. Prescott N. Dunbar, ed. Graham A. Loud (Woodbridge, 2004).

Ambroise, *The History of the Holy War: Ambroise's Estoire de la guerre sainte*, ed. Marianne Ailes and Malcolm Barber, 2 vols. (Woodbridge, 2003).

Analecta Leodiensia, seu Collectio Documentorum Quorumdam, ad Res Ludovici Borbonii et Joannis Hornaei Temporibus Gestas Spectantum, in *Documents relatifs aux troubles du Pays de Liège*, ed. Ram.

Anna Comnena, *The Alexiad of Anna Comnena*, trans. E. R. A. Sewter (Harmondsworth, 1969).

Anselmi de Ribodi Monte ad Manassem, archiepiscopum Remensem, epistola, RHC Oc. 3 (Paris, 1866), pp. 890–6.

Arena, Antoine, *Meygra Entrepriza catoliqui imperatoris …*, ed. Norbert-Alexandre Bonafous (Aix, 1860).

Arnold of Lubeck, *Arnoldi abbatis Lubecensis chronica Slavorum*, ed. Georgius H. Pertz (Hanover, 1978 [1868]).

Aubigny, Bérault Stuart, lord of, *Traité sur l'art de la guerre*, ed. Elie de Commingnes (Hague, 1976).

Avesbury, Robert de, *De gestis mirabilibus Regis Edwardi tertii*, ed. Edward M. Thompson (Nendeln, 1965).

Bahā' al-Dīn ibn Shaddād, *Kitāb sīrat Salāh al-Dīn al-Ayyūbī: al-Nawādir al-sultāniyya wa'l-mahāsin al-yūsufiyya* (Cairo, 1927).

—— *The Rare and Excellent History of Saladin, or al-Nawadir al-Sultaniyya wa'l-Mahasin al-Yusufiyya*, trans. Donald S. Richards (Aldershot, 2001).

Baker, Geoffrey le, *Chronicon Galfridi le Baker de Swynebroke*, ed. Edward M. Thompson (Oxford, 1889).

Baldry of Dol, *Historia Jerosolimitana*, RHC Oc. 4 (Paris, 1879), pp. 1–111.

Balduini III, Hierosolymitani Latinorum regis quarti, Historia Nicaena vel Antiochena necnon Jerosolymitana, RHC Oc. 5 (Paris, 1895), pp. 139–85.

Barber, Malcolm and Keith A. Bate (eds.), *The Templars: Selected Sources* (Manchester and New York, 2002).

Bar Hebraeus, Gregory Abu al-Faraj, *The Chronography of Gregory Abu'l Faraj*, ed. and trans. Ernest A. W. Budge, 2 vols. (Amsterdam, 1976 [1932]).

Basin, Thomas, *Histoire des règnes de Charles VII et de Louis XI*, ed. J. Quicherat, 4 vols. (Paris, 1855–9).

Bonenfant, Paul (ed.), *Actes concernant les rapports entre les Pays-Bas et la Grande Bretagne* ... in *Bulletin de la Commission Royale d'Histoire* 109 (1944): 53–125.

Bonivard, François, *Chroniques de Genève*, ed. Micheline Tripet, 3 vols. (Geneva, 2001–).

Bower, Walter, *Scotichronicon*, ed. Donald. E. R. Watt *et al.*, 9 vols. (Aberdeen, 1989–98).

Brantôme, Pierre de Bourdeille, Abbot of, *Œuvres complètes de Pierre de Bourdeille, seigneur de Brantôme*, ed. Ludovic Lalanne, 11 vols. (Paris, 1864–82).

Der Briefwechsel Karls des Kühnen (1433–1477), ed. Werner Paravicini, 2 vols. (Frankfurt am Main, 1995).

Brocardus, *Directorium ad passagium faciendum*, RHC Ar. 2 (Paris, 1906), pp. 367–517.

Buser, B., *Die Beziehungen der Mediceer zu Frankreich während der Jahre 1434–1494 in ihrem Zusammenhang mit den allgemeinen Verhältnissen Italiens* (Leipzig, 1879).

But, Adrien de, *Chronique des religieux des Dunes*, ed. Kervyn de Lettenhove, in *Chroniques relatives à l'histoire de la Belgique sous la domination des ducs de Bourgogne*, 3 vols. (Brussels, 1870), vol. 1.

Cafarus, *Genuensis consulis de liberatione civitatum orientis*, RHC Oc. 5 (Paris, 1895), pp. 41–73.

Catalogue des actes de François Ier, ed. Paul Marichal, 10 vols. (Paris, 1887–1908).

La Chanson du Chevalier au Cygne et de Godefroid de Bouillon, ed. Célestin Hippeau, 2 vols. (Geneva, 1969 [Paris, 1852–77]).

Charny, Geoffroi de, *The 'Book of Chivalry' of Geoffroi de Charny: Text, Context, and Translation*, ed. and trans. Richard W. Kaeuper and Elspeth Kennedy (Philadelphia, 1996).

Le Charroi de Nîmes: Chanson du geste de XII siècle, ed. J.-L. Perrier (Paris, 1982 [1931]).

Chartier, Jean, *Chronique de Charles VII, Roi de France*, ed. Auguste Vallet de Viriville, 3 vols. (Paris, 1868).

Chastellain, George, *Œuvres*, ed. Kervyn de Lettenhove, 8 vols. (Geneva, 1971 [Brussels, 1863–6]).

Chronicle of the Third Crusade: A Translation of the Itinerarium Peregrinorum et Gesta Regis Ricardi, ed. and trans. Helen J. Nicholson, Crusade Texts in Translation 3 (Aldershot, 1997).

Chronicon Angliae, ab anno domini 1328 usque ad annum 1388, auctore monacho quodam Sancti Albani, ed. Edward M. Thompson (Nendeln, 1965 [London, 1874]).

La Chronique de Lorraine: Les opérations des feus ducs de Loheregne, commenceant à duc Jehan, fils à duc Raoul …, ed. L. Marchal (Nancy, 1859).

Chronique de Michel le Syrien, Patriarche Jacobite d'Antioche (1166–1199), ed. and trans. J.-B. Chabot, 4 vols. (Brussels, 1963).

Chronique d'Ernoul et de Bernard le Trésorier, ed. Louis de Mas Latrie (Paris, 1871).

Chronique des quatre premiers Valois, 1327–1393, ed. Siméon Luce (Paris, 1862).

'Chronique de Terre-Sainte (1131–1224)', in *Gestes des Chiprois*, ed. Raynaud, pp. 1–24.

'Chronique du Templier de Tyr (1242–1309)', in *Gestes des Chiprois*, ed. Raynaud, pp. 139–334.

Chronique Normande du XIVe siècle, ed. Auguste and Émile Molinier (Paris, 1882).

Chroniques de Yolande de France, duchesse de Savoie, sœur de Louis XI, ed. L. Ménabréa (Paris, 1859).

Chronographia Regum Francorum, ed. H. Moranville, 3 vols. (Paris, 1891–7).

Commynes, Philippe de, *Mémoires*, ed. Emilie L. M. Dupont, 3 vols. (Paris, 1840–7).

——*Mémoires*, ed. B. de Mandrot, 2 vols. (Paris, 1901–3).

Corpus Documental de Carlos V, ed. Manuel F. Álvarez, 5 vols. (Salamanca, 1973–81).

Correspondance de Joachim de Matignon, ed. L.-H. Labande (Paris, 1914).

Correspondance du Cardinal François de Tournon, 1521–1562, ed. Michel François (Paris, 1946).

Correspondenz des Kaisers Karl V, ed. Karl Lanz, 3 vols. (Frankfurt, 1966).

Dépêches des ambassadeurs milanais en France sous Louis XI et François Sforza, ed. Bernard de Mandrot and Charles Samaran, 4 vols. (Paris, 1916–25).

Dépêches des ambassadeurs milanais sur les campagnes de Charles-le-Hardi, duc de Bourgogne, de 1474 à 1477, ed. Frédéric de Gingins La Sarra, 2 vols. (Paris and Geneva, 1858).

Diesbach, Ludwig von, Die autobiographischen Aufzeichnungen Ludwig von Diesbachs: Studien zur spätmittelalterlichen Selbstdarstellung im ober-deutschen und schweizerischen Raume, ed. Urs M. Zahnd (Bern, 1986).

Documents relatifs aux troubles du Pays de Liège sous les princes-évêques Louis de Bourbon et Jean de Horne, 1455–1505, ed. P. F. X. de Ram (Brussels, 1844).

Du Bellay, Martin, and Guillaume du Bellay, *Mémoires (1513–47)*, ed. V.-L. Bourrilly and Fleury Vindry, 4 vols. (Paris, 1908–19).

Du Clercq, Jacques, *Mémoires de J. du Clercq*, ed. F. A. F. T. de Reiffenberg, 4 vols. (Brussels, 1835–6).

Du glorieux retour de Lempereur de Prouence, par ung Double de lectres, escriptes de Bouloigne à Romme a Labbe de Caprare. Translate Dytalien en Francoys. Adiouste le double du dicton prononce a la Condempnation de Lempoisonneur de feu monsieur le Dauphin de France (Lyon?, 1537).

Edbury, Peter W. (ed.), *The Conquest of Jerusalem and the Third Crusade: Sources in Translation* (Brookfield, 1996).

Ekkehard of Aura, *Hierosolymita*, RHC Oc. 5 (Paris, 1895), pp. 1–39.

d'Escouchy, Mathieu, *Chronique de Mathieu d'Escouchy*, ed. G. du Fresne de Beaucourt, 3 vols. (Paris, 1863–4).

Etterlin, Petermann, *Kronica von der loblichen Eydtgnoschaft, jr harkommen und sust seltzam strittenn und geschichten*, ed. Eugen Gruber (Aarau, 1965).

'Excerpts of Polyaenus', in Polyaenus, *Stratagems of War*, ed. and trans. Peter Krentz and Everett L. Wheeler, 2 vols. (Chicago, 1994), 2:851–1004.

Fantosme, Jordan, 'Chronicle of the War between the English and the Scots in 1173 and 1174', in *Contemporary Chronicles of the Middle Ages: Sources of Twelfth-Century History*, trans. Joseph Stephenson (Felinbach, 1988), pp. 77–120.

'The First and Second Crusades from an Anonymous Syriac Chronicle', ed. and trans. A. S. Tritton and Hamilton A. W. Gibb, *Journal of the Royal Asiatic Society* 92 (1933): 69–101, 273–306.

Fordun, John, *Chronica gentis Scotorum*, ed. William F. Skene, 2 vols. (Edinburgh, 1871–2).

Froissart, Jehan, *Chroniques de J. Froissart*, ed. Simeon Luce, 12 vols. in 14 parts (Paris, 1869–1931).

—— *Œuvres de Froissart: Chroniques*, ed. Kervyn de Lettenhove, 25 vols. in 26 parts (Brussels, 1867–77).

—— *Voyage en Béarn*, ed. A. H. Diverres (Manchester, 1953).

Frontinus, Sextus Julius, *The Stratagems*, ed. Mary B. McElwain and trans. Charles E. Bennett (London, 1969 [1925]).

Fulcher of Chartres, *Fulcheri Carnotensis Historia Hierosolymitana (1095–1127)*, ed. Heinrich Hagenmeyer (Heidelberg, 1913).

—— *A History of the Expedition to Jerusalem, 1095–1127*, ed. Harold S. Fink and trans. Frances R. Ryan (Knoxville, 1969).

Gabrieli, Francesco, *Arab Historians of the Crusades: Selected and Translated from the Arabic Sources*, trans. E. J. Costello (London, 1969).

Galbert de Bruges, *Histoire du meurtre de Charles le Bon Comte de Flandre (1127–1128)*, ed. Henri Pirenne (Paris, 1891).

Gesta Francorum et aliorum Hierosolymitanorum, ed. and trans. Rosalind Hill (London, 1962).

Gesta Francorum expugnantium Iherusalem, RHC Oc. 3 (Paris, 1866), pp. 487–543.

Gesta Stephani: The Deeds of Stephen, ed. and trans. Kenneth R. Potter (London, 1955).

Les Gestes des Chiprois: Recueil de chroniques françaises écrites en Orient aux XIIIᵉ et XIVᵉ siècles: Philippe de Navarre et Gérard de Monréal, ed. Gaston Raynaud, Publications de la Société de l'Orient Latin, Série historique 5 (Geneva, 1887).

Gilo of Paris, *Historia Gilonis Cardinalis Episcopi de Via Hierosolymitana*, RHC Oc. 5 (Paris, 1895), pp. 725–800.

Gruel, Guillaume, *Chronique d'Arthur de Richemont, connétable de France, duc de Bretagne*, ed. Achille le Vavasseur (Paris, 1890).

Guibert de Nogent, *Dei Gesta per Francos*, ed. R. B. C. Huygens (Turnholt, 1996).

Guillaume de Tyr et ses Continuateurs, ed. Paulin Paris, 2 vols. (Paris, 1879–80).

Guyard, Stanislas, 'Un Grand Maître des Assassins au temps de Saladin', *Journal Asiatique* ser. VII, 9 (1877): 324–489.

Guyon, Fery de, *Mémoires de Fery de Guyon*, ed. A.-P.-L. de Robaulx de Soumoy (Brussels, 1858).

Hagenmeyer, Heinrich, *Epistulae et chartae ad historiam primi Belli Sacri spectantes quae supersunt aevo aequales ac genuinae: Die Kreuzzugsbriefe aus den Jahren 1088–1100* (Innsbruck, 1901).

Haynin, Jean de, *Mémoires de Jean, Sire de Haynin et de Louvignies, 1465–1477*, ed. Dieudonné Brouwers, 2 vols. (Liège: 1905–6).

Henrici de Merica, *Compendiosa Historia de Cladibus Leodiensium*, in *Documents relatifs aux troubles du Pays de Liège*, ed. Ram.

Henry of Huntingdon, *De captione Antiochiae a Christianis*, RHC Oc. 5 (Paris, 1895), pp. 374–9.

Historia Gotfridi, RHC Oc. 5 (Paris, 1895), pp. 439–523.

Ibn al-Athīr, 'Izz al-Dīn, *Min kitāb kāmil al-tawārīkh*, RHC Or. 1 (Paris, 1872), pp. 187–744; RHC Or. 2 , part 1 (Paris, 1887), pp. 4–180.

Ibn al-Qalānisī, Hamza ibn Asad, *The Damascus Chronicle of the Crusades*, ed. and trans. Hamilton A. R. Gibb (London, 1932).

Istore et Croniques de Flandres, ed. Kervyn de Lettenhove, 2 vols. (Brussels, 1879–80).

Itinerarium peregrinorum et gesta regis Ricardi, ed. William Stubbs (London, 1864).

Johnston, Ronald Carlyle (ed.), *The Crusade and Death of Richard I* (Oxford, 1961).

Joinville, Jean de, *Vie de Saint Louis*, ed. and trans. Jacques Monfrin (Paris, 1995).

Journal d'un bourgeois de Paris, 1405–1449, ed. Alexandre Tuetey (Paris, 1881).

Les Journaux du trésor de Philippe VI de Valois, suivis de l'Ordinarium thesaurii de 1338–1339, ed. Jules É. M. Viard (Paris, 1899).

Juvaini, 'Ala-ad-Din 'Ata-Malik, *The History of the World-Conqueror*, trans. John A. Boyle, 2 vols. (Manchester, 1958).

Kamāl al-Dīn ibn al-'Adīm, *Extraits de la Chronique d'Alep*, RHC Or. 3 (Paris, 1884).

al-Kātib al-Isfahānī, 'Imād al-Dīn Muhammad ibn Muhammad, *Conquête de la Syrie et de la Palestine par Saladin*, trans. Henri Massé (Paris, 1972).

La Marche, Olivier de, *Mémoires d'Olivier de la Marche, maître d'hôtel et capitaine des gardes de Charles le téméraire*, ed. Henri Beaune and Jules d'Arbaumont, 4 vols. (Paris, 1883–8).

Langtoft, Pierre de, *The Chronicle of Pierre de Langtoft, in French Verse, from the Earliest Period to the Death of King Edward I*, ed. Thomas Wright, 2 vols. (Nendeln, 1964 [London, 1866–8]).

La Noue, François de, *Discours politiques et militaries*, ed. Frank E. Sutcliffe (Paris, 1967).

Le Bel, Jean, *Chronique de Jean le Bel*, ed. Jules Viard and Eugène Déprez, 2 vols. (Paris, 1904–5).

Lefèvre de St Rémy, Jean, *Chronique de Jean le Fèvre, seigneur de Saint Remy*, ed. François Morand, 2 vols. (Paris, 1876–81).

Leo VI, 'Stratagems', in Polyaenus, *Stratagems of War*, ed. and trans. Peter Krentz and Everett L. Wheeler, 2 vols. (Chicago, 1994), 2:1005–75.

Lescot, Richard, *Chronique de Richard Lescot*, ed. Jean Lemoine (Paris, 1896).

Lettres de Louis XI, roi de France, ed. Joseph Vaesen and Etienne Charavay, 11 vols. (Paris, 1883–1909).

Lettres de rois, reines et autres personnages des cours de France et d'Angleterre, depuis Louis VII jusqu'a Henri IV, ed. J.-J. Champollion-Figeac, 2 vols. (Paris, 1839–47).

Lettres-missives originales du chartier de Thouars, ed. Paul Marchegay ([n.p.], 1873).

Lewis, Bernard, 'Kamāl al-Dīn's Biography of Rāshid al-Dīn Sinān', *Arabica: Revue d'études arabes et islamiques* 13 (1966): 225–67.

Linden, Herman Vander, *Itinéraires de Charles, Duc de Bourgogne, Marguerite d'York et Marie de Bourgogne (1467–1477)* (Brussels, 1936).

—— *Itinéraires de Philippe le Bon, Duc de Bourgogne (1419–1467) et de Charles, Comte de Charolais (1433–1467)* (Brussels, 1940).

Los, Johannis de, *Chronicon rerum gestarum ab anno MCCCCLV ad annum MDXIV*, in *Documents relatifs aux troubles du Pays de Liège*, ed. Ram.

Machiavelli, Niccolò, *Art of War*, ed. and trans. Christopher Lynch (Chicago, 2003).

Malaterra, Gaufredo, *De rebus gestis Rogerii Calabriae et Siciliae comitis et Roberti Guiscardi ducis fratris eius*, ed. Ernesto Pontieri (Bologna, 1928).

Matthew of Edessa, *Armenia and the Crusades, Tenth to Twelfth Centuries: The Chronicle of Matthew of Edessa*, ed. and trans. Ara Edmond Dostourian (New York, 1993).

Maupoint, Jean, *Journal parisien de Jean Maupoint, prieur de Sainte-Catherine-de-la-Couture, 1437–1469*, ed. Gustave Fagniez, Mémoires de la Societe de l'histoire de Paris et de l'Île de France 4 (Paris, 1878), pp. 1–113.

Miolo, Gianbernardo, *Cronaca*, in *Miscellanea di storia italiana*, 5 series, 79 vols. (Turin, 1862–1968), series I, vol. I.

Molinet, Jean, *Chroniques de Jean Molinet*, ed. Georges Doutrepont and Omer Jodogne, 3 vols. (Brussels, 1935–7).

Monluc, Blaise de, *Commentaires, 1521–1576*, ed. Paul Courteault (Paris, 1964).

—— *The Habsburg–Valois Wars and the French Wars of Religion*, ed. Ian Roy and trans. Charles Cotton (London, 1971).

Monstrelet, Enguerran de, *La Chronique d'E. de Monstrelet*, ed. L. Douët-d'Arcq, 6 vols. (Paris, 1857–62).

More, Thomas, *Utopia*, trans. Paul Turner (Harmondsworth, 1965).

Muisit, Gilles le, *Chronique et Annales de Gilles le Muisit, abbé de Saint-Martin de Tournai*, ed. Henri Lemaître (Paris, 1906).

Murimuth, Adam, *Adae Murimuth Continuatio Chronicarum: Robertus de Avesbury de gestis mirabilibus Regis Edwardi tertii*, ed. Edward M. Thompson (Nendeln, 1965 [London, 1889]).

Nouvelle collection des mémoires pour servir à l'histoire de France, depuis le XIIIe siècle jusqu'à la fin du XVIIIe, ed. Joseph F. Michaud and Jean J. F. Poujoulat, 3 series, 32 vols. (Paris, 1836–9).

Novare, Philippe of, 'Estoire de la guerre qui fu entre l'empereor Federic & Johan d'Ibelin', in *Gestes des Chiprois*, ed. Raynaud, pp. 25–138.

Onofrio de Santa Croce, *Mémoire du légat Onufrius sur les affaires de Liège*, ed. Stanislas Bormans (Brussels, 1885).

Oudenbosch, Adriaan van, *Chronique d'Adrien d'Oudenbosch*, ed. C. de Borman (Liège, 1902).

Pauwels, Theodoric, *Historia de Cladibus Leodensium*, in *Documents relatifs aux troubles du Pays de Liège*, ed. Ram.

Peter Tudebode, *Historia de Hierosolymitano itinere*, RHC Oc. 3 (Paris, 1866), pp. 3–117.

Pizan, Christine de, *The Book of Deeds of Arms and of Chivalry*, ed. Charity Cannon Willard and trans. Sumner Willard (University Park, 1999).

Polyaenus, *Stratagems of War*, ed. and trans. Peter Krentz and Everett L. Wheeler, 2 vols. (Chicago, 1994).

Primi Belli Sacri Narrationes Minores, RHC Oc. 5 (Paris, 1895), pp. 341–98.

La Prince noir, poème du Héraut d'armes Chandos, ed. Francisque Michel (London, 1883).

Ralph of Caen, *Gesta Tancredi*, RHC Oc. 3 (Paris, 1866), pp. 587–715.

Ralph of Coggeshall, *Chronicon Anglicanum, de Expugnatione terrae Sanctae libellus*, ed. Joseph Stevenson (Nendeln, 1965 [London, 1875]).

Ralph of Diceto, *Radulphi de Diceto Decani Lundoniensis Opera Historica*, ed. William Stubbs, 2 vols. (Nendeln, 1965 [London, 1876]).

Raymond of Aguilers, *Le 'Liber' de Raymond d'Aguilers*, ed. John Hugh and Laurita L. Hill and trans. Philippe Wolff (Paris, 1969).

Récits d'un bourgeois de Valenciennes, ed. Kervyn de Lettenhove (Geneva, 1979 [1877]).

La Regle du Temple, ed. Henri de Curzon (Paris, 1977 [1886]).

Robert the Monk, *Historia Iherosolimitana*, RHC Oc. 3 (Paris, 1866), pp. 717–881.

Rochechouart, Guillaume de, *Mémoires de messire Guillaume de Rochechouart*, in *Nouvelle collection des mémoires*, ed. Michaud and Poujoulat, ser. 1, vol. 8, pp. 597–605.

Roger of Howden, *Chronica Magistri Rogeri de Houedene*, ed. William Stubbs, 4 vols. (Nendeln, 1964 [London, 1868–71]).

Rotuli Scotiae, ed. David Macpherson, John Caley and William Illingworth, 2 vols. (London, 1814–19).

Roye, Jean de, *Journal de Jean de Roye, connu sous le nom de chronique scandaleuse, 1460–1483*, ed. Bernard de Mandrot, 2 vols. (Paris, 1894–6).

Rymer, Thomas, *Foedera, Conventiones, literae, et Cujuscunque generis Acta publica inter Reges Angliae …*, 3rd edn, 40 vols. in 10 parts (Farnborough, 1967 [Hague, 1739–45].

Sandoval, Fray Prudencio de, *Historia de la Vida y Hechos del Emperador Carlos V: Maximo, Fortisimo, Rey catolico de Esoana y de las Indias, Islas y tierra firme del Mar Oceano*, ed. Carlos Seco Serrando, Biblioteca des Autores Españoles 80–82 (Madrid, 1955–6).

Schertlin, Sebastian von Burtenbach, *Leben und Thaten des weiland wohledlen und gestrengen Herrn Sebastian Schertlin von Burtenbach, durch ihn selbst deutsch beschrieben*, ed. Ottmar F. H. Schönhuth (Münster, 1858).

Schilling, Diebold, *Die Berner Chronik des Diebold Schilling*, ed. Gustav Tobler, 2 vols. (Bern, 1897–1901).

Sharon, Ariel and David Chanoff, *Warrior: The Autobiography of Ariel Sharon* (New York, 1989).

Speierische Chronik, 1406–1476, in *Quellensammlung der badischen Landesgeschichte*, ed. F. J. Mone, 4 vols. (Karlsruhe, 1848–67), 1:367–520.

Stephani, comitis Carnotensis, ad Adelam, uxorem suam, epistolae, RHC Oc. 3 (Paris, 1866), pp. 885–90.

Tavannes, Jean de Saulx, Viscount of, *Mémoires de tres-noble et tres-illustre Gaspard de Saulx, seigneur de Tavanes …*, in *Nouvelle collection des mémoires*, ed. Michaud and Poujoulat, ser. 1, vol. 8, pp. 1–434.

Three Byzantine Military Treatises, ed. and trans. George T. Dennis (Washington, DC, 1985).

Usāmah ibn-Munqidh, *Kitāb al-I'tibār: An Arab-Syrian Gentleman & Warrior in the Period of the Crusades, Memoires of Usamah Ibn-Munkidh*, trans. Philip K. Hitti (New York, 2000).

Valbelle, Honorat de, *Histoire journalière d'Honorat de Valbelle (1498–1539): journal d'un bourgeois de Marseille au temps de Louis XII et de François Ier*, ed. Victor-Louis Bourrilly, Roger Duchêne, Lucien Gaillard and Charles Rostaing, 2 vols. (Aix-en-Provence, 1985).

Vegetius, *Epitome of Military Science*, ed. and trans. N. P. Milner (Liverpool, 1993).

Venette, Jean de, *The Chronicle of Jean de Venette*, ed. Richard A. Newhall and trans. Jean Birdsall (New York, 1953).

Vieilleville, François de Scepeaux, Lord of, *Mémoires de la vie de François de Scepeaux, sire de Vieilleville et Comte de Durestal, Mareschal de France*, in *Nouvelle collection des mémoires*, ed. Michaud and Poujoulat, ser. 1, vol. 9.

Vitalis, Ordericus, *The Ecclesiastical History of Orderic Vitalis*, ed. and trans. Marjorie Chibnall, 6 vols. (Oxford, 1969–79).

Walsingham, Thomas, *Historia Anglicana*, ed. Henry T. Riley, 2 vols. (New York, 1965 [London, 1863–4]).

Walter of Coventry, *Memoriale Fratris Walteri de Coventria*, ed. William Stubbs, 2 vols. (Nendeln, 1965 [London, 1872–83]).

Wavrin, Jehan de, *Recueil des croniques et Anchiennes Istories de la grant Bretaigne, a present nommee Engleterre*, ed. William Hardy, 5 vols. (London, 1864–91).

William of Apulia, *La Geste de Robert Guiscard*, ed. Margerite Mathieu (Palermo, 1961).

William of Tyre, *La Continuation de Guillaume de Tyr, 1184–1197*, ed. Margaret Ruth Morgan (Paris, 1982).

—— *Historia rerum in partibus transmarinis gestarum*, RHC Oc. 1–2 (Paris, 1844).

Wyntoun, Andrew of, *Androw of Wyntoun's Orygynale Cronykil of Scotland*, ed. David Laing, 3 vols. (Edinburgh, 1872–9).

Secondary Sources

Alban, J. R., and Christopher T. Allmand, 'Spies and Spying in the Fourteenth Century', in *War, Literature and Politics in the Late Middle Ages*, ed. Christopher T. Allmand (Liverpool, 1976), pp. 73–101.

Allmand, Christopher T., 'Intelligence in the Hundred Years War', in *Go Spy the Land: Military Intelligence in History*, ed. Keith Neilson and B. J. C. McKercher (Westport, 1992), pp. 31–47.

—— (ed.), *Society at War: The Experience of England and France during the Hundred Years War* (Rochester, 1998).

Amitai, Reuven, 'Mamluk Espionage among Mongols and Franks', in *The Medieval Levant: Studies in Memory of Eliyahu Ashtor (1914–1982)*, ed. Benjamin Z. Kedar and Abraham K. Udovitch, Asia and Africa Studies 22 (Haifa, 1988), pp. 173–81.

Anglo, Sydney (ed.), *Chivalry in the Renaissance* (Woodbridge, 1990).

Archer, John Michael, *Sovereignty and Intelligence: Spying and Court Culture in the English Renaissance* (Stanford, 1993).

Arnold, Thomas F., 'Fortifications and the Military Revolution: The Gonzaga Experience, 1530–1630', in *The Military Revolution Debate: Readings on the Military Transformation of Early Modern Europe*, ed. Clifford J. Rogers (Boulder, 1995), pp. 201–26.

——'War in Sixteenth-Century Europe: Revolution and Renaissance', in *European Warfare, 1453–1815*, ed. Jeremy Black (New York, 1999), pp. 23–44.

Arquilla, John (ed.), *From Troy to Entebbe: Special Operations in Ancient and Modern Times* (Lanham, 1996).

Arthurson, Ian, 'Espionage and Intelligence from the Wars of the Roses to the Reformation', *Nottingham Medieval Studies* 35 (1991): 134–54.

Asbridge, Thomas S., *The Creation of the Principality of Antioch, 1098–1130* (Woodbridge, 2000).

——*The First Crusade: A New History* (Oxford, 2004).

Ayton, Andrew, 'English Armies in the Fourteenth Century', in *Arms, Armies and Fortifications in the Hundred Years War*, ed. Anne Curry and Michael Hughes (Woodbridge, 1994), pp. 21–38.

Bachrach, Bernard S., 'Logistics in Pre-Crusade Europe', in *Feeding Mars: Logistics in Western Warfare from the Middle Ages to the Present*, ed. John A. Lynn (Boulder, 1993), pp. 57–78.

——'Medieval Siege Warfare: A Reconnaissance', *Journal of Military History* 58 no. 1 (1994): 119–33.

——'The Siege of Antioch: A Study in Military Demography', *War in History* 6 no. 2 (1999): 127–46.

Bachrach, David Steward, 'The Military Administration of England: The Royal Artillery (1216–1272)', *Journal of Military History* 68 no. 4 (2004): 1083–1104.

——'Origins of the Crossbow Industry in England', *Journal of Medieval Military History* 2 (2003): 73–88.

Barnett, Frank R., B. Hugh Tovar and Richard H. Shultz (eds.), *Special Operations in US Strategy* (Washington, DC, 1984).

Bartlett, W. B., *The Assassins: The Story of Medieval Islam's Secret Sect* (Phoenix Mill, 2001).

Beaune, Colette, *The Birth of an Ideology: Myths and Symbols of Nation in Late-Medieval France*, ed. Fredric L. Cheyette and trans. Susan Ross Huston (Berkeley, 1991).

Bittmann, K., *Ludwig XI und Karl der Kühne: die Memoiren des Philippe de Commynes als historische Quelle* (Göttingen, 1964–70).

Black, Jeremy, *European Warfare, 1494–1660* (London, 2002).

—— 'Introduction', in *The Origins of War in Early Modern Europe*, ed. Jeremy Black (Edinburgh, 1987), pp. 1–27.

—— *Why Wars Happen* (New York, 1998).

Bohrer, David, *America's Special Forces* (Osceola, 1998).

Bonenfant, Paul, *Philippe le Bon: sa politique, son action* (Brussels, 1996).

—— and Jean Stengers, 'Le rôle de Charles le Téméraire dans le gouvernment de l'état bourguignon en 1465–1467', *Annales de Bourgogne* 25 (1953): 7–29, 118–33.

Bouche, Honoré, *La chorographie ou description de Provence et l'histoire chronologique du mesme pays*, 2 vols. (Aix, 1664).

Bouchier, E. S., *A Short History of Antioch, 300 B.C. – A.D. 1268* (Oxford, 1921).

Boulton, D'Arcy D. J., *The Knights of the Crown: The Monarchical Orders of Knighthood in Later Medieval Europe, 1325–1520* (New York, 1987).

Bricard, Georges, *Un serviteur et compère de Louis XI: Jean Bourré, seigneur du Plessis, 1424–1506* (Paris, 1893).

Bradbury, Jim, *The Medieval Siege* (Woodbridge, 1992).

—— *Philip Augustus: King of France, 1180–1223* (London, 1998).

Braudy, Leo, *From Chivalry to Terrorism: War and the Changing Nature of Masculinity* (New York, 2003).

Brown, Gordon S., *The Norman Conquest of Southern Italy and Sicily* (Jefferson, 2003).

Brown, Reginald A., Howard M. Colvin and Alfred J. Taylor, *The History of the King's Works*, vols. 1–2: *The Middle Ages* (London, 1963).

Brundage, James A., *Richard Lion Heart* (New York, 1974).

Bully, Philippe, *Charles VII: le 'Roi des merveilles'* (Paris, 1994).

Burne, Alfred Higgins, *The Agincourt War: A Military History of the Latter Part of the Hundred Years War, from 1369 to 1453* (London, 1956).

Burns, Robert I., '100,000 Crossbow Bolts for the Crusader King of Aragon', *Journal of Medieval Military History* 2 (2004): 159–64.

Cahen, Claude, *La Syrie du nord à l'époque des croisades et de la principauté franque d'Antioche* (Paris, 1940).

Cauchies, Jean-Marie, *Louis XI et Charles le Hardi: de Peronne à Nancy (1468–1477): le conflit* (Brussels, 1996).

Cazelles, Raymond, *Société politique, noblesse et couronne sous Jean le Bon et Charles V* (Paris, 1982).

Chase, Kenneth Warren, *Firearms: A Global History to 1700* (Cambridge, 2003).

Chaunu, Pierre, and Michele Escamilla, *Charles Quint* (Paris, 2000).

Chevedden, Paul E., 'Fortifications and the Development of Defensive Planning in the Latin East', in *The Circle of War in the Middle Ages: Essays on Medieval Military and Naval History*, ed. Donald J. Kagay and L. J. Andrew Villalon (Woodbridge, 1999), pp. 33–44.

——, Les Eigenbrod, Vernard L. Foley and Werner Soedel, 'The Trebuchet', *Scientific American* 273 no. 1 (July 1995): 66–71.

Collard, Franck, 'L'Assassinat manqué de Charles le Téméraire', *L'Histoire* 165 (April 1993): 6–11.

Contamine, Philippe, 'Les compagnies d'aventure en France pendant la guerre de Cent ans', *Mélanges de l'École française de Rome, Moyen Age, Temps modernes* 87 (1975): 365–96.

——'Geoffroy de Charny (début du xiv⁰ siècle–1356), "Le plus prudhomme et le plus vaillant de tous les autres"', in *Histoire et société: Mélanges Georges Duby, II, Le tenancier, le fidèle et le citoyen*, ed. J. J. N. Palmer (Aix-en-Provence, 1992), pp. 107–21.

—— *War in the Middle Ages*, trans. Michael Jones (New York, 1984).

Courteault, Paul, *Blaise de Monluc historien: étude critique sur le texte et la valeur historique des Commentaires* (Paris, 1908).

Crawford, Steve, *The SAS Encyclopedia* (Miami, 1998).

Crook, David, 'The Confession of a Spy, 1380', *Historical Research* 62 (1989): 346–50.

Daftary, Farhad, *The Assassin Legends: Myths of the Isma'ilis* (London, 1994).

Dahl, Per F., *Heavy Water and the Wartime Race for Nuclear Energy* (Bristol, 1999).

Dam, Poul, *Niels Bohr (1885–1962): Atomic Theorist, Inspirator, Rallying Point*, trans. Gitte and Norman Shine (Copenhagen, 1987).

Davies, R. R., *The Age of Conquest: Wales, 1063–1415* (Oxford, 1987).

Davis, Alex, *Chivalry and Romance in the English Renaissance*, Studies in Renaissance Literature 11 (Cambridge, 2003).

Dawson, Graham, *Soldier Heroes: British Adventure, Empire, and the Imagining of Masculinities* (London, 1994).

Day, J. F. R., 'Losing One's Character: Heralds and the Decline of English Knighthood from the Later Middle Ages to James I', in *Chivalry, Knighthood, and War in the Middle Ages*, ed. Susan J. Ridyard, Sewanee Mediaeval Studies 9 (Sewanee, 1999), pp. 97–116.

Decrue de Stoutz, Francis, *Anne de Montmorency, grand maître et connétable de France: à la cour, aux armées, et au conseil du roi François Iᵉʳ* (Geneva, 1978).

DeVries, Kelly, 'Catapults are not Atomic Bombs: Towards a Redefinition of "Effectiveness" in Premodern Military Technology', *War in History* 4 no. 1 (1997): 454–70.

——'Gunpowder and Early Gunpowder Weapons', in *Gunpowder: The History of an International Technology*, ed. Brenda Buchanan (Bath, 1996), pp. 121–35.

——'Gunpowder Weaponry and the Rise of the Early Modern State', *War in History* 5 no. 2 (1998): 127–45.

——'Gunpowder Weapons at the Siege of Constantinople, 1453', in *War and Society in the Eastern Mediterranean, 7th–15th Centuries*, ed. Yaacov Lev (Leiden, 1997), pp. 343–62.

——'Hunger, Flemish Participation and the Flight of Philip VI: Contemporary Accounts of the Siege of Calais, 1346–1347', *Studies in Medieval and Renaissance History* 12 (1991): 133–79.

——'The Impact of Gunpowder Weaponry on Siege Warfare in the Hundred Years War', in *The Medieval City under Siege*, ed. Ivy A. Corfis and Michael Wolfe (Woodbridge, 1995), pp. 227–44.

——*Infantry Warfare in the Early Fourteenth Century: Discipline, Tactics, and Technology* (Woodbridge, 1996).

——*Medieval Military Technology* (Peterborough, 1992).

——'The Technology of Gunpowder Weaponry in Western Europe during the Hundred Years War', in *XXII. Kongress der Internationalen Kommission für Militärgeschichte Acta 22: Von Crécy bis Mohács Kriegswesen im späten Mittelalter (1346–1526)* (Vienna, 1997), pp. 285–98.

——'The Use of Gunpowder Weaponry by and against Joan of Arc during the Hundred Years War', *War and Society* 14 (1996): 1–15.

Dewald, Jonathan, *Aristocratic Experience and the Origins of Modern Culture: France, 1570–1715* (Berkeley, 1993).

Dockery, Kevin, and Elaine Abbrecht, *Special Forces in Action: Missions, OPS, Weapons, and Combat, Day by Day* (New York, 2004).

Doig, James A., 'A New Source for the Siege of Calais in 1436', *English Historical Review* 110 (1995): 405–16.

Dufayard, Charles, *Histoire de Savoie* (Paris, 1930).

Duffy, Christopher, *Siege Warfare: The Fortress in the Early Modern World, 1494–1660* (London, 1997).

Dufournet, Jean, *La destruction des mythes dans les Mémoires de Ph. de Commynes* (Genève, 1966).

Dunnigan, James F., *The Perfect Soldier: Special Operations, Commandos, and the Future of U.S. Warfare* (New York, 2003).

Dvornik, Francis, *Origins of Intelligence Services: The Ancient Near East, Persia, Greece, Rome, Byzantium, the Arab Muslim Empires, the Mongol Empire, China, Muscovy* (New Brunswick, 1974).

Edgington, Susan B., 'Albert of Aachen and the *Chansons de Geste*', in *The Crusades and their Sources: Essays Presented to Bernard Hamilton*, ed. John France and William G. Zajac (Aldershot, 1998), pp. 23–38.

El-Azhari, Taef Kamal, *The Saljūqs of Syria: During the Crusades, 463–549 A.H./1070–1154 A.D.* (Berlin, 1997).

Ellenblum, Ronnie, 'Frankish and Muslim Siege Warfare and the Construction of Frankish Concentric Castles', in *Dei gesta per Francos: Études sur les Croisades dédiées à Jean Richard*, ed. M. Balard, J. Riley-Smith and B. Z. Kedar (Aldershot, 2001), pp. 211–22.

——*Frankish Rural Settlement in the Latin Kingdom of Jerusalem* (Cambridge, 1998).

——'Were there Borders and Borderlines in the Middle Ages? The Example of the Latin Kingdom of Jerusalem', in *Medieval Frontiers: Concepts and Practices*, ed. David Abulafia and Nora Berend (Aldershot, 2002), pp. 105–19.

Eltis, David, *The Military Revolution in Sixteenth-Century Europe* (London, 1995).

Emerson, Catherine, *Olivier de la Marche and the Rhetoric of Fifteenth-Century Historiography* (Woodbridge, 2004).

Fairon, Emile, 'Les six cents Franchimontois', *Wallonia* 22 (1914): 136–55.

Fallows, Noel, 'Knighthood, Wounds, and the Chivalric Ideal', in *Chivalry, Knighthood, and War in the Middle Ages*, ed. Susan J. Ridyard, Sewanee Mediaeval Studies 9 (Sewanee, 1999), pp. 117–36.

Favier, Jean, *Louis XI* (Paris, 2001).

Ferguson, Arthur B., *The Chivalric Tradition in Renaissance England* (Washington, DC, 1986).

Ford, Franklin L., *Political Murder: From Tyrannicide to Terrorism* (Cambridge, MA, 1985).

Fowler, Kenneth, *Medieval Mercenaries*, vol. 1: *The Great Companies* (Oxford, 2001).

France, John, 'The Anonymous *Gesta Francorum* and the *Historia Francorum qui ceperunt Iherusalem* of Raymond of Aguilers and the *Historia Hierosolymitano itinere* of Peter Tudebode: An Analysis of the Textual Relations between Primary Sources of the First Crusade', in *The Crusades and their Sources: Essays Presented to Bernard Hamilton*, ed. John France and William G. Zajac (Aldershot, 1998), pp. 39–70.

——'The Departure of Tatikios from the army of the First Crusade', *Bulletin of the Institute of Historical Research* 44 (1971): 131–47.

——'The Fall of Antioch during the First Crusade', in *Dei Gesta per Francos: Études sur les croisades dédiées à Jean Richard*, ed. Michel Balard, Benjamin Z. Kedar and Jonathan Riley-Smith (Aldershot, 2001), pp. 13–20.

——'Recent Writing on Medieval Warfare: From the Fall of Rome to c. 1300', *Journal of Military History* 65 no. 2 (2001): 441–73.

—— *Victory in the East: A Military History of the First Crusade* (Cambridge, 1994).

—— *Western Warfare in the Age of the Crusades, 1000–1300* (Ithaca, 1999).

François, Michel, *Le Cardinal François de Tournon: homme d'état, diplomate, mécène et humaniste (1489–1562)* (Paris, 1951).

Friedman, Yvonne, *Encounter between Enemies: Captivity and Ransom in the Latin Kingdom of Jerusalem* (Leiden, 2002).

——'Women in Captivity and their Ransom during the Crusader Period', in *Cross Cultural Covergences in the Crusader Period: Essays Presented to Aryeh Grabois on his Sixty-fifth Birthday*, ed. Michael Goodich, Sophia Menache and Sylvia Schein (New York, 1995), pp. 75–87.

Gabotto, Ferdinando, *Lo stato sabaudo da Amedeo VIII ad Emanuele Filiberto*, 3 vols. (Turin, 1892–5).

Geary, Patrick J., *Furta Sacra: Thefts of Relics in the Central Middle Ages* (Princeton, 1978).

Ghazarian, Jacob G., *The Armenian Kingdom in Cilicia During the Crusades: The Integration of Cilician Armenians with the Latins, 1080–1393* (Richmond, 2000).

Gillingham, John, *Richard Cœur de Lion: Kingship, Chivalry and War in the Twelfth Century* (London, 1994).

—— *Richard I* (New Haven, 1999).

——'Richard I and the Science of War in the Middle Ages', in Gillingham, *Richard Cœur de Lion*, pp. 211–26.

——'The Unromantic Death of Richard I', *Speculum* 54 (1979): 18–41.

——'"Up with Orthodoxy!": In Defense of Vegetian Warfare', *Journal of Medieval Military History* 2 (2004): 149–58.

——'War and Chivalry in the *History of William the Marshal*', in Gillingham, *Richard Cœur de Lion*, pp. 227–42.

——'William the Bastard at War', in *Studies in History Presented to R. Allen Brown*, ed. C. Harper-Bill, J. Holdsworth and J. Nelson (Woodbridge, 1986), pp. 141–58.

Glete, Jan, *War and the State in Early Modern Europe: Spain, the Dutch Republic and Sweden as Fiscal-Military States, 1500–1660* (London, 2002).

Goodman, Jennifer R., *Chivalry and Exploration, 1298–1630* (Woodbridge, 1998).

Grant, Alexander, *Independence and Nationhood: Scotland, 1306–1469*, The New History of Scotland 3 (London, 1984).

Groebner, Valentin, *Defaced: The Visual Culture of Violence in the Late Middle Ages*, trans. Pamela Selwyn (New York, 2004).

Grummitt, David, 'The Financial Administration of Calais during the Reign of Henry IV, 1399–1413', *English Historical Review* 113 (1998): 277–99.

Guichonnet, Paul, *Histoire de Genève*, 3rd edn (Toulouse, 1986).

Gunn, Steven, 'The French Wars of Henry VIII', in *The Origins of War in Early Modern Europe*, ed. Jeremy Black (Edinburgh, 1987), pp. 28–51.

Hale, John R., *War and Society in Renaissance Europe, 1450–1620*, 2nd edn (Guernsey, 1998).

Hall, Bert S., 'The Changing Face of Siege Warfare: Technology and Tactics in Transition', in *The Medieval City under Siege*, ed. Ivy A. Corfis and Michael Wolfe (Woodbridge, 1995), pp. 257–76.

—— *Weapons and Warfare in Renaissance Europe: Gunpowder, Technology, and Tactics*, Johns Hopkins Studies in the History of Technology 22 (Baltimore, 1997).

Hamilton, Ian R., *No Stone Unturned: The Story of the Stone of Destiny …* (London, 1952).

Harari, Yuval Noah, 'The Concept of "Decisive Battles" in World History', *Journal of World History* [forthcoming].

—— 'Inter-Frontal Cooperation in the Fourteenth Century and Edward III's 1346 Campaign', *War in History* 6 no. 4 (1999): 379–95.

—— 'Martial Illusions: War and Disillusionment in Twentieth-Century and Renaissance Military Memoirs', *Journal of Military History* 69 no. 1 (2005): 43–72.

—— 'The Military Role of the Frankish Turcopoles: A Reassessment', *Mediterranean Historical Review* 12 no. 1 (1997): 75–116.

—— *Renaissance Military Memoirs: War, History and Identity, 1450–1600* (Woodbridge, 2004).

—— 'Strategy and Supply in Fourteenth-Century Western European Invasion Campaigns', *Journal of Military History* 64 no. 2 (2000): 297–334.

Harclerode, Peter, *Fighting Dirty: The Inside Story of Covert Operations from Ho Chi Minh to Osama Bin Laden* (London, 2001).

—— *Secret Soldiers: Special Forces in the War against Terrorism* (London, 2001).

Harriss, G. L., 'The Struggle for Calais: An Aspect of the Rivalry between Lancaster and York', *English Historical Review* 75 (1960): 30–53.

Haynes, Alan, *Invisible Power: The Elizabethan Secret Services, 1570–1603* (Stroud, 1992).

Hewitt, Herbert J., 'The Organisation of War', in *The Wars of Edward III: Sources and Interpretations*, ed. Clifford J. Rogers (Woodbridge, 1999), pp. 285–302.

—— *The Organization of War under Edward III, 1338–62* (Manchester, 1966).

Hindley, Geoffrey, *Saladin* (London, 1976).

Hodgson, Frances Coterrell, *The Early History of Venice from the Foundation to the Conquest of Constantinopole*, A.D. 1204 (London, 1901).

Howard, Michael E., *The Causes of Wars and Other Essays* (Cambridge, MA, 1983).

—— *Weapons and Peace* (London, 1983).

Isaac, Steven, 'The Problem with Mercenaries', in *The Circle of War in the Middle Ages: Essays on Medieval Military and Naval History*, ed. Donald J. Kagay and L. J. Andrew Villalon (Woodbridge, 1999), pp. 101–10.

Jackson, Richard A., *Vive le Roi! A History of the French Coronation from Charles V to Charles X* (Chapel Hill, 1984).

Janowitz, Morris, and Edward A. Shils, 'Cohesion and Disintegration in the Wehrmacht in World War II', *Public Opinion Quarterly* 12 no. 2 (1948), 280–313.

Jones, Richard L. C., 'Fortifications and Sieges in Western Europe, c.800–1450', in *Medieval Warfare: A History*, ed. Maurice H. Keen (Oxford, 1999), pp. 163–85.

Kagay, Donald J., 'A Shattered Circle: Eastern Spanish Fortifications and their Repair during the "Calamitous Fourteenth Century"', *Journal of Medieval Military History* 2 (2004): 111–36.

Kaeuper, Richard W., *Chivalry and Violence in Medieval Europe* (Oxford, 1999).

Kedar, Benjamin Z., *Crusade and Mission: European Approaches toward the Muslims* (Princeton, 1984).

—— 'The Subjected Muslims of the Frankish Levant', in *Muslims under Latin Rule, 1100–1300*, ed. James M. Powell (Princeton, 1990), pp. 135–74.

Keegan, John, *A History of Warfare* (New York, 1993).

Keen, Maurice H., 'The Changing Scene: Guns, Gunpowder, and Permanent Armies', in *Medieval Warfare: A History*, ed. Maurice H. Keen (Oxford, 1999), pp. 273–92.

—— *Chivalry* (New Haven, 1984).

—— 'Chivalry, Nobility and the Man-at-Arms', in *War, Literature and Politics in the Late Middle Ages*, ed. Christopher T. Allmand (Liverpool, 1976), pp. 32–45.

——'Huizinga, Kilgour and the Decline of Chivalry', *Medievalia et Humanistica* new ser. 8 (1977): 1–20.

—— *The Laws of War in the Late Middle Ages* (London, 1965).

Kendall, Paul M., *Louis XI* (London, 1971).

Kiras, James D., *Rendering the Mortal Blow Easier: Special Operations and the Nature of Strategy* (Reading, 2004).

Klein, Aaron J., *Striking Back: The 1972 Munich Olympics Massacre and Israel's Deadly Response*, trans. Mitch Ginsburg (New York, 2005).

Knecht, R. J., *Renaissance Warrior and Patron: The Reign of Francis I* (Cambridge, 1994).

Kurth, Godefroid J. F., *La cité de Liège au Moyen Âge*, 3 vols. (Brussels, 1910).

La Monte, John L., *Feudal Monarchy in the Latin Kingdom of Jerusalem, 1100 to 1291*, Monographs of the Medieval Academy of America 4 (Cambridge, MA, 1932).

Landau, Alan M., et al., *U.S. Special Forces: Airborne Rangers, Delta & U.S. Navy SEALs* (Osceola, 1999).

Le Cam, Anne, *Charles le Téméraire: un homme et son rêve* (Ozoir-la-Ferriere, 1992).

Le Gras, Joseph, *Blaise de Monluc: héros malchanceux et grand écrivain: portraits et documents inédits* (Paris, 1926).

Lewis, Bernard, *The Assassins: A Radical Sect in Islam* (New York, 1968).

Lockhart, James, *The Men of Cajamarca: A Social and Biographical Study of the First Conquerors of Peru*, Latin American Monographs (ILAS) 27 (Austin, 1972).

Loud, G. A., *The Age of Robert Guiscard: Southern Italy and the Norman Conquest* (Harlow, 2000).

Luard, Evan, *War in International Society: A Study in International Sociology* (London, 1986).

Lynn, John A., *Bayonets of the Republic: Motivation and Tactics in the Army of Revolutionary France, 1791–94* (Boulder, 1996 [Urbana, 1984]).

—— *Giant of the Grand Siècle: The French Army, 1610–1715* (Cambridge, 1997).

——'The *trace italienne* and the Growth of Armies: The French Case', in *The Military Revolution Debate: Readings on the Military Transformation of Early Modern Europe*, ed. Clifford J. Rogers (Boulder, 1995), pp. 169–200.

McCormack, John, *One Million Mercenaries: Swiss Soldiers in the Armies of the World* (London, 1993).

McGlynn, Sean, 'The Myths of Medieval Warfare', *History Today* 44 no. 1 (1994), 28–34.

McRaven, William H., *Spec Ops: Case Studies in Special Operations Warfare: Theory and Practice* (Novato, 1996).

Maleissye, Jean de, *Histoire du poison* (Paris, 1991).

Mallett, Michael, 'Mercenaries', in *Medieval Warfare: A History*, ed. Maurice H. Keen (Oxford, 1999), pp. 209–29.

—— 'Siegecraft in Late Fifteenth-Century Italy', in *The Medieval City under Siege*, ed. Ivy A. Corfis and Michael Wolfe (Woodbridge, 1995), pp. 245–56.

Mandrot, Bernard de, 'Jean de Bourgogne, duc de Brabant, comte de Nevers et le procès de sa succession', *Revue Historique* 93 (1907): 1–44.

Marquis, Susan Lynn, *Unconventional Warfare: Rebuilding U.S. Special Operations Forces* (Washington, DC, 1997).

Marshall, Christopher, *Warfare in the Latin East, 1192–1291* (Cambridge, 1992).

Marshall, Samuel Lyman A., *Men against Fire: The Problem of Battle Command in Future War* (Gloucester, MA, 1978 [Washington, DC, 1947]).

Mayer, Hans Eberhard, *The Crusades*, trans. John Gillingham, 2nd edn (Oxford, 1990).

Mirza, Nasih Ahmad, *Syrian Ismailism: The Ever Living Line of the Imamate, AD 1100–1260* (Richmond, UK, 1997).

Molin, Kristian, 'The Non-Military Functions of Crusader Fortifications, 1187 – c. 1390', *Journal of Medieval History* 23 (1997): 367–88.

Morillo, Stephen, 'Battle Seeking: The Contexts and Limits of Vegetian Strategy', *Journal of Medieval Military History* 1 (2002): 21–41.

—— *Warfare under the Anglo-Norman Kings, 1066–1135* (Woodbridge, 1994).

Morris, John E., *The Welsh Wars of Edward I: A Contribution to Mediaeval Military History, Based on Original Documents* (New York, 1969 [1901]).

Mott, Lawrence V., 'The Battle of Malta, 1283: Prelude to a Disaster', in *The Circle of War in the Middle Ages: Essays on Medieval Military and Naval History*, ed. Donald J. Kagay and L. J. Andrew Villalon (Woodbridge, 1999), pp. 145–72.

Munro, John H., 'An Economic Aspect of the Collapse of the Anglo-Burgundian Alliance, 1428–1442', *English Historical Review* 85 (1970): 225–44.

Murray, Alan V., '"Mighty Against the Enemies of Christ": The Relic of the True Cross in the Armies of the Kingdom of Jerusalem', in *The Crusades and their Sources: Essays Presented to Bernard Hamilton*, ed. John France and William G. Zajac (Aldershot, 1998), pp. 217–38.

Neillands, Robin, *The Hundred Years War* (London, 1991).

—— *In the Combat Zone: Special Forces since 1945* (New York, 1998).

Newsinger, John, *Dangerous Men: The SAS and Popular Culture* (London, 1997).

Nicholson, Helen, *Medieval Warfare: Theory and Practice of War in Europe, 300–1500* (New York, 2004).

Nicholson, Ranald Grange, *Scotland: The Later Middle Ages* (Edinburgh, 1974).

Nicholson, Robert L., *Joscelyn I, Prince of Edessa*, Illinois Studies in the Social Sciences 34.4 (Urbana, 1954).

——*Joscelyn III and the Fall of the Crusader States, 1134–1199* (Leiden, 1973).

Norwich, John J., *The Normans in the South, 1016–1130* (London, 1967).

—— *Venice: The Rise to Empire* (London, 1977).

Oman, Charles W. C., *A History of the Art of War in the Middle Ages*, 2 vols. (London, 1991 [1924]).

—— *A History of the Art of War in the Sixteenth Century* (London, 1937).

Paravicini, W., *Guy de Brimeu: der burgundische Staat und seine adlige Führungsschicht unter Karl der Kühnen* (Bonn, 1975).

—— *Karl der Kühne: das Ende des Hauses Burgund* (Göttingen, 1976).

Paris, Michael, *Warrior Nation: Images of War in British Popular Culture, 1850–2000* (London, 2000).

Parker, Geoffrey, *The Army of Flanders and the Spanish Road, 1567–1659: The Logistics of Spanish Victory and Defeat in the Low Countries' Wars* (Cambridge, 1975).

—— *The Military Revolution: Military Innovation and the Rise of the West, 1500–1800* (Cambridge, 1988).

——'The Military Revolution, 1560–1660 – a Myth?', in *The Military Revolution Debate: Readings on the Military Transformation of Early Modern Europe*, ed. Clifford J. Rogers (Boulder, 1995), pp. 37–54.

——'The Political World of Charles V', in *Charles V 1500–1558 and his Time*, ed. Hugo Soly *et al.*, trans. Suzanne Walters *et al.* (Antwerp, 1999), pp. 113–226, 513–19.

Parrott, David, *Richelieu's Army: War, Government, and Society in France, 1624–1642* (Cambridge, 2001).

Parrott, David A., 'Strategy and Tactics in the Thirty Years' War: The "Military Revolution"', in *The Military Revolution Debate: Readings on the Military Transformation of Early Modern Europe*, ed. Clifford J. Rogers (Boulder, 1995), pp. 227–52.

Payne, Robert, *The Crusades: A History* (Ware, 1998 [1994]).

Perjés, G., 'Army Provisioning, Logistics, and Strategy in the Second Half of the Seventeenth Century', *Acta Historica Academiae Scientiarum Hungaricae* 16 (1970): 1–52.

Perret, Paul-Michel, *Histoire des relations de la France avec Venise: du XIIIe siècle a l'avènement de Charles VIII*, 2 vols. (Paris, 1896).

Pipes, Daniel, *Slave Soldiers and Islam: The Genesis of a Military System* (New Haven, 1981).

Plancher, Urbain, *Histoire générale et particulière de Bourgogne …*, 4 vols. (Dijon, 1739–81).

Potter, David, 'The duc de Guise and the Fall of Calais, 1557–1558', *English Historical Review* 98 (1983): 481–512.

Pounds, Norman J. G., *The Medieval Castle in England and Wales: A Social and Political History* (Cambridge, 1990).

Power, Eileen, 'The English Wool Trade in the Reign of Edward IV', *Cambridge Historical Journal* 2 (1926): 17–35.

Powers, James F., 'Life on the Cutting Edge: The Besieged Town on the Luso-Hispanic Frontier in the Twelfth Century', in *The Medieval City under Siege*, ed. Ivy A. Corfis and Michael Wolfe (Woodbridge, 1995), pp. 17–34.

Prawer, Joshua, *A History of the Latin Kingdom of Jerusalem*, 3 vols. (Jerusalem, 1984 [Hebrew]).

Prestwich, J. O., 'Military Intelligence under the Norman and Angevin Kings', in *Law and Government in Medieval England and Normandy: Essays in Honour of Sir James Holt*, ed. George Garnett and John Hudson (Cambridge, 1994), pp. 1–30.

Prestwich, Michael, *Armies and Warfare in the Middle Ages: The English Experience* (New Haven, 1996).

—— *The Three Edwards: War and State in England, 1272–1377* (London, 1980).

—— *War, Politics and Finance under Edward I* (Totowa, 1972).

Pringle, Denys, 'Town Defences in the Crusader Kingdom of Jerusalem', in *The Medieval City under Siege*, ed. Ivy A. Corfis and Michael Wolfe (Woodbridge, 1995), pp. 69–122.

Procacci, G., 'La Provence à la veille des Guerres de Religion: une periode décisive, 1535–1545', *Revue d'histoire modern et contemporaine* 5 (1958): 241–64.

Redlich, Fritz, *The German Military Enterpriser and his Work Force: A Study in European Economic and Social History*, vol. 1 (Weisbaden, 1964).

Rice, Tamara Talbot, *The Seljuks in Asia Minor* (London, 1961).

Richard, Jean, *The Crusades, c. 1071 – c. 1291*, trans. Jean Birrell (Cambridge, 1999).

——'Philippe Auguste, la croisade et le royaume', in *Croisés, missionaires et voyageurs: les perspectives orientales du monde latin medieval*, ed. Jean Richard (London, 1983), pp. 411–24.

Riley-Smith, Jonathan, 'Casualties and the Number of Knights on the First Crusade', *Crusades* 1 (2002): 13–28.

—— *The First Crusade and the Idea of Crusading* (London, 1986).

—— *The First Crusaders, 1095–1131* (Cambridge, 1997).

——'Raymond IV of St Gilles, Achard of Arles and the Conquest of Lebanon', in *The Crusades and Their Sources: Essays Presented to Bernard Hamilton*, ed. John France and William G. Zajac (Aldershot, 1998), pp. 1–8.

Roberts, Michael, 'The Military Revolution, 1560–1660: An Inaugural Lecture Delivered before the Queen's University of Belfast', in *The Military Revolution Debate: Readings on the Military Transformation of Early Modern Europe*, ed. Clifford J. Rogers (Boulder, 1995), pp. 13–35.

Robertson, William, *The History of the Reign of the Emperor Charles the Fifth*, 2 vols. (Philadelphia, 1890).

Rogers, Clifford J., 'The Vegetian "Science of Warfare" in the Middle Ages', *Journal of Medieval Military History* 1 (2002): 1–19.

—— *War Cruel and Sharp: English Strategy under Edward III, 1327–1360* (Woodbridge, 2000).

—— (ed.), *The Wars of Edward III: Sources and Interpretations* (Woodbridge, 1999).

Rogers, Randall, *Latin Siege Warfare in the Twelfth Century* (Oxford, 1992).

Rosenthal, Franz, *The Herb: Hashish versus Medieval Muslim Society* (Leiden, 1971).

Ruff, Julius R., *Violence in Early Modern Europe* (Cambridge, 2001).

Runciman, Steven, *A History of the Crusades*, 3 vols. (Harmondsworth, 1971 [Cambridge, 1951]).

Sanok, Catherine, 'Almoravides at Thebes: Islam and European Identity in the *Roman de Thebes*', *Modern Language Quarterly* 64 no. 3 (September 2003): 277–98.

Sarkesian, Sam C., *The New Battlefield: The United States and Unconventional Conflicts*, Contributions in Military Studies 54 (New York, 1986).

Schramm, Percy Ernst, *A History of the English Coronation*, trans. Leopold G. Wickham Legg (Oxford, 1937).

Sheldon, Rose Mary, *Espionage in the Ancient World: An Annotated Bibliography of Books and Articles in Western Languages* (Jefferson, 2002).

Showalter, Dennis E., 'Caste, Skill, and Training: The Evolution of Cohesion in European Armies from the Middle Ages to the Sixteenth Century', *Journal of Military History* 57 no. 3 (1993): 407–30.

Simon, Kate, *A Renaissance Tapestry: The Gonzaga of Mantua* (New York, 1988).

Smail, R. C., *Crusading Warfare, 1097–1193*, 2nd edn (Cambridge, 1995).

Smith, Robert D., 'Artillery and the Hundred Years War: Myth and Interpretation', in *Arms, Armies and Fortifications in the Hundred Years War*, ed. Anne Curry and Michael Hughes (Woodbridge, 1994), pp. 151–9.

Sournia, Jean-Charles, *Blaise de Monluc: soldat et écrivain (1500–1577)* (Paris, 1981).

Strachan, Hew, 'The Experience of Two World Wars: Some Historiographical Comparisons', in *Time to Kill: The Soldier's Experience of War in the West, 1939–1945*, ed. Paul Addison and Angus Calder (London, 1997), pp. 369–78.

Strickland, Matthew, 'Securing the North: Invasion and the Strategy of Defence in Twelfth-Century Anglo-Scottish Warfare', in *Anglo-Norman Warfare: Studies in Late Anglo-Saxon and Anglo-Norman Military Organization and Warfare*, ed. Matthew Strickland (Woodbridge, 1992), pp. 208–29.

—— *War and Chivalry: The Conduct and Perception of War in England and Normandy, 1066–1217* (Cambridge, 1996).

Sumption, Jonathan, *The Hundred Years War*, 2 vols. (London, 1990–9).

Taillon, J. Paul de B., *The Evolution of Special Forces in Counter-Terrorism: The British and American Experiences* (Westport, 2001).

Tallett, Frank, *War and Society in Early Modern Europe, 1495–1715* (London, 1992).

Thomas, David, 'The Importance of Commando Operations in Modern Warfare, 1939–82', *Journal of Contemporary History* 18 no. 4 (October 1983): 689–718.

Thomas, Heinz, 'Französische Spionage im Reich Ludwigs des Bayern', *Zeitschrift für Historische Forschung* 5 (1978): 1–21.

Thomas, Hugh, *The Conquest of Mexico* (London, 1993).

Thomson, Robert W., 'The Crusaders through Armenian Eyes', in *The Crusades from the Perspective of Byzantium and the Muslim World*, ed. Angeliki E. Laiou and Roy Parviz Mottahedeh (Washington, DC, 2001), pp. 71–82.

Toch, Michael, 'The Medieval German City under Siege', in *The Medieval City under Siege*, ed. Ivy A. Corfis and Michael Wolfe (Woodbridge, 1995), pp. 35–48.

Tracy, James D, *Emperor Charles V, Impresario of War: Campaign Strategy, International Finance, and Domestic Politics* (Cambridge, 2002).

Tuchman, Barbara W., *A Distant Mirror: The Calamitous 14th Century* (New York, 1978).

Turnbull, Stephen, *Ninja: The True Story of Japan's Secret Warrior Cult* (Poole, 1991).

Turner, Ralph V., and Richard R. Heiser, *The Reign of Richard Lionheart: Ruler of the Angevin Empire, 1189–1199* (New York, 2000).

Vale, Malcolm, *War and Chivalry: Warfare and Aristocratic Culture in England, France, and Burgundy at the End of the Middle Ages* (Athens, GA., 1981).

Van Creveld, Martin, *Command in War* (Cambridge, MA, 1985).

——*Fighting Power: German and US Army Performance, 1939–1945* (London, 1983).

Vandenbroucke, Lucien S., *Perilous Options: Special Operations as an Instrument of U.S. Foreign Policy* (New York, 1993).

Vann, Theresa M., 'Twelfth-Century Castile and its Frontier Strategies', in *The Circle of War in the Middle Ages: Essays on Medieval Military and Naval History*, ed. Donald J. Kagay and L. J. Andrew Villalon (Woodbridge, 1999), pp. 21–32.

Vaughan, Richard, *Charles the Bold: The Last Valois Duke of Burgundy* (London, 1973).

——*John the Fearless: The Growth of Burgundian Power* (London, 1966).

——*Philip the Good: The Apogee of Burgundy* (London, 1970).

—— *Valois Burgundy* (London, 1975).

Waller, Douglas C., *The Commandos: The Inside Story of America's Secret Soldiers* (New York, 1994).

Warner, Philip, *Sieges of the Middle Ages* (London, 1968).

Weale, Adrian, *Secret Warfare: Special Operations Forces from the Great Game to the SAS* (London, 1998).

Webster, Bruce, *Medieval Scotland: The Making of an Identity* (London, 1997).

White, Terry, *Swords of Lightning: Special Forces and the Changing Face of Warfare* (New York, 1992).

Wilson, Peter, 'European Warfare, 1450–1815', in *War in the Early Modern World*, ed. Jeremy Black (Boulder, 1999), pp. 177–206.

Wilson, Peter L., 'Secrets of the Assassins', in *Scandal: Essays in Islamic Heresy* (New York, 1988), pp. 33–66.

Wolfe, Michael, 'Siege Warfare and the *Bonnes Villes* of France during the Hundred Years War', in *The Medieval City under Siege*, ed. Ivy A. Corfis and Michael Wolfe (Woodbridge, 1995), pp. 49–68.

Yewdale, Ralph Bailey, *Bohemond I, Prince of Antioch* (Princeton, 1924).

Film bibliography

Black Hawk Down, Jerry Bruckheimer, Ridley Scott *et al.* (producers), dir. Ridley Scott (USA, 2001).

Executive Decision, Joel Silver *et al.* (producers), dir. Stuart Baird (USA, 1996).

Lord of the Rings: The Fellowship of the Ring, Bob Weinstein, Harvey Weinstein *et al.* (producers), dir. Peter Jackson (New Zealand & USA, 2001).

Lord of the Rings: The Two Towers, Bob Weinstein, Harvey Weinstein *et al.* (producers), dir. Peter Jackson (New Zealand, USA & Germany, 2002).

Lord of the Rings: The Return of the King, Bob Weinstein, Harvey Weinstein *et al.* (producers), dir. Peter Jackson (New Zealand, USA & Germany, 2003).

Mission: Impossible (TV), Bruce Geller *et al.* (producers), created by Bruce Geller (USA, 1966–73).

Proof of Life, Taylor Hackford *et al.* (producers), dir. Taylor Hackford (USA, 2000).

Raiders of the Lost Ark, Frank Marshall, George Lucas *et al.* (producers), dir. Steven Spielberg (USA, 1981).

Saving Private Ryan, Ian Bryce, Mark Gordon, Gary Levinsohn, Steven Spielberg *et al.* (producers), dir. Steven Spielberg (USA, 1998).

Star Wars, Gary Kurtz and George Lucas (producers), dir. George Lucas (USA, 1977).

The Terminator, John Daly, Derek Gibson and Gale Anne Hurd (producers), dir. James Cameron (USA, 1984).

Terminator II: Judgment Day, James Cameron, Gale Anne Hurd and Mario Kassar (producers), dir. James Cameron (USA & France, 1991).

Terminator III: Rise of the Machines, Moritz Borman *et al.* (producers), dir. Jonathan Mostow (USA, UK & Germany, 2003).

Twelve Monkeys, Robert Cavallo *et al.* (producers), dir. Terry Gilliam (USA, 1995).

Wag the Dog, Michael De Luca, *et al.* (producers), dir. Barry Levinson (USA, 1997).

Index

WARFARE IN HISTORY